Loch

Human Sexuality
and Personhood

Human Sexuality and Personhood

Proceedings of the Workshop for the Hierarchies of
the United States and Canada Sponsored by
the Pope John Center Through a Grant
from the Knights of Columbus

Dallas, Texas, February 2-6, 1981

Pope John Center
St. Louis

Nihil Obstat:
    Rev. Robert F. Coerver, C.M., S.T.D.
    Censor Deputatus

Imprimatur:
    + John N. Wurm, S.T.D., Ph.D.
    Vicar General of St. Louis

January 16, 1981

The Nihil Obstat and Imprimatur are a declaration that a book or pamphlet is considered to be free from doctrinal or moral error. It is not implied that those who have granted the Nihil Obstat and Imprimatur agree with the contents, opinions or statements expressed.

Copyright 1981
by
The Pope John XXIII Medical-Moral
Research and Education Center
St. Louis, Missouri 63104

Library of Congress Catalog Card Number: 80-85411
ISBN 0-935372-09-1

Distributors for the Trade:
    FRANCISCAN HERALD PRESS
    1434 West 51st St.
    Chicago, IL 60609

PREFACE

In October 1980, for the fifth time since the Vatican Council ended in 1965, an international Synod of Bishops met in Rome. The Synod bishops reviewed the Church's special role in protecting the dignity of marriage and the transmission of human life because conjugal love is a participation in the very mystery of God's Life and Love. Human sexuality permeates human personhood, enabling human sexual love to reflect the infinite love within the Trinity.

While renewing the Church's challenging doctrine that conjugal love must be fully human, exclusive, and open to new life, in their "Message to Christian Families in the Modern World" the Synod bishops recognized that God's plan for marriage and the family can only be fully understood, accepted, and lived by persons who have experienced conversion of heart. They discussed the development of a pastoral theology of human sexuality reflecting the normative moral teaching of the Church. Pope John Paul II in his closing homily at the Synod described the "law of gradualness" or gradual progress in accepting the plan of God.

Eight months before the Synod, a large majority of the 122 bishops from the United States and Canada who had attended a Workshop on "New Technologies of Birth and Death," sponsored by the Pope John Center, indicated their preference that the next workshop discuss "Human Sexuality and Personhood." Like the Synod bishops and the Holy Father, they were recognizing the need of a more positive theology of human sexuality and a more effective pastoral ministry in a person-centered context.

The Pope John XXIII Medical-Moral Research and Education Center presented that Workshop on "Human Sexuality and Personhood" for two hundred bishops in Dallas, Texas, February 2 through 6, 1981. The Center's mission is to assist the Church in responding to the new challenges our technological culture presents to a Catholic theology of life, health, and procreation. The Workshop was made possible by a grant from the Knights of Columbus with additional assistance from Mr. Frank J. Schneider, a Member of the Board of the Pope John Center.

This book contains the proceedings of that Workshop. The authors were doing their research and writing during the Synod. In their work we note the same two hinges of discussion that Pope John Paul II cited in the Synod's own deliberations: fidelity toward the plan of God for the family, and a pastoral way of acting. These scholars set out to present a contemporary and balanced theology of human sexuality and marriage in the light of magisterial teaching and the Christian theology of the person.

The "Introduction" by the Reverend James Gill, S.J., M.D., reflects his keynote address at the Workshop. Part One contains a brief historical overview of Church teaching on human sexuality from the Biblical period until 1918. These three essays were distributed to the bishops before the Workshop and were not actually presented by the three authors in Dallas.

Part Two contains the survey of contemporary scientific and philosophical approaches to human sexuality which several scholars prepared. Paul Peachey, the sociologist in the group, strikes a basic theme in the conclusion of his chapter. "Nowhere is the miscarriage of individuation processes more evident," he says, "than in the crisis of sexuality. Older norms have collapsed more rapidly than new ones have grown. The real sexual revolution still lies in the future."

Part Three surveys contemporary Catholic moral theology and Church teaching on human sexuality and marriage since 1918. These essays capture the ecclesial and theological context in which the Synod deliberated in October 1980. The Reverend Benedict Ashley states succinctly the reason for the enduring sexual teaching of the Church when he writes that "Jesus bases His interpretation of the sixth commandment on God's original reason for creating the two sexes, because this original purpose of God's is universal and enduring, transcending the historical situations of particular human cultures . . . ."

The Reverend Francis Meehan points out in his earlier essay that the Church's doctrine involved in the contraceptive debate goes much deeper than merely an ethical teaching. "It is a theological anthropology," he says, "about the meaning of human love imaging forth the divine love." The people of God are looking for this biblically inspired understanding of their own sexuality and personhood.

The Pope John Center gladly offers this volume in sequence to the work of the Fifth International Synod in the spirit of the ancient motto, *Pro Deo et Ecclesia.*

The Most Reverend Bernard F. Law, D.D.
Bishop of Springfield-Cape Girardeau
Chairman of the Board
Pope John Center

TABLE OF CONTENTS

Introduction

Sexuality and Pastoral Rapport

The Reverend James J. Gill, S.J., M.D.

I consider this opportunity to offer these introductory remarks both a privilege and a challenge. This chance to make some small contribution to the pastoral effectiveness of so many Church leaders all at one time is a joy I certainly welcome, but I find myself puzzled about what it might be that a priest who also happens to be a psychiatrist could say that would, in the long run, prove helpful.

The issue we are to address here in Dallas is a complex, timely and enormously important one; no one needs to remind any bishop of that. (I suppose there has never been a day in history, nor will there ever be one, when that same statement could not be truthfully made.) Sexuality is such a central, powerful and crucial aspect of our humanity that the topic deserves every bit of time, attention and reflection we can devote to it. Certainly it will come as no surprise to the Catholic laity that their bishops are gathering to discuss the manifold aspects of sex; they know the theme has been a clergy-preoccupying one down through the ages, particularly its moral and ethical dimensions. As a matter of fact, it would probably be accurate to estimate that most Catholics in the United States believe that in the minds of the majority of men who have been ordained to the priesthood, the sexual behavior of their parishioners, penitents, and young people especially is already claiming too prominent a place. They hear us speak and find us writing so frequently about such issues as contraception, homosexuality, abortion, and premarital sex that it would be impossible for them not to realize how seriously we are inclined to view all matters sexual, since these are related to what life is given for – human relationships, love and salvation. What Catholics must wonder is whether we also keep in mind the beauty, the humor, the spirituality, the fun, the therapeutic and the other facets of sexuality, to give the balance to our natural and inevitable concern about its potentially destructive features related to sin.

It is the realization that millions of those whom the Lord has given to you as your pastoral flock have been raised since childhood to think of Catholic clergymen as being moralistic in regard to sex which prompts me to offer, by way of introduction, just one simple recommendation as you begin to consider and discuss the presentations to follow. This suggestion would probably never have entered my mind had I not been given, in God's providence, the chance to study medicine and practice psychiatry after ordination. I hope it won't sound presumptuous on my part to offer it now.

First of all, we are – as preachers of the Gospel of Jesus Christ – aware of the importance He and His Church have always attached to sexuality in relation to personal salvation; it is our responsibility and mission to proclaim His teaching about it. Like Moses, we hold up the Sixth Commandment we have received from God and call for observance. And we make the gravity of the matter apparent, just as Jesus did, by insisting that our human propensity to transgress in this precarious area of life is perilous enough to result – given a don't-care attitude on one's part – in an eternal loss of the face-to-Face sharing of life with God for which we were lovingly created. Putting it bluntly, we threaten the deliberate sexual sinner with damnation. And since sin of this sort is so difficult for so many to avoid, at least during certain seasons of their life, our message is received as a distressing one. As you know so well, adolescents particularly are inclined to experience our call for sexual abstinence, when we couple it with a threat of possible loss of God's love and heaven, as emotionally unbearable, in

4

view of the strength of their sexual impulses and the difficulty they so often experience in controlling them. In an unconsciously defensive manner, countless thousands of them have resorted automatically to the use of a mental mechanism that serves to remove their anxiety and guilt; they simply *deny* that they believe in the God-Church-sin complex which is so threatening to them. They "drop out" over sex, many of them never to return, as far as we can see.

What I would want to recommend, as you reflect on human sexuality during the days ahead and while you are considering ways of helping young people especially to understand and follow the Lord's teaching, is based on a fact every psychiatrist, psychologist or other practicing clinician learns gradually through experience to appreciate; there is also ample research evidence to substantiate it. The fact is this: people who feel threatened when in contact with an authority figure tend to become defensive, block communication, and withdraw from the relationship to whatever extent is required to eliminate their emotional distress. (When I say *threatened* I mean that they feel anxious and insecure, as if they are about to experience some painful injury or harm.) People do feel threatened inevitably, at least at the unconscious level of their personality, when a person with authority holds up an ideal and links it with a warning of personal suffering if they choose to transgress. Their anxiety is heightened when they are aware of deep and at times intense, difficult-to-control yearnings and impulses within themselves toward the forbidden behavior. Our proclaiming the ideals of Christian sexual morality, perhaps more than any other preaching or teaching we do, is likely to trigger the undesirable response pattern: hearing, feeling threatened, becoming defensive, backing off, and, finally, denying the existence of the realities that occasioned the discomfort (namely God and sin).

What can we do to prevent people from being thus "turned off" by our preaching with regard to sexuality? Again, theory and practice within the various helping professions suggest an answer. It is one that certainly does not entail terminating our presentation of ideals. Rather, it grows out of an appreciation of the fact that, since no one on earth is perfect but many desire to attain, step-by-step, as mature a level of moral behavior as they can, while realizing that arriving at that point in a single leap is impossible, one who desires to be helpful – instead of promising or implying dire consequences if their behavior falls short of the ideal – must show convincingly an awareness and

5

acceptance (not a condoning) of their current stage of moral development, refrain from responding in what sounds like a blaming manner, and offer to help find a way so that the next step in the direction of progress can be taken with reasonable hope of success.

Underlying his approach to the task of facilitating human development is a well researched truth about our nature: you are not likely to help anyone face the fact that he is falling short of his goal, without his feeling judged by you to be a less-than-fully acceptable and good person, unless you already have a solidly established relationship with him and he trusts you as being interested only in helping him to make progress, not at all disposed to hurt him in any way. In other words, he needs to feel that you are at his side, an ally in rapport with him, with only one desire on your part, to assist him to take his own steps toward the goal he has deliberately made his own and is striving to attain. If he hesitates out of anxiety (over what he might lose) to give up his current mode of moral behaving in order to ascend to a new and as yet untried level of functioning, he needs to feel certain that you are going to be understanding, not judgmental, impatient, or rejecting, and still respectful and hopeful in his regard. Anything less than this attitude on the helping person's part, research has shown, tends to rupture the relationship and render further efforts to be helpful very unlikely to succeed.

The point I want to make is not that bishops and other clergy should take seriously and give convincing evidence of heeding Jesus' injunction, "Judge not and you will not be judged"; neither am I advocating that the best pastoral approach to fostering a mature, Christian morality in the sexual sphere of a person's life is a developmental step-by-step one within the context of a mutually trustful "helping relationship." Reminders like these are hardly necessary at this point in the Church's history of pastoral ministry. I see no need, moreover, to encourage any American bishop to view his role as one that entails helping his people to discover effective ways to advance *on their own initiative,* both spiritually and morally, in line with the teachings of the Lord and His Church, with responsibility for listening to these teachings, deciding to pursue the Christian ideals and finding suitable means of growth resting squarely on their, not the bishop's, shoulders. We all know that no clergyman can live his people's lives for them, or coerce them into holiness; he can just, like Christ, stand ready to assist them to achieve the growth and behavior

6

he prescribes and models for them, successful only to the extent that they will permit and welcome him.

Then what is it I want to recommend? Simply this: teach your people to learn to regard you as present and ready to *assist* them in their own, self-chosen pursuit of advancement in morality, especially in regard to sexuality; help them see that their growth and their ideals are *their* responsibility to make deliberately their own. Many, if not most, of the Catholics whom I encounter are at the present time failing to see you clearly as playing this helping role in their lives. They have not as yet assumed full responsibility, out of love for God, for pursuing the ideals the Church proposes, and they view you as inclined to impose a burdensome morality upon them. They have not as yet been enabled by you to develop a sense of alliance with you, a rapport that is perhaps best pictured as you walking at their side, lending your strong support, as they struggle to reach a mature level of sexuality they themselves deeply desire and consider worth pursuing at any price.

But please don't take my word for this; ask your people. Ask whether they have, in fact, firmly committed themselves to becoming more and more deeply and maturely moral because they know and love Jesus Christ, and whether they see you, and our Holy Father, and all of us priests as caringly present, missioned by our Lord to assist them in whatever way we can – not to function as towering "authority figures" in their lives. What will you hear from most? My hunch is that they will tell you they look upon bishops as persons who feel responsible before God to hold up sexual and other moral ideals that are often extremely difficult if not impossible for them to attain (just recall their response to *Humanae Vitae*) and who place upon them the burden of living up to the requirements the Church enunciates, with an implication of loss of salvation if they do not comply. Below the level of their conscious awareness, I would bet, most of them still regard you, and all of us priests, as parental figures, who – if we were to witness their sexual transgressions – would be inclined to regard them judgmentally as less worthy of our respect and love because they are weak, morally flawed or reprehensible as they stand in the sight of God. You and I know that you and I don't look upon our people this way. My point is that in the way we talk to them, write to them, and deal with them, we need to give them *evidence* that we don't.

I think that perhaps the majority of adolescents and adults in our

7

country today need a new experience of their bishops in relation to sexual morality. They react to pastoral sexual teaching in too great numbers (recall the Roman document on "certain questions," including premarital sex, masturbation and homosexuality) in unheeding or even resentful ways which, I believe, reveal their current inability to perceive bishops and priests as compassionate fellow-strugglers, striving just as they are to live up to Christian sexual ideals which we too find difficult. They need to see us trying to learn to relate to others of both sexes in such a way that our own sexuality is integrated into a life of strong and deep human love. They need, too, to find us transparently seeking to understand our sexuality, accept it, and love it as a gift God gives to make our love for each other and for Him more possible, more intense and more creative. They need, I think, to hear from us how much we want this week of discussion here in Dallas to improve our understanding of the nature of sexuality, the appropriate role it should be playing in all our lives, and how we can help others to grow to full Christian sexual maturity. Perhaps then they will want us to walk beside them helpfully, not by commanding, but by inviting them to learn to be fully sexual and fully alive as Christian persons, each according to his or her own vocation. Perhaps, too, they will all soon recognize that we celibates are trying to become such persons ourselves, for God's greater glory and out of love for *them*.

Part One:
A Brief Historical Overview: Catholic Teaching from the Biblical Period to 1918

A Brief Historical Overview: Catholic Teaching from The Biblical Period to 1918

How did the Catholic Church's Magisterial teaching on human sexuality get to be the way it is? To understand well and in depth the meaning of that teaching requires not only a grasp of the current formulations as expressed in various official documents but also some appreciation of its roots and its subsequent development over the centuries as it was shaped by a variety of factors – theological, cultural, psychosocial, historical.

The following three short essays seek to provide a brief sketch of that development from Old and New Testament times through the patristic, medieval and Renaissance periods to the time of the 1918 *Code of Canon Law*.

The Reverend Joseph Jensen, O.S.B., Associate Professor in the School of Religious Studies, The Catholic University of America, and Executive Secretary of the Catholic Biblical Association, was invited to provide a very brief study on the contribution of the Sacred Scriptures to the Church's teaching on sexual morality. After surveying the Old Testament teachings with regard to fornication, prostitution, adultery and homosexuality, Father Jensen contrasts them with the New Testament revelation. Although Jesus expected His disciples to follow many of the moral norms laid down in the Old Testament, the early Church — as noted particularly in St. Paul's writings – did not hold the Christian to the Mosaic Law precisely as law. Because the Christian has been saved by the graciousness of Jesus Christ, the disciple is not held to the demands of the letter of the Law, but instead is to walk in the Spirit and respond in all matters according to the demands of love in the manner of Jesus' own love. Such Christlike fidelity to love results in a sexual morality which goes beyond what the Old Testament demanded but which requires the free and mature judgment of a disciple totally dedicated to the Person of Jesus.

During the early Church's life, the teaching of the Scriptures on sexual morality underwent some development and articulation. The Reverend Francis Firth, C.S.B., Professor of Theology at St. Joseph College of the University of Alberta in Edmonton, traces some of this development in the second essay. One of the pitfalls of studies of the early Church is the variety of ways in which the same word is used by different writers. The Greek word *porneia* is one such, and even the biblical author St. Paul used the same word to mean at various times fornication, adultery, incest, or sexual immorality in general. A similar problem arises in dealing with the patristic and medieval periods. After sketching the contributions made by the Greek philosophers, Father Firth outlines the major contributions of St. Augustine and St. Thomas Aquinas, who picked up the lead from the biblical authors and developed more specific statements regarding the morality of various forms of sexual behavior.

The third essay, prepared by Dr. James Hitchcock, Professor of History at Saint Louis University, covers the span of time from 1300 to 1918. After the highwater mark of scholastic theology in the thirteenth century, theological activity in the Church went into a period of decline, wherein nominalism had a significant impact on the thinking of the day. A stress on voluntaristic interpretation of God's relationship to humans was one result. From that perspective, moral laws were seen as expressions of God's almost arbitrary manner of dealing with human behavior: supposedly an act was morally evil because God decreed that it was so; He could have decreed the opposite.

In the area of sexual morality, Catholic doctrine during this period continued the previous teaching and held with continuing insistence that sexual intercourse be directed to the procreation of children. Therefore, sexual intercourse could only take place within a marriage and in a manner which would not deliberately prevent conception. All uses of the sexual faculties which did not meet these two requirements were prohibited. Recurring debates among theologians regarding other justifying reasons for sexual intercourse (aside from the procreation of children), such as the fostering of mutual love and the degree and type of procreative intent, marked this period.

With the advent of the Protestant reformers of the sixteenth century, the primacy of celibacy over marriage as a state of life was denied. While supporting in general the sacredness of the family hearth, the displacement of celibacy from its privileged position placed marriage in a differently nuanced position in Christian society.

The rise in society of a merchant class (the middle class), the rapidly increasing industrialization of Europe and America, the move from rural to urban forms of living, the secularization of society, all contributed to the increasing burden experienced by couples having many children and trying to raise them adequately. Concurrently with the increasing secularization of Western Christianity, the relative torpidity of Catholic theology of the 1800's was unable to deal effectively with the increasing number of Catholic couples who practiced some form of "family planning" – natural or otherwise.

For almost two thousand years, the authentic teaching of the Catholic Church developed organically. No basic discontinuity in that growth can be discovered. It is clear that the Church, taking its cue from the various scriptural statements on sexuality, regarded human sexuality as a good from God, but one which could be easily corrupted because of the power and pleasure with which this faculty is endowed. Clearly, sexuality and marriage were honored in and by the Church, but their relationship to human procreation was determinative. In the midst of what seemed to be clear and compelling principles regarding the use of human sexual faculties, the evident and great difficulty experienced by all persons in abiding by those moral demands required that the pastors of the Church find pastoral solutions to complex and painful human problems. This challenge continues – perhaps with greater urgency – in the contemporary world.

Chapter 1

Human Sexuality
in the
Scriptures

The Reverend Joseph Jensen, O.S.B., S.T.D.

Twentieth-century moral theology asks many questions about matters which arise from modern biology or medical technology, questions relating to birth control, artificial insemination, etc. In many cases the Scriptures give no answers because the questions being asked lay outside the knowledge and/or concerns of the inspired writers. Many of the principles contained in the Bible undoubtedly have implications for modern problems, and it is the role of moral theologians to work out their applications. The following pages are intended primarily to present and analyze the contents of Scripture and to set forth at least some modest conclusions of a general nature. No attempt is made to bring together the unitive and procreative aspects of sex here; both aspects are known in the Bible, but no explicit concern to correlate them appears.

The Creation Accounts: General Comments

It is of interest, however, that the two Creation accounts contained in the early chapters of Genesis do highlight the procreative and unitive aspects of marriage, respectively. In Genesis 1 the creation of mankind comes as the climax of all the other creative works, is preceded by a divine deliberation ("let us make mankind in our image . . ."), and is formulated (unlike the rest of the account) in poetic lines:

> God made mankind in his image
>> in the image of God he created him
> male and female he created them (v. 27).

Nothing here suggests anything other than equality and equal dignity of the two sexes. Then follows the blessing: "And God blessed them and said to them, 'Be fruitful and multiply and fill the earth and subdue it'" (v. 28). It is to be noted that this is a blessing rather than a command[1] (cf. the similar formula pronounced over the fish and birds in v. 22, though they are not given dominion as mankind, made in God's image, is). This is in line with the Old Testament's high regard for fertility, considering it a gift from God, just as barrenness was considered a curse.

The account in chapter 2, as already suggested, highlights the unitive aspects of the marriage relationship. This is seen, first of all, in the divine reflection that "it is not good for man to be alone." The animals are then formed from the earth, as the man had been, but nonetheless none of them are apt as his helpmate; a special creation is called for. The account then tells of the woman being formed from the very substance of the man's own body; thus is acknowledged the special closeness of man and woman in the marriage relationship: it is as though in this union they are returning to an original unity from which the two were formed. Now it is the advent of the woman alone which is greeted in poetic lines:

> This one, at last, is bone of my bones,
>> and flesh of my flesh;
> this one shall be called "woman"
>> for out of "her man" was she taken (v. 23).

The unitive aspect is again underlined as the author reflects that "for this reason a man leaves his father and mother and clings to his wife, and the two become one flesh."

As in the case of the first account, there is no suggestion of inequality; on the contrary, the description of the woman being made from the very substance of the man and being placed at his side to perform a function that the animals cannot suggests just the opposite. It is the advent of sin which occasions accusation and recrimination (3:12) and the domination to which woman becomes subject (3:16). This is not to condone woman's subjection to man; the author who sees this as a departure from the ideal, original state, precisely through the presence of sin in the world, clearly indicates it is a bad thing. In this account fertility appears as a mixed blessing (v. 16).

This solemn and sublime bringing together of the first couple in effect makes God the author of marriage. The "two in one flesh" imagery strongly suggests that monogamy is here considered the ideal, even though it was not the invariable rule in Israel. Of Lamech it is specifically noted that he took two wives (4:19), but he was a violent, unprincipled character (4:23-24).

Many other Old Testament passages attest to one or the other of these two important aspects of marriage. The desire for children and the conviction that fruitfulness or barrenness are in God's hands is a frequent theme, e.g., in the cases of Sarah (Gen. 16:1-2; 18:14; 21:1-2), Rebekah (Gen. 25:21), Leah and Rachel (Gen. 29:31, 32; 30:2, 6, 17, 22-24), Ruth (Ru. 4:13), and Hannah (1 Sam. 1:5, 11, 19-20). The tenderer aspects of human love are also alluded to, as when the seven years Jacob served in order to obtain Rachel as his wife seemed but a few days because of the greatness of his love (Gen. 29:20). In the Canticle of Canticles deep tenderness, and eroticism as well, are brought to expression. Marriage was the norm. The single life, as a free choice, was virtually unknown, though Jeremiah was told to remain unmarried as a sign that the begetting of children was pointless, in view of the calamities to come (Jer. 16:1-4), and Judith, the widow, chose not to remarry even though she was greatly sought after (Jdt. 16:22).

Monogamy may be suggested as an ideal in the second Creation account, but it was not imposed by Israel's mores or customs. Abraham took Hagar, Sarah's maid, in an attempt to circumvent Sarah's barrenness, and Jacob married two sisters and likewise their two maids; Elkanah had another wife, Peninnah, besides Hannah; David married a number of wives, and Solomon is said to have had a sizeable harem. It is not clear, however, how widely polygamy was practiced; since acquiring a wife involved paying a bridal price to the woman's family, as well as supporting the woman herself, economic necessity alone probably dictated monogamy in the vast number of cases. The instances of concubinage with slave girls (as Abraham with Hagar, Jacob with Zilphah and Bilhah) should not be construed as an indication that casual sex was countenanced, for such unions tended to be stable.[2] From the Code of Hammurabi we know that marriage unions with slaves were often the subject of legal safeguards,[3] while in the Old Testament offspring of such unions often figure in genealogies and are not considered illegitimate. The case is often otherwise with the children of harlots.[4] According to Ex. 21:7-11 the slave concubine has rights that cannot be diminished, even if another wife is taken, and she cannot be sold.[5] Thus we are dealing with a type of marriage, not with extramarital affairs.

The lawfulness of divorce is presupposed in the Old Testament. The one legal text that deals with it explicitly, Dt. 24:1-4, seeks to regulate the practice in two ways: it provides that the man who sends his wife away must give her a document to show that such is the case (she is then considered free to marry) and it forbids the original husband to take the woman back as his wife once she has been married to another. The reason given for the prohibition is that the woman, having been intimate with another man, is now defiled with respect to the first one. The wording of the law does not suggest that it intends to establish what the lawful grounds for divorce are, but presupposes that the husband has found something unworthy about the woman, though there is no general agreement on what the Hebrew phrase in question (*'erwat dabar*) means. The prophet Jeremiah seems to be alluding to this law when he refers to the difficulty of Israel's returning to the Lord after her infidelities (Jer. 3:1). The prophet Malachi condemns the divorce which brings misery upon the repudiated wife, "the wife of your youth," calling it a breach of faith (Mal. 2:13-16). Since the broader context (vv. 10-12) includes a condemnation of marriage with pagan wives, what seems to be envisioned here is a repudiation of an Israelite wife in favor of a pagan. Although marriage seems here to be referred to as a covenant ("the wife of your covenant" – v. 14), it has been argued that the covenant in question is that of Sinai (*cf.* "the covenant of our fathers" in v. 10), the term thus distinguishing the Israelite wife from the pagan.[6] Even if this is correct, marriage must have been conceived of in convenantal terms since the prophets, from Hosea on, compared Israel's bond to Yahweh with the marital union,

18

each demanding comparable loyalty. When Ezekiel, using this marriage allegory, has God say, "I swore an oath to you and entered into a covenant with you" (Ezel. 16:8), the words would appear to be equally applicable to marriage and to Israel's situation. The Malachi text refers to "godly offspring" (literally "seed – or offspring – of God") as what is sought from marriage, but what is probably intended is the distinction between the children of the union with an Israelite wife ("godly offspring") and those born of union with an idolatrous wife. The Hebrew of the text is rather difficult and in part corrupt.

Sexual Morality in the Old Testament

Since this presentation is written from a Christian standpoint, it is the New Testament that is considered normative. This approach takes into account not only the development that is found beyond Old Testament perspectives but also the fact that at least some of the New Testament writers no longer take the Mosaic law as normative. Nevertheless, the Old Testament is of great importance in understanding New Testament moral teaching, because there is a good deal of continuity in content (which in the Old Testament is far broader than the Mosaic law), the New Testament authors frequently supposing and sometimes citing it; indeed, even the double commandment of love of God and love of neighbor comes from the Old Testament (Dt. 6:4-5; Lev. 19:18). There is also the fact that in each case we are dealing with a covenant morality, which means that the behavior of the members of the covenant community is understood as grateful response to the covenant Lord who has already won redemption for them. Thus morality is thought of not in terms of a natural law equally imposed on all mankind, but in terms of covenant loyalty on the part of the redeemed; morality is not a private matter, for each individual lives out his or her life in the context of the covenant community. The community has a certain right, under God, to define at least certain minimum standards for those who would number themselves as its members.

Of the numerous Old Testament laws (later Judaism counted 613 commandments), many deal with sexual matters in a variety of areas. Some of them impart high moral attitudes while others rest on little more than taboos. Examples of the latter would be those laws which see uncleanness involved in a woman's menstrual flow, a defilement which is communicated to everyone and everything she touches (Lev.

15: 19-27), or in giving birth (Lev. 12:1-5), or in a man's genital discharge (Lev. 15:16-17), even when it is continuous through some bodily defect or illness (Lev. 15:1-3) – again an uncleanness that is communicated to anyone who touches him or anything he has touched (Lev. 15:4-12). Sexual intercourse also involved both man and woman in a state of uncleanness (Lev. 15:18). Intercourse during menstruation was forbidden under the extreme penalty of being "cut off from the people" (Lev. 18:19, 29).

Other laws, however, reflect much better the social, familial, and basic human values that the Old Testament so often concerns itself with – the sort of concerns that produced legislation that commands helping an enemy when he is in need (Ex. 23:4-5), protects the widow, orphan, and alien (Ex. 22:20-23), forbids interest on a loan to a poor man (Ex. 22:24), provides that gleanings be left for the poor (Lev. 19:9-10), and commands love for neighbor (Lev. 19:18) and even for the alien sojourner (Lev. 19:34). It has been properly pointed out that some of these matters are not really capable of being legislated and that what is being inculcated are attitudes and ideals. Thus it is not to be thought that in Israel's sexual legislation the primary concern was with economic interests (e.g., in the case of the seduction of a virgin daughter) or with a clear line of inheritance (as in the case of adultery), as has sometimes been asserted. Israelite ideals in the area of sexual morality were fairly strict, especially considering the laxity of the cultures around them. We will review Israelite attitudes in the areas of fornication and prostitution, adultery, and homosexuality. It will be necessary to broaden the picture beyond legislation, however, for the Old Testament law codes are neither complete nor systematic, and a clearer picture of Israel's response under the covenant emerges when other materials, too, are taken into account. Historical narratives (taking "historical" in the broad sense) illuminate some areas more clearly than the laws do, and the wisdom tradition is also an important witness to Israel's sexual ethic.

Fornication and Prostitution

Since the Old Testament does not contain legislation that specifically forbids fornication, some have concluded that it was not frowned upon. But it should be noted that the legal expectation that a girl be a virgin when she came to marriage was so strong and the sanctions so severe that legislation concerning specific facts was hardly needed. It was the custom in Israel for the parents to preserve the garment or sheet of the wedding night as a proof of their daughter's virginity. If the man to whom she had been given claimed she was not a virgin, and the parents could not produce proof to the contrary, the girl was to be stoned to death (Dt. 22:13-21).[7]

There was a tendency to equate extramarital intercourse with prostitution. Thus, in the Deuteronomy text just referred to, the girl's crime is described as "playing the harlot," though the only evidence of misconduct is non-virginity. In the same manner Dinah's brothers claim that she had been "treated as a harlot" by Shechem (Gen. 34:31), even though it was a once-only affair and he ardently desired marriage.[8] Fornication is also compared to adultery in that the two are treated in parallel fashion in Sir. 42:10, which expresses a father's concern for his daughter:

> While unmarried, lest she be seduced,
>   or, as a wife, lest she prove unfaithful;
> Lest she conceive in her father's home,
>   or be sterile in that of her husband.

Sir. 9:3-9 weaves together warnings against adultery, fornication, and prostitution in a way that indicates they are comparable kinds of misbehavior.

Old Testament attitudes on extramarital intercourse are conveyed in its use of the Hebrew term *nĕbalâ*. Literally the word means "foolishness," but the contexts show it was a strong term, which most modern translations regularly render by "outrage," "crime," or something equally strong. In the Dt. 22:13-21 text referred to above, the girl found to be non-virgin is put to death for having done *nĕbalâ* in Israel. Dinah's enraged brothers ultimately kill Shechem because his rape is *nĕbalâ* "in Israel" (even though Shechem was not an Israelite) (Gen. 34:7), and Tamar pleads with Amnon not to commit *nĕbalâ* by raping her (2 Sam. 13:12).[9] Clearly finances were not the overriding concern in the Shechem-Dinah incident. Shechem willingly consents to a financial settlement most favorable to Jacob, but his sons' desire to avenge the wrong done to their sister leads to the act which makes Jacob's situation odious (Gen. 34:30).

The most explicit Old Testament legal text relevant to prostitution is Lev. 19:29, where the father is commanded "do not profane your daughter by making her a harlot," and the motivation given is that otherwise the land would be full of lewdness. The terminology suggests religious concern. The term for "to profane" (ḥalal) regularly has to do with the profanation of holy things or persons (the sanctuary, God's name, the covenant, the priest, etc.). That the obligation is laid first of all on the father, rather than on the girl, simply reflects the social realities of the time. But the motivation given ("else the land will become corrupt and full of lewdness") indicates the general result of prostitution and therefore makes it clear that commerce with a prostitute would be reprehensible also for the man. [10]

In fact, it is to the man that the warning is addressed in Pr. 23:37 ("For the harlot is a deep ditch, and the adulteress a narrow pit"), a text which treats of adultery and prostitution in parallel fashion. This suggests that prostitution, contrary to the suggestions of some, was regarded as quite reprehensible, a kind of behavior comparable to adultery. [11]

Adultery

The prohibition of adultery in Israel is well-known, it being one of the provisions of the Decalogue. The penalty was death for both the man and the woman involved (Lev. 20:10). The formulation in Lev. 20:10 ("if a man commits adultery with the wife of his neighbor . . .") indicates that the law safeguarded the rights of a husband but did not recognize parallel rights of a wife. The formulation of Lev. 20:10 addresses itself only to the man, and Nielsen may be right in arguing that the omission of "your neighbor's wife" in the Sixth Commandment of the Decalogue has the effect of addressing it to the wife as well as to the husband. [12]

The motivation behind the prohibition of adultery was not simply to safeguard the legitimacy of a man's line of descent, as pointed out above, nor did the prohibition relate merely to social responsibilities owed to members of the same community, as has sometimes been alleged. The story of Joseph and Potiphar's wife shows both that religious considerations were prominently present and that the prohibition regarded others than simply fellow Israelites. Joseph's response to the Egyptian woman's solicitation was that it would be "great wickedness" and a "sin against God" (Gen. 39:9). The same conclusions can be drawn from the Abimelech story. This pagan is depicted as protesting to God that he had acted "in the integrity of my heart and the innocence of my hands" in regard to Sarah (Gen. 20:5), and Abraham gives as his excuse for misleading Abimelech the suspicion that "there is no fear of God in this place" (v. 11). The probity expressed in terms such as integrity, innocence, and fear of God was expected of Israelites and looked for also in pagans.

Thus the historical narratives help to put Israel's legislation in perspective. Additional dimensions are seen when Israel's wisdom literature is brought in, especially when diachronic development is noted. In Sir. 23:22-23 legitimacy of offspring is listed only as a third consideration after "disobeyed the law of the Most High" and "wronged her husband." A clear religious note is found in Pr. 2:17, where the crime of the adulteress consists in "forgetting the covenant with her God." Development is seen also in Sir 23:16-21, in that it threatens the *man* "who dishonors his marriage bed."

Homosexuality

The Old Testament does not appear to distinguish between homosexual orientation and homosexual acts. Sodomy is forbidden in Lev. 18:22 ("you shall not with a male as with a woman; such a thing is an abomination") and Lev. 20:13 ("if a man lies with a male as with a woman, both of them shall be put to death for their abominable deed; they have forfeited their lives"). In each case the law is contained within a longer series and followed by the explanation that such acts represented the kind of behavior the Canaanites were guilty of, for which reason the Lord drove them out (*cf.* Lev. 18:24-30; 20:22-26). The conclusion is justified that the Israelites found such acts morally reprehensible in that they relate to a perversion of normal sexual activity.

Those who wish to weaken this conclusion often allege that homosexual relations were forbidden only because of the connection of such behavior with pagan cult (*i.e.,* that it related to male prostitution that was carried out in a pagan cultic context). This position is frequently argued solely or in part by the assertion that the term which designates homosexual intercourse as an "abomination" (*tô'ebâ*) is a term derived from the sphere of the cult and designates especially idolatry and anything connected with it. Both parts of the argument are faulty.

On the first point, there is no reason to doubt that the Israelites would have been familiar with non-cultic homosexual activity. There is plenty of evidence from non-biblical sources that homosexuality was known, in addition to its cultic forms, as a merely secular phenomenon in the ancient Near East, as can be seen in the many examples given by Bottéro-Petschow.[13] The existence of non-cultic homosexuality is also attested in the Middle Assyrian Laws #19 and #20.[14] The latter has to do with homosexual rape and prescribes castration as the punishment. The former fixes a severe fine for an unproved accusation against someone of habitually playing the passive role in homosexual acts. With this as background it is significant to note that in their prohibition of homosexual intercourse neither Lev. 18:22 nor Lev. 20:13 uses terminology that suggests cultic personages, even though such terminology did exist,[15] but refer only to a male (*zākār*) or man (*'îš*) who lies with a male as with a woman.

The provisions of Leviticus cannot be dismissed on the plea that its concerns are cultic, not ethical, for some parts of it contain very lofty precepts, including those of love of neighbor, provision for the poor, impartiality in judgment, and respect for the aged, as well as prohibitions of stealing and lying, oppression of neighbor or servant, mistreatment of deaf and blind, and wronging of a resident alien (*cf.* esp. Lev. 19:9-34). The constant admonition of the Holiness Code, "Be holy, for I Yahweh, your God, am holy," is not exhausted in cultic concerns. It embraces everything, on the negative side, that would make Israel unworthy of living in Yahweh's land and, positively speaking, would advance them towards that consecration as God's people to which they were called.

The second point referred to above has to do with the assertions that "abomination" *(tô'ebâ)* is a term derived from the sphere of the cult and designates idolatrous practices, that therefore homosexuality is designated as abomination because of its connection with ritual prostitution in the Canaanite fertility cult. In fact, this "abomination" terminology is far more broadly based than this sort of assertion would lead one to suspect. An equivalent term (though not etymologically related) is found in early Egyptian wisdom texts, where it can have to do with speaking false words or, more directly relevant, to misbehavior with the women in a house one happens to frequent.[16] Obviously such usage does not relate to Israel's cultic sphere at all. The use of "abomination" in Proverbs is also clearly not dependent on cult of any kind; it can be used without reference to God or divine things, as when wrongdoing, arrogance, and the evildoer are said to be an abomination, respectively, to the king, to men, and to the just (Pr. 16:12; 24:9; 29:27). As in Egyptian wisdom, falsehood and lying is an abomination to God (12:22). A numerical proverb can tie together under the same "abomination" rubric such things as lying, shedding innocent blood, plotting wicked schemes, and sowing discord (6:16-19). When Proverbs does use "abomination" with some reference to the cult, it has to do with legitimate sacrifice which is made an abomination by the wickedness of the one who offers it (15:8, 21:27; cf. 28:9). Isaiah's use of the term in Is. 1:13 is very similar to this, and Jeremiah can combine under "abomination" false worship as well as stealing, murder, adultery, and false swearing (Jer. 7:9-10).

The legal tradition does not stand apart from such wisdom and prophetic diction. The use of false weights and measures is condemned as "abomination" in Dt. 25:13-16 just as it is in Pr. 11:1; 20-10, 23. There is no reason to hold, therefore, that the use of "abomination" to condemn homosexual intercourse relates it to pagan cult.

This understanding of the legal texts is confirmed by two narrative passages, namely, the cursing of Canaan (Gen. 9:20-27) and the destruction of Sodom (Gen. 19:1-25), both of which make reference to the sexual perversion of those who had lived in the land before Israel and neither of which betrays cultic interest. On the latter text Bruce Vawter comments that individual biblical authors used the example of the fearful destruction of the cities of the plain for "unspecified but notorious offenses" by assigning "to the old saga the parabolic role of defining a clear and present evil" and that "there is no doubt about what the Yahwist believed that evil to have been."[17]

A final point to be made here is that the attempt to place sole responsibility on the Bible for the opprobrium associated with homosexuality is hardly justified. The Old Testament considered sodomy a serious evil and attached a death penalty to it (as it did to other matters considered serious crimes, e.g., adultery and breaking the Sabbath), and it was of course denied any place in the cult. But the Bible nowhere witnesses to the sort of contempt directed at the homosexual in Mesopotamia. There those who had homosexual cultic functions were called "effeminate," partly because some of them were victims of castration, but mainly, it would seem, because of their comportment: sometimes functioning as the female in sexual relations, sometimes bearing feminine names, wearing feminine clothes, and carrying the distaff. They were referred to by the designation "female dog," and were considered men who had been turned into women by the curse of Ishtar. Although as an institution both male and female cult prostitutes were an important element in this culture, as individuals they were held in contempt, as were their non-cultic counterparts; this did not result from moral scruples but from the conviction that they had departed from what nature intended them to be.[18] The Old Testament, as was pointed out above, does not seem to distinguish between homosexual orientation and homosexual behavior, but there is no reason to suppose that the motive for condemning homosexual acts goes beyond the act itself. Unlike Mesopotamia and other cultures, the Old Testament says nothing to diminish the dignity of the individual.

The Scriptures have little to say directly to the burning issues of birth control, masturbation, and abortion. The incident of the sin of Onan, who "destroyed (his seed) to the ground" (Gen. 38:9 – the term "his seed" does not appear in the text but is presumably to be supplied from the context) relates to his failure to fulfill his duty to raise up offspring to the name of his dead brother. Masturbation may be included in the various terms for sexual immorality in St. Paul's vice lists (see below, pp. 30, 32), though this would be difficult to demonstrate. Abortion, to the extent that one can know when human life is present in the womb, would of course fall under the prohibition of murder.

Sexual Morality in the New Testament

To pass from the Old Testament to the New Testament in this sort of material is to face the problem of the continuity and discontinuity between the Old and New Testaments in its most acute form. On the one hand, the New Testament, as witnessed in the words of Jesus and many of the New Testament writers, clearly expects that Christian behavior will follow many of the norms recognized by Israel. On the other hand, there early arose the conviction that the Christian was not bound by the Mosaic law.

The Christian and the Old Law

Let us take the second point first. It emerges with as much clarity as can be wished for in the writings of St. Paul. The question seems to have arisen first of all with reference to Gentile converts who, as

Gentiles, were not required to obseve the Mosaic law when they became Christians. When certain Jewish Christians attempted to insist on observance of the law for them, the matter was taken to Jerusalem to be decided, where the judgment went in favor of freedom (Acts 15), the operative theological principle being "our belief is . . . that we are saved by the favor of the Lord Jesus and so are they" (v. 11), only certain obligations being imposed to ease table-fellowship between Jewish Christian and Gentile Christian. St. Paul gives much attention to this matter in some of his epistles, notably Romans and Galatians. In Rom. 7-8 he contrasts the two regimes of the flesh and the Spirit, in which contrast the regime of the flesh is identical with that of the law — a dispensation from which the Christian has been delivered in being transferred into the regime of the Spirit. In Galatians Paul wages a sometimes bitter polemic against those who would submit to the law, urging them that since "it was for liberty that Christ freed us" they should "not take on yourselves the yoke of slavery a second time" (Gal. 5:1).

Our faith in the inspired character of the Bible persuades us that Paul was not a corrupter of the teaching of Jesus. And, although Jesus might generally have been characterized and regarded as an observant Jew, He acts with complete sovereignty with reference to the law as it was interpreted and observed in His day. The gospels present Him as coming into early conflict with the Jewish leaders on the question of Sabbath observance, and one of the sayings attributed to Him in effect cuts the ground out from under the whole system of Mosaic dietary laws (Mk. 7:14-15), a consequence that the evangelist is not slow to point out (Mk. 7:19). Jesus does indeed cite a number of provisions of the law to the rich man who asked Him about eternal life, but He goes on to say that something still is lacking, that only radical discipleship to Himself will do; and when the man "who has kept all these since his childhood" turns away, Jesus comments on the difficulty of entering the Kingdom of God (Mk. 10:17-31). And in the antitheses of the Sermon on the Mount, Jesus shows that some of the Old Testament laws are only a starting point (Mt. 5:21-30) whereas others are set aside as inadequate (vv. 1-47).[19]

The later Christian tradition, in spite of some ambivalences along the way, shows it does not accept the Old Testament in its force of law. Thus Christians do not feel themselves bound by Mosaic dietary laws, nor by rules of ritual cleanness having to do with genital discharges, prohibitions of intercourse during menstruation (on all of which see above), prohibitions of weaving garments of two kinds of thread, sowing two kinds of seed in the same field, or breeding two different kinds of animals together (Lev. 19:19), nor even by the prohibition of partaking of blood (Lev. 17:10), even though this pertains to the so-called Noachic covenant (Gen. 9:4). It is not a matter of distinguishing between ritual and ethical commandments, for even those which are highly ethical in content (e.g., the prohibition of taking interest on loans – Ex. 22:24; Dt. 23:20-21) are not considered binding as law on Christians. As Fitzmyer points out, "Except for a few passages where *nomos* is qualified either explicitly . . . or by the context . . . , *ho nomos* or simply *nomos* otherwise always means for Paul the Mosaic Law, without any distinction being made between cultic or ritual commandments or ethical requirements."[20]

It follows that even the Decalogue, however venerable it may be and however great a use it may have had as a catechetical tool, does not oblige the Christian in its force of law. This is clear from the fact that the Church does not scruple to permit (even – or especially – within the Vatican!) those sort of plastic representations of the divine that are strictly forbidden by the First Commandment, from the fact that the Sabbath commandment is no longer observed,[21] and from the fact that many of the other provisions of the Decalogue are "observed" only by a radical reinterpretation of their original meaning.[22] That Paul does not exempt the Decalogue from what he has to say about the Christian's deliverance from the law is clear from the fact that it is precisely through an example taken from the Decalogue ("you shall not covet") that he argues in Romans 7 (vv. 7-11).*

---

*Some New Testament scholars would want to interpret St. Paul somewhat differently and make a distinction:

Christians are freed from the law according to St. Paul in two senses. First, the Christian does not look to the law for salvation but to the grace of God in Jesus Christ; hence, he is freed to obey the Law no longer as an exterior imposition of God's will, but from the interior motives of faith, hope, and love inspired by the Holy Spirit. Second, the law given to the Jews is universalized for all humanity, and is thus freed of all those ceremonial and political requirements proper to the Jewish nation, such as circumcision and the dietary laws. The universal moral law, however, because it expresses God's wisdom and loving care for the welfare of all humanity and the rights of every human being remains perennially valid in the New Testament and has been restored by Jesus to its original force, demanding more of us than did the Old Law. –*Ed.*

Christian Freedom

The fundamental situation of the Christian is that of freedom, and Paul exhorts the Galatians, as a means of fulfilling their vocations, to stand fast in the freedom for which Christ had freed them. This is a freedom not only from the law, but from sin, death, the flesh, and even the mysterious "elements of this world" (Gal. 4:9) as well. It is a freedom that can be easily surrendered, and that is why St. Paul urges the Galatians to "stand fast" in it (Gal. 5:1). The danger he perceives comes not only from the law but also from the flesh.[23] In dealing with the latter he cites the commandment of love, urges them to "walk by the Spirit," and gives a list of the "works of the flesh," warning that those who do such things are excluded from God's Kingdom.

These three elements are absolutely typical of what the New Testament has to say about the Christian moral life. Matthew's version of Jesus' citation of the double commandment of love of God and love of neighbor adds the important assertion, "on these two commandments depend all the law and the prophets" (Mt. 22:40). Elsewhere, too, the New Testament has the love commandment bear all the weight, as when Paul says, "He who loves his neighbor has fulfilled the law. The commandments . . . are summed up in this sentence,'You shall love your neighbor as yourself.' Love does no harm to a neighbor; therefore love is the fulfilling of the law" (Rom. 13:8-10 – see also Gal. 5:14). And according to John, in Jesus' final address to His disciples, He tells them, "This is my commandment, that you love one another as I have loved you" (Jn. 15:12). The Christian is able to live up to the demands of love because he or she has been transferred into the sphere of the Spirit (Rom. 8:1-17), and it is the Spirit which is the source of love and light and strength.[24]

New Testament Moral Teaching

All of this leaves the matter of what is expected of the Christian in the concrete somewhat vague.[25] In fact, however, this is not where the matter is left. It is here that the many paraenetic passages of the New Testament come in. First of all, it is to be noted that the Christian's response in obedience is absolutely required. Those who hear Christ's words and do not carry them out build on sand and prepare for ruin (Mt. 7:24-27). The one who does not abide in Christ "is like a withered, rejected branch, picked up to be thrown in the fire and burnt" (Jn. 15:6). In a context which deals with temptations, Jesus leaves only the alternatives of entering into life and being cast into gehenna (Mt. 18:7-9), and Paul lists vices that he sees excluding one from God's Kingdom (1 Cor 6:9; Gal. 5:21).

When we turn to passages such as the Sermon on the Mount and other passages that contain Jesus' teachings in the gospels, the epistolary vice lists, and the other New Testament materials that contain exhortations to right living, the kind of sexual morality that emerges is very similar to that found in the Old Testament. Adultery is proscribed (Mk. 7:22; Mt. 15:19; 1 Cor. 6:9), commerce with prostitutes (1 Cor. 6:2-20), fornication,[26] and sodomy (Rom. 1:27; 1 Cor. 6:9), as are adulterous looks (Mt. 5:28).

In matters such as these there is good continuity in content and attitude with the Old Testament materials reviewed above.[27] The New Testament does not have a developed teaching on marriage. On the one hand Paul accords it a high dignity in comparing the union of Christ and His Church to it, describing the relationship in a beautiful manner (Eph. 5:21-33), though not in a manner that recognizes the equality of husband and wife. On the other hand he seems to accord it only grudging approval as a necessary means of avoiding unchastity for those who cannot remain celibate (1 Cor. 7:1-5). This apparent lack of enthusiasm for marriage as a vocation probably is conditioned by his preference for the single life as a condition for serving the Lord without distraction (1 Cor. 7:6-7, 32-35), a decided change from the Old Testament, a change probably occasioned in part by the personal relationship the Christian enjoys with the Lord Jesus, in part by the expectation of an imminent parousia. Yet too much should not be made of the latter point either in regard to Paul's teaching on celibacy nor in regard to his teaching on sexual morality in general. John Meier has well said:

> A further point on Paul concerns the relation of Pauline eschatology to Pauline moral imperatives. Eschatology is certainly basic to Paul's thought. Christian life, Christian sexual activity, and Christian virginity are all eschatological modes of existence. Yet how much of this vision really depends for its validity on the idea of an imminent return of Christ? If an imminent return drops out as a dominant theme – as it does by the time of the Epistle to the Romans (compare 1 Thessalonians!) how much of Paul's vision is necessarily changed? Perhaps not all

that much. The unique eschatological quality of Christian existence is determined primarily by the already/not-yet tension in which the Christian lives – and not by a particular timetable for the parousia.[28]

Certainly the New Testament departs from the Old Testament convictions that marriage is the only acceptable state of life, and there is little in the New Testament of the Old Testament desire for numerous progeny and the blessing of fertility.

The Divorce Question

Another departure from the Old Testament is found in Jesus' prohibition of divorce.[29] The saying is reported in different contexts (Mt. 5:32; 19:3-12; Mk. 10:2-12; Lk. 16:18; 1 Cor. 7:10-11), sometimes with substantial variations. There are many disputed points in these texts, but what does emerge with a fair degree of clarity is that Jesus' words imply the indissolubility of marriage *and* that He is speaking of marriage in general, not of Christian or sacramental marriage. The latter point is clear for three reasons: (1) Jesus is addressing a first-century Palestinian Jewish audience; (2) in the Mt. 19:3-12 and Mk. 10:2-12 versions, which are disputation sayings, the question is raised by Jewish teachers and there is specific reference to the Mosaic law of Dt. 24:1-4; (3) for justification for His teaching Jesus points simply to the nature of marriage as it came from God, as described in the second Creation account of Genesis 2. These are points on which virtually all modern commentators agree. In spite of the clarity of Jesus' teaching, there emerges already in the New Testament the tendency to adapt it in various ways. The earliest of these is St. Paul's use of the logion in 1 Cor. 7:10-16. He would have it applied literally in the case of believers, but allows a dissolution of the marriage in the case of a mixed marriage in which the non-Christian party wishes to separate. In that case, Paul says, the Christian is "not bound," though he does not say to what he or she is not bound. The usual interpretation is that they are not bound to remain single (thus the "Pauline privilege"), and this may well be what is intended. However, it does constitute a departure from the universal application of the word of Jesus.

In addition, in each of the two Matthean passages there is found a clause apparently intended as an exception – *parektos tou porneias* in 5:32, *me epi porneia* in 19:9 – usually translated "except for unchastity"

31

or something similar. The clause is not found in Mark, Luke, or Paul and is therefore almost certainly an addition in Matthew. The import of the insertion continues to be debated, but the present consensus recognizes that an exception is being made, now presumably within the Christian community.[30] The words of Jesus continue to be understood to represent the ideal of marriage, but they are adapted to new situations, as indeed are many of the other words of Jesus found in the gospels. This is often found difficult to accept, but there is the fact that the Church has more latitude in this matter than it is willing to accept.

Conclusions

This paper can end with three conclusions.

1. The New Testament seriously intends the proclamation of Christian freedom which it makes, a point which emerges with unmistakable clarity in the letters of Paul. No arbitrary or unfounded obligations may be laid upon the Christian. This does not imply license, for Paul would see everything the Christian does being subject to the test of the law of love; what the Christian does must harm no one and should tend to build up the community. Because the law of love is general and humans are prone to self-deception, what is proper Christian behavior is often specified in many sayings of Jesus' and in other New Testament sources.

2. In spite of the many exhortations to right conduct, any attempt to find a comprehensive list of do's and don'ts would be in vain. This emerges in part from the nature of the sources, but there are other reasons, too. The Sermon on the Mount, basic as it is to Christian instruction, contains many sayings difficult to interpret or paradoxical or so idealistic that the Church does not interpret them literally (e.g., "do not swear at all" – Mt. 5:34; who can "give to all who ask of you"? – 5:42). Many of these sayings are more in the way of wisdom instruction than of legislation. So also St. Paul's vice lists (1 Cor. 6:9-10; Gal. 5:19-21; Eph. 5:3-7; and other passages that resemble these) compile terms that refer to sins that exclude from God's Kingdom (1 Cor. 6:9; Gal. 5:21; Eph. 5:5), and merit God's wrath (Eph. 5:6), though it is no easier to make precise distinctions among some of the Greek terms than it is to distinguish precisely the English terms to translate them (immorality, lewd conduct, promiscuousness, uncleanness), nor is it easy to know when economy turns into greed or

when a banquet becomes an orgy. And what is the "silly talk" that merits exclusion from God's Kingdom (Eph. 5:4)?

The fact is, that to go that route is to fall back into what St. Paul wanted us freed from. Obviously there is an appearance of security in having morality summed up in 613 commandments, and many Christians hanker after it. But even this is a deceptive appearance. Ultimately Judaism's desire to understand the commandments generated the vast body of literature of the Talmud (to begin with) and begot such divergent schools of interpretation as those of Shammai and Hillel.

3. It would be pastorally more effective and truer to Scripture to make people aware of issues and choices than to confront them with lists of commandments. There may appear to be risk involved in this approach. But if we can properly speak of moral chaos in our times, it is because by and large the contemporary world is rejecting the Christian message as they see it presented, not because here or there someone has made a faulty judgment about the morality of a particular act.

Notes

1. Rabbinic interpretation sees here a commandment, but this is not the literal import of the Old Testament text. See David Daube, *The Duty of Procreation* (Edinburgh: Edinburgh University Press, 1977).

2. The slave concubines given Jacob by Rachel and Leah become a stable part of Jacob's household and are regularly named along with Jacob's other wives, even though the point was that their children should be reckoned as offspring of Rachel and Leah (Gen. 29:31-30:24; 33:1-3, 6-7; 46:8-27).

3. See laws ## 119, 170, and 171.

4. *Cf.* the situation of Jephtah in Jg. 11:1-2.

5. So also the prisoner of war taken as a wife may not later be sold as a slave, even though she loses her husband's favor; *cf.* Dt. 21:10-14.

6. So also in Pr. 2:17, "the covenant of her God," which the adulteress forgets can refer to Israel's covenant rather than to marriage.

7. Rabbinic interpretation explains the severity of the punishment by asserting that the girl's lapse takes place between betrothal and marriage (thus being the equivalent of adultery), but of this there is no hint in the text. The description of the manner of reaching a judgment in the case rules out any detailed knowledge of the circumstances. The case does illustrate how later interpretation could come to mitigate the rigor of the law.

8. This sort of assimilation can also be seen in that simple fornication is understood to involve a defilement similar to that of prostitution, both cases being covered by the Hebrew term *ḥalal* in the Masoretic text and by *bebeloun* in the Greek of the Septuagint.

9. The case is complicated both by the fact that it was a matter of rape and that Amnon is Tamar's half-brother. However, since she argues that David will give her to him as wife if Amnon only asks, the act is *nĕbālâ* because, in the present circumstances, there is no marriage.

10. There is no reason to assert that the concern here has to do with cultic prostitution of a pagan sort. The Hebrew terminology employed (the verb *zāna*) does not suggest that.

11. The tendency to equate prostitution and adultery occurs repeatedly. Sometimes it is a question of two distinct crimes which are nevertheless treated in parallel fashion, as in Pr. 23:27,

cited above (cf. also Jer. 5:7), though sometimes the parallelism tends to blur the distinction, as though different terms were used to describe the same crime (Jer. 3:8-9; Hos. 4:13-14). For a fuller treatment of the material covered in this section, see J. Jensen, "Does *porneia* Mean Fornication? A Critique of Bruce Malina," *Novum Tetamentum* 20 (1978): 162-184.

12. Eduard Nielsen, *The Ten Commandments in New Perspective* (SBT 2/7; Naperville, IL: Allenson, 1968), 105-08. On the other hand, H. Schungel-Straumann, *Der Dekalog – Gottes Gebote?* (Stuttgarter Bibelstudien 67; Stuttgart: KBW, 1973), p. 51, is correct in rejecting Nielsen's further contention that the omission of the object "came in this way to be directed not only against every form of sexual offense (including sodomy and homosexuality) but also against religious apostasy" (Nielsen, p. 107).

13. See J. Bottéro and H. Petschow, "Homosexualität," *Reallexikon der Assyriologie und Vorderasiatischen Archäologie* 4 (Berlin/New York: Walter de Gruyter, 1972-75): 459-68. Among other examples listed, they give erotic dreams of men dreaming they are copulating with a god, the king, another prominent person, the man's father-in-law, another person's son, a young man, an infant, and a cadaver. A treatise in which divination is based on incidents in the subject's sex life includes four references to male intercourse: once with a social equal, once with a male cult prostitute, and twice with household members, free servant and slave. They note also a series of prayers with respect to love of a man for a woman, of a woman for a man, and of a man for a man; the same verb, which expresses the warm and sentimental side of attachment to others, is used in all three cases.

14. These can be found in J. B. Pritchard, ed., *Ancient Near Eastern Texts Relating to the Old Testament* (2d ed.; Princeton, NJ: Princeton University Press, 1955), p. 181.

15. The usual term for a male cult prostitute was *qādēš*, the masculine form of *qedēšâ*, "holy one," applied first to Ishtar, the goddess of love and fertility, and then, by way of identification, to female cult prostitutes. The term is found in passages such as 1 Kg. 15:12; 22:47; 2 Kg. 23:7. One text, Dt. 23:18-19, uses the term "dog" (*keleb*), a mode of designation found in Mesopotamia.

16. These texts can be found in Pritchard's *Ancient Near Eastern Texts*, pp. 423 and 413, respectively.

17. Bruce Vawter, *On Genesis: A New Reading* (Garden City, NY: Doubleday, 1977), pp. 233-36.

18. Bottéro-Petschow, pp. 463-67.

19. For one view on the difficult verses of Mt. 5:17-19, which seem to insist on the continuing validity of the Mosaic law, see especially John Meier, *The Vision of Matthew: Christ, Church, and Morality in the First Gospel* (New York: Paulist, 1979), pp. 222-36. Because this book is concerned with morality and was prompted in part by the CTSA report, *Human Sexuality* (New York: Paulist, 1977), it is relevant in its entirety.

20. Joseph A. Fitzmyer, "Pauline Theology," *The Jerome Biblical Commentary*, edited by R. E. Brown *et al.* (Englewood Cliffs, NJ: Prentice-Hall, 1968), 79:106.

21. Not only is the change from the seventh day to the first day a substantive one, but the manner of observance – which in the Old Testament consisted especially in repose from most physical activities, including lighting fires and cooking – has been radically reinterpreted.

22. See further, J. Jensen, "Old Testament, New Testament, and Christian Morality," *The Living Light* 12 (1975): 491-93.

23. "As Paul sees it, there are two dangers threatening the Christian freedom of the Galatians: (1) the acceptance of the Jewish Torah (5:2-12), and (2) the corruption of their life by the 'flesh' (5:13-24)." H. D. Betz, *Galatians: A Commentary on Paul's Letter to the Churches in Galatia* (Philadelphia: Fortress, 1979), p. 258.

24. In Ga. 5:16 Paul says that those who live in accord with the Spirit do not yield to the cravings of the flesh, and in vv. 22-23 he lists the "fruits of the Spirit," which are the antithesis of the "works of the flesh" (vv. 19-21). The "works of the flesh" include carnal sins, of course, but the range of reference includes all the sins of weak and fallen human nature, including envy, jealousy, etc.

25. Betz suggests that Paul's Judaizing opponents in Galatia were able to persuade the Christians there to accept the Torah precisely because of this difficulty: they were left with the Spirit and freedom but had no law to tell them what was right or wrong (Gal. 8-9).

26. The Greek term *porneia* is notoriously difficult, since it includes a wide range of meanings, including prostitution, marriage within forbidden degrees of kinship, and (figuratively) idolatry. Yet in a large number of passages *porneia* refers to wanton sexual behavior, perhaps in a more generalized sense but certain including fornication: *cf.* Mk. 7:21/Mt. 15:19; 1 Cor. 5:9-11; 7:2; 2 Cor. 12:21; Gal. 5:19, Eph. 5:3, 5; etc.

27. It is perhaps continuity with the Old Testament that leads Paul to come down so hard on the "incestuous Corinthian" (Paul calls it *porneia*) in 1 Cor. 5:1-5. The man had apparently taken his step-mother, a union forbidden by Lev. 18:8, though in modern Catholic parlance this would be affinity and the impediment could receive a dispensation.

28. From an article that has not yet appeared in print.

29. Whether this is totally new to Judaism is disputed. Joseph Fitzmyer, "The Matthean Divorce Texts and Some New Palestinian Evidence," *Theological Studies* 37 (1976): 197-226, finds that divorce was forbidden in certain circles of first-century Palestinian Judaism, but this reading of the evidence is questioned by Bruce Vawter, "Divorce and the New Testament," *Catholic Biblical Quarterly* 39 (1977): 528-42.

30. The matter is touched upon by both Fitzmyer and Vawter in the articles cited above. See also the excellent discussion on this point and on the whole matter of divorce in the New Testament by George MacRae, "New Testament Perspectives on Marriage and Divorce," in *Divorce and Remarriage in the Catholic Church,* edited by L. G. Wrenn (New York: Newman, 1973), pp. 1-15.

Chapter 2

Catholic Sexual Morality in the Patristic and Medieval Periods

The Reverend Francis Firth, C.S.B., S.T.D.

One of the first problems which confronts the researcher in this field, as in the biblical field, is the correct meaning of the terms used by various authors. For example, the Greek word *porneia,* derived from *pornē* (prostitute), is usually translated by the Latin word *fornicatio* and has come to be understood as "sexual intercourse between unmarried persons." However, this word in ancient times meant first of all "prostitution" and then came to be used more generally for sexual immorality. Thus it is used by St. Paul in 1 Cor. 5:1 to describe a union which is objectionable because incestuous. So when early Christian writers condemn both adultery and fornication as seriously sinful, it cannot immediately be concluded that all sexual intercourse between unmarried persons comes under that condemnation.

However, there is considerable evidence that many writers in the early Church did regard such intercourse as seriously wrong. For example, Tertullian, writing as a Montanist (member of a rigorist sect alienated from the Catholic Church) early in the third century, included all such intercourse among the sins for which the Church should grant no absolution, but should only urge the sinner to do penance in the hope of obtaining pardon ultimately from God.[1] Of course Tertullian as a Montanist was more rigorous than the Catholic Church of his time, but he could hardly have regarded this sin as beyond absolution if the Church had not traditionally regarded it as serious.

Again, St. Ambrose warns a maiden against glancing at the face of a youth lest she be caught in the sin of which Our Savior warned: "If anyone shall look at a woman to lust after her, he has already committed adultery with her in his heart."[2] And St. Augustine in a letter relates that he once questioned Count Marcellinus with pastoral solicitude lest he should perhaps have committed some sin that might require the remedy of public penance. He received the following reply: "I swear . . . that I have never had sexual intercourse outside my marriage, either before or after it."[3] In fact, a careful reading of St. Augustine's *Confessions* shows that when he says to God, "You enjoin continence," he understands that our Creator requires human beings to abstain from all extra-marital intercourse.[4]

In the early Church, pardon for very grave external sins could be obtained only by a process of public penance. A long period of fasting was required, followed by a public ceremony of reconciliation. This reconciliation would normally be granted only once in a lifetime. Those who fell seriously again were urged to enroll as penitents and hope for pardon from God.

This penance was generally only for external sins. While wicked thoughts and desires were understood to exclude one from the Kingdom of Heaven, yet it was considered sufficient to repent seriously for these and do some private penance before returning to communion. Now, while "fornication" was often listed among the gravest of crimes requiring solemn penance and even sometimes lifelong penance, some authorities considered that intercourse with only one person followed by marriage with that same person should be treated in somewhat the same way as sins of thought. Thus the Council of Elvira (Illiberis), a strict early council (about 300-303 A.D.) that followed even earlier traditions, demanded very severe penances, many of them lifelong, for various crimes. But it decreed as follows regarding pre-marital intercourse:

> Virgins who have not preserved their virginity, if they have married and remained with the same men who have had intercourse with them, because they have violated only the law of marriage are to be reconciled after a year without penance; or if they have had intercourse with other men, because they have committed adultery, it was decreed that only after five years and the completion of legitimate penance may they be reconciled.[5]

So pre-marital intercourse was considered as serious; it excluded one from the Eucharist for a year. But solemn penance was not always required.

Early Christian authorities were most concerned about complete intercourse, with some attention also to other sexual intimacies. So when St. Cyprian, Bishop of Carthage (249-258 A.D.), heard that some consecrated virgins were cohabiting with and even sleeping with men, he condemned such conduct and demanded that it be stopped at once. Those who disobeyed were to be excommunicated until they should reform and, if stubborn, might even be required to do public penance. However, if they obeyed at once and upon inspection by midwives the women were found to be still virgins, they could be admitted to communion. Only if their consecrated virginity was found to have been violated were the obedient ones required to do solemn penance. So St. Cyprian indicated that other sexual intimacies could be seriously sinful, but only for completed intercourse was public penance strictly required.[6]

In the early part of the Middle Ages many "penitential books" were written to instruct confessors concerning the penance to be imposed. These penances imply certain moral evaluations about the sins for which they are imposed. In these books much attention is paid to various sexual crimes, such as adultery, incest, etc. But grave penances are imposed also for intercourse between unmarried persons.[7]

When St. Thomas Aquinas, a little past the middle of the thirteenth century, comes to discuss the morality of such intercourse he analyzes the need for union of male and female human beings in marriage. He finds that the rearing and education of human offspring requires a much longer time than that of other animals and requires, if it is to be done well, the support of both father and mother. Hence he finds it wrong and against the purpose of sexual activity to perform the act by which offspring are generated except in a marriage. This is the general situation, he says, and the law, the universal law of morality, must conform to the general needs of the human race.[8] In this discussion St. Thomas finds reasonable grounds for the Christian moral teaching of centuries.

Of course adultery is condemned in all Christian tradition. In most of the Old Law, adultery is seen as violation of a man's exclusive right to his wife, but Christ and the whole Christian tradition regard intercourse of a married man with any woman (not his wife) as adultery. Christian marriage is monogamous and the husband is equally obliged to fidelity; this has been maintained throughout the whole history of the Church.[9]

Both the Jewish and the Greco-Roman backgrounds of Christianity condemned incest as very wicked, especially between close relatives. The early Christians followed this, for example, St. Paul in 1 Cor. 5:1-5. After some centuries, by reason of a certain confusion between the Roman and the Germanic methods of counting degrees of relationship, incest came to be extended to the seventh degree; marriage was considered by Church authorities as immoral and invalid with one's sixth cousin. Furthermore, affinity (relationship with in-laws) was considered on the authority of 1 Cor. 6:16 to be based on intercourse rather than on marriage. If one had heterosexual intercourse with someone, one immediately became brother or sister-in-law to that person's brothers and sisters and cousin-in-law to his or her cousins to the seventh degree. Unconsummated marriage or solemn engagement created a lesser, but real, impediment called public decency. Moreover, the impediment of spiritual relationship, between baptizers and sponsors at baptism or confirmation on the one hand and the baptized or confirmed person on the other, was extended to the children: if one's natural parent had been sponsor for someone, one might not marry that person; neither might one marry the god-parent of one's own child.[10]

All of this made it rather difficult to find a legitimate marriage partner, both among the nobility who were constrained by social convention to marry within their own class, and among the common people who were constrained by their lords to marry within the estate. As a result, the law came to be generally disregarded in the more remote degrees and the Church came to tolerate such marriages once they had been established. At the same time this law could be grounds for annulment. The result was a kind of divorce-by-annulment which became somewhat common for a few centuries until in 1215 the Fourth Lateran Council reduced the degrees of impediment to the fourth, at the same time insisting that the law be observed.[11] Thereafter legally recognized exceptions to this law could be only by papal dispensation.

Sexual morality then is closely connected with marriage; to understand Christian teaching about sex, we must try to understand Christian teaching about marriage. Generally early Christians were severe and ascetic. Virginity consecrated to God was seen as something especially pleasing to Him, a way of following the crucified Christ which had some affinity to martyrdom. Hence, with the notable exception of Clement of Alexandria (writing about 200 A.D.), practically all orthodox writers in the early Church who considered the matter evaluated celibacy undertaken for such motives as superior to the married life. This attitude continued all through the Middle Ages, in fact was intensified by medieval esteem for the monastic and religious life.

But there was another attitude to counterbalance this one. The Church from very early in its existence had to deal with various kinds of heretics who thought that matter was evil, not created by the good God. Hence, flesh was seen as evil as was all sexual activity. Other groups, besides, such as Encratites and Montanists, depreciated the value of marriage. Against all these, orthodox Christians had to defend the sanctity and positive value of marriage as something established by God and even the moral rightness of sexual activity as part of married life. This feature of the Church's teaching is succinctly expressed by a ruling of a council held at Gangra in Asia Minor about 340 A.D.: "If anyone is virgin or celibate, shunning marriage as something abominable and not on account of the very beauty and holiness of virginity, let him be anathema."[12]

Respect for marriage as something good and part of God's plan continued right through the Middle Ages. Sometimes when we read the enthusiastic praise of Christian authors for celibacy, this respect seems to have been forgotten, but orthodox writers were always careful to make clear that marriage was something good. This esteem was further encouraged by the necessity of combatting various heretical groups, such as in the twelfth and thirteenth centuries the

Albigensians, a kind of revival of the ancient Manichees.[13]

Of course the main basis for Christian esteem of marriage is found in the texts of Scripture which speak of its Divine origin, its renewal by Christ, and its symbolizing the union of Christ and His Church.[14] For these reasons most patristic writers speak of Christian marriage as something holy, differing in this from marriages of other persons. Because it is a symbol of Christ and His Church, it is in a special way indissoluble.[15] But a full development of the theology of marriage as one of the seven sacraments could not come until the twelfth century, when the definition of a sacrament as a "sacred sign" by which God confers grace had been worked out in the schools.[16]

In the course of this development two elements became especially clear in Western theology and canon law, as well as in the juridicial decisions of the Church courts, especially of the papal court. First, marriage is essentially a contract; hence it is produced by the free consent of the two parties. Provided that they freely consent to a monogamous, permanent union according to God's plan and the laws of the Church, no authority of parents, bishops or lords can render it invalid. Without this consent these authorities cannot bring it about.[17] Secondly, sexual intercourse has a central place in this affair. If sexual intercourse is impossible, the marriage is invalid. Mere sterility does not have this effect. The final, completely indissoluble character of this union is somehow brought about by sexual intercourse within the marriage.[18] It is marriage so conceived which came to be recognized in the twelfth century as one of the seven sacraments.

This brings us then to the morality and proper motivation of intercourse in marriage. Early Christian apologists boasted: "We do not marry except in order to bring up children, or else, renouncing marriage, we live in perfect continence."[19] Other early Christian writers expressed similar views, often restating them directly from the books of Stoic philosophers. They did not borrow such positions indiscriminately, however; they only took what they found to be in conformity with the gospel of Christ. The Stoic reasoning which they followed was very simple. It is obvious that the Creator has given us our sexual powers so that the human race may continue and the world be populated. To use these powers in a passionate way for mere pleasure to make oneself a slave of one's own body. Instead of reasonable control according to nature, this is degrading submission to irrational desires. Hence, these activities must be practiced only with

41

moderation for the purpose for which they were intended.[20] To have intercourse when the woman was already pregnant obviously cannot contribute to the increase of the human race. Hence some early Christian writers condemned this practice. Intercourse during either menstruation or pregnancy was also considered as dangerous for any child being conceived or brought to birth.[21]

One important factor in the early Christians' insistence on the procreative purpose of intercourse was their opposition to gnostic heretics who considered it wicked to beget a child and so imprison another spirit in matter.[22] The Manichees, successors to earlier Gnostics, were still more strongly opposed to this.

St. Augustine, great opponent of the Manichees, writing about 400 A.D., analyzed this matter more fully. Unlike the Greek Fathers, who under neoplatonic influences had interpreted Genesis as implying that the division of humanity into male and female was in view of the future Fall, Augustine in his later writings interpreted Genesis to mean that sexual intercourse between man and woman was according to God's original plan for the human race, and hence was something good of itself, even though, because of original sin, people were impelled towards it by "concupiscence" or disordered love, an evil effect of Adam's sin. However, in marriage intercourse was rendered free from sin, he said, by the three "goods" of marriage: offspring (their generation, nurture and education), fidelity (both to render the "debt" of marital intercourse when required and to abstain from intercourse with anyone else) and *sacramentum,* the sacred character of Christian marriage which renders it an indissoluble symbol of Christ's union with His Church.[23] This act is completely good only if performed for the right motives:

> The intercourse necessary for generation is without fault and it alone belongs to marriage. The intercourse that goes beyond this necessity no longer obeys reason, but passion. Still, not to demand this intercourse but to render it to a spouse, lest he sin by fornication, concerns the married person. But if both are subject to such concupiscence, they do something that manifestly does not belong to marriage.[24]

This reasoning may seem rather strange unless it is understood in relation to Augustine's understanding of morality in general. Right morality, he maintains, is essentially a rightly ordered love. This means first of all loving God with one's whole heart and soul so that whatever else is loved in any way is loved for God's sake and according to the order which He has established. So Augustine could write: "That person loves you (God) too little who loves along with you anything which he does not love for your sake."[25] In fact, he even goes so far as to say only the Three Persons of the Holy Trinity may legitimately be enjoyed. All other beings are to be used, not enjoyed, since they are to be loved only for God.[26] Hence in his *Confessions* he laments the disordered attraction he has to creatures for their own sake, for example, the joy he finds in the melody of hymns.[27]

It is not surprising, then, if he finds it not quite morally right to seek to have intercourse merely out of the attraction of its pleasure. To satisfy this attraction in marriage is venially sinful because it is a kind of moral weakness; in fact this is one of the purposes of marriage, to turn this moral weakness of carnal or youthful incontinence to a good purpose, the begetting of children, and to dignify intercourse by making it the action of parents.[28] This purpose of marriage, *remedium concupiscientiae,* is the basis of the duty of the *debitum*: the serious obligation of complying with any reasonable request of one's partner for intercourse; husband and wife in this matter have equal rights.[29]

St. Augustine finds still another purpose for marriage: natural companionship between the two sexes; this is most evident in the marriage of old people where other reasons may be lacking. But this is a purpose for marriage, not for intercourse. He would hope that such people by mutual consent would learn to refrain from intercourse and so dignify their union even more.[30]

In the Venerable Bede's *Historia Ecclesiastica Gentis Anglorum,* completed by 731 A.D. there is quoted a letter purported to have been sent by Pope St. Gregory the Great over a hundred years earlier in answer to some questions said to have been sent to him from St. Augustine of Canterbury in England. In this letter, whose authenticity has been seriously contested but not disproved,[31] it is said that marital intercourse which takes place under the impulse of "fleshly desire" is in some sense sinful, and those who engage in it are to abstain from entering a church and from reception of the Eucharist for a short time. If, however, not sexual impulse but the desire to beget children dominates, there is no sin and one may enter the church and partake of the Eucharist at once.[32] The writer of this letter seems to be interpreting St. Augustine's understanding of ordered and disordered love. However, this point was generally missed by subsequent medieval writers who used isolated sentences and short passages from this letter in their collections of texts and decrees. The substitution of *voluptas* (pleasure) for *voluntas* (desire) soon gave the impression that Pope Gregory had said that sexual pleasure itself was sinful. Since intercourse cannot take place without this pleasure, some authors came to claim that intercourse, even in marriage, could not take place without some sin, at least venial.[33] The same letter forbade intercourse during pregnancy and after childbirth until the child was weaned, also during times of menstruation. In all of this the influence of the Old Testament is clear. However, the author of the letter rejected many Old Testament strictures no longer applicable in the time of Christ's Kingdom.[34]

The penitential books of the Middle Ages often contained directives derived from this letter. After intercourse, unless performed purely for the purpose of generating children, one might not enter a church or partake of the Eucharist for a time. The act came to be forbidden on Sundays and feast days, in Lent and on days of fasting; both feast days and fast days came to be multiplied. This emphasis on sexual abstinence before communion was probably based on notions of ritual purity which in the Old Testament required priests to abstain before performing the sacred rites and to St. Paul's remark in I Cor. 7:5 about abstaining for the sake of prayer. At the same time it was emphasized that neither married partner might abstain without the other's consent. Some books even insisted that this obligation would override considerations of sacred time and place.[35]

St. Thomas Aquinas in the thirteenth century comes to essentially the same conclusions as St. Augustine about the morality of intercourse in marriage. Unless it is motivated by the purpose of procreation or performed in response to a demand of one's married partner, then at least venial sin is involved.[36] However, he does maintain that if one perceives one's partner needs or wants to have intercourse, but is too shy to ask, one would be obliged to propose it.[37] Such intercourse would no doubt be free of sin on one's own part.

All of this is based on a theory of total love for God which is very like that of Augustine's, but with some differences. According to Aquinas, God has put real goodness into creatures; this goodness comes from God and is directed to Him as Ultimate Goal.[38] Hence creatures should be loved for their own goodness, not merely used.[39] However, this love, like all human love, should ultimately be for love of God.[40] By charity one is oriented to God and lives for Him.[41] Pleasure, as Aquinas sees it, is good if it is connected with an activity that is itself good.[42] Hence the pleasure of legitimate, rightly motivated intercourse may reasonably be willed.[43] Aquinas taught that there would have been sexual intercourse even if there had been no sin and that it would have been more pleasurable than now, because he considered pleasure as the proper overflow of natural and virtuous actions.[43a] Pleasure of itself, in his view, is not a proper goal of activity, but is the rest of the appetite in a good possessed. It gets its whole value from some worthwhile good, such as health or understanding of the truth, in which one finds satisfaction.[44]

However, Aquinas refuses to say that intercourse in marriage performed merely for pleasure is necessarily a mortal sin. It would be mortally sinful if a man in this regarded his wife just as any woman, and were prepared to act that way with any woman. But if he regards her as his wife, with whom he is one flesh, the deordination of the act towards pleasure is not serious.[45]

It might seem, then, that the marriage act could be free from all sin if motivated by some worthwhile good, such as health or legitimate relaxation, other than the matrimonial goods of offspring and fidelity. But Aquinas does not agree:

> Although to intend the conservation of health is of itself not evil, nevertheless this intention becomes evil if health is sought from something that is not of itself ordained for this, just as if someone were to seek from the sacrament of baptism only bodily health.[46]

Aquinas seems to find ordinary human life shot through with easy opportunities for venial deordination of the human will, but under God's grace this does not prevent Christians from living primarily for God in charity.[47] Like many medieval theologians, he saw that it was not easy even for virtuous married people to be free of selfishness in the way they conduct marital relations. The same is true of most human activities where pleasure plays an urgent role.

Since Christians have insisted so strongly down through the history of the Church on the orientation of sexual intercourse towards procreation and educational rearing of children, it is not surprising to find them condemning contraception. What is surprising is that many of the earliest writers are not so clear on this point. This can be attributed to a number of factors. First, their condemnation of contraception is often associated with their condemnation of homicide and sometimes it is hard to distinguish which is meant. Infanticide and abortion were all too common in the Greco-Roman civilization of ancient times.[48] Some of the potions condemned had or were thought to have the effect of producing both abortion and sterility; it is not always clear whether or not both abortion and sterilization were considered wrong.[49] There is another problem with potions. Many poisons and similar drugs were considered to work by some kind of magic. For Christians this meant by the power of evil spirits. To look for efficacy from this source was usually considered as a form of idolatry. It is often hard to tell whether potions are condemned for this reason or because of the effect they are thought to produce.[50]

When it comes to aberrations from the regular forms of intercourse, again it is often not clear whether "unnatural" practices as anal or oral intercourse are meant or an action like that of Onan or something else.[51] When texts do refer to Onan it is often uncertain whether he is blamed for frustrating the effect of intercourse or for injustice to his dead brother in not acting so as to fulfill the purpose of the Levirate law.[52] Also, a number of ancient and medieval authorities followed the Old Testament in condemning intercourse during menstruation; some considered it wrong during pregnancy, and some also during lactation. These prohibitions were perhaps intended as a kind of protection for the mother in her weakened condition or for the child. Some ancient medical opinions considered that children conceived during menstruation were likely to be deformed; or the danger of harming an unborn child was feared.[53] But intercourse during pregnancy was sometimes condemned because it could not lead to procreation; it was like seeding a field that was already producing a crop.[54]

It is not surprising, then, if scholars disagree about the moral stand of early Christian writers about contraception. A study published about eighteen years ago by A.-M. Dubarle finds no certain condemnation of this practice before St. Augustine.[55] Two other studies, by R. S. Callewaert and John T. Noonan, published about two years later, do find several of the earlier writers condemning some form of contraception.[56] All of them agree that St. Augustine of Hippo is quite explicit in his condemnation. He denounces the Manichean practice of avoiding intercourse when, according to their theory, a woman is likely to conceive, although here it seems to be their determination to avoid all offspring that is most at fault. He condemns also "poisons of sterility" and the method of Onan.[57] Similar views were expressed by his slightly later contemporary, St. Cyril of Alexandria.[58] About a hundred years later St. Caesarius of Arles in southern France inculcated Augustine's views with pastoral zeal.[59] This teaching, given a sharper edge by the constant danger from some form of the Manichean heresy, became established in medieval pastoral writing, especially in the penitential books.[60]

In his logical analysis of the reasons for monagamous marriage, St. Thomas Aquinas says:

> It is good for everything to gain its end and evil for it to be diverted from its due end. But as in the whole, so also in the parts, our endeavour should be that every part of the human being and every act of his may attain its due end. Now though the semen is superfluous for the preservation of the individual, yet it is necessary to him for the propagation of the species. . . . The emission of semen then ought to be so directed as that both proper generation may ensue and the education of the offspring be secured.
>
> Hence it is clear that every emission of the semen is contrary to the good of man which takes place in a way whereby generation is impossible; and if this is done on purpose, it must be a sin. I mean a way in which generation is impossible *in itself*, as is the case in every emission of the semen without the natural union of male and female; wherefore such sins are called "sins against nature." But if it is *by accident* that generation cannot follow from the emission of the semen, the act is not against nature on that account, nor is it sinful; the case of the woman being barren would be a case in point. . . .
>
> The inordinate emission of the semen [as in fornication] is repugnant to the good of nature, which is the conservation of the species. Hence after the sin of murder, whereby a human nature already in existence is destroyed, this sort of sin seems to hold second place, whereby the generation of human nature is precluded.[61]

This analysis might seem to presuppose some premises now known to be false, namely the desirability of producing as many human beings as possible and the relative scarcity of semen available. As regards the first of these, as John T. Noonan has pointed out,[62]

Aquinas does not make indefinite reproduction an absolute good; for in this same discussion he judges that it is seriously wrong to have intercourse according to nature except within a marriage, where in the normal course of events the rearing and education of the offspring can be properly provided for. As regards the relative scarcity of semen, this is not his only consideration in demanding proper orientation for sexual activity. Elsewhere he says:

> No wise person should allow himself to lose something except for some compensation of an equal or better good. Therefore the choice of something that has a loss attached to it needs to have some good connected with it which by compensating for that loss makes the thing ordinate and right. Now there is a loss of reason incidental to the union of man and woman, both because the reason is carried away entirely on account of the vehemence of the pleasure, so that it is unable to understand anything at that time, as the Philosopher says (Aristotle, *Ethics*, 7.11.4; 1152b18), and because of the *tribulation of the flesh* which such persons have to suffer from solicitude for temporal things, as is explained in 1 Cor. 7.18. Consequently the choice of this union cannot be made ordinate except by certain compensations whereby that same union is righted; and these are the goods which excuse marriage and make it right.[63]

These are the three "goods of marriage" explained by St. Augustine: offspring, fidelity and *sacramentum:* they are intrinsic to Christian marriage. Hence intercourse outside of marriage, as also any intercourse which is not in harmony with these features and goals of marriage, is disordered and sinful. It is incompatible with a properly ordered love for God and for those creatures which God has made in His own image and likeness, destined to share in His glory.[64]

This applies then, not only to deliberate frustration of procreation within marriage, but even more to actions such as bestial or homosexual or anal or oral intercourse.[65] These have been regarded as wicked in the whole history of Christian moral teaching.[66] Masturbation, however, did not come in for much notice or condemnation until the medieval penitential books began to appear; therein the penance for it, especially for boys, was much lighter than for other sins.[67] However, according to St. Thomas Aquinas' logical analysis, masturbation by its nature would be a more serious sin than fornication.[68]

Concluding Remarks

Catholic sexual morality thus has its beginning from the gospel message and from Christian consciences appreciating its teaching about God's love for humankind and the love that people should have for God and for one another and about sex and marriage, their purposes and their place in human life. These insights have been expanded and developed with the help of Greek philosophy. In this they are like many other items of Christian and Catholic teaching; for example, our notion of spiritual substance, a reality without size or shape or colour, comes from Greek philosophy. The question is not: "Does it come from Greek philosophy?" Rather we ask: "Is this a legitimate and true insight into the real meaning of the gospel message and has it been so accepted and taught by the Church of Christ?" What has been so taught must still be true.

One of the most important insights of both Augustine's and Aquinas' is their understanding of "natural law." This is not so much a "law" in the juridical sense as a truth, or complexus of moral truths, about the purpose of human life and the rightness of human activity. These have their source in the eternal plan of God's for His creation; this plan has been implanted into the natures of things in the creation and can be perceived, with considerable difficulty, by human minds who perceive what things are and how they are intended to interact.[69] Especially it is the nature of human beings that must be understood, their orientation and purpose, and how they ought to use their powers and relate to one another according to what it right and reasonable. St. Thomas at the beginning of the long discussion quoted above puts it this way:

> God has care of everything according to what is good for it. Now it is good for everything to gain its end, and evil for it to be diverted from its due end.[70]

This moral insight of St. Thomas Aquinas' comes from his own understanding of Christian truth, especially as taught by St. Augustine,[71] and from his analysis of human nature with the help of Aristotle's philosophy.

Notes

1. ". . . a man who has intercourse outside of marriage makes himself guilty of adultery and fornication, wheresoever the place and whosoever the woman." *De pudicitia (On Purity)* c. 4, translated by William P. LeSaint, in *Ancient Christian Writers* 28 (Baltimore: Newman Press,

1959): 61-62. The passage is puzzling in some ways and in part speaks of violent assault, but an examination of the whole context supports this rendering.

2. Mt. 5:28; see Ambrose, *De paenitentia* 1.14.68, in *Sources chretiennes* 179, edited by Roger Gryson (Paris: Cerf, 1971): 110.

3. Epist. 151 *Ad Caecilianum* 3, translated by Sister Wilfrid Parsons, in *The Fathers of the Church* 20:276.

4. See *Confessions*, Book 2.1-3.1.8; Book 4.2.2; Book 6.15.25; Book 10.29.40. Augustine, after some youthful irregularities, remained true to one concubine for about eleven years until separated from her under the influence of his mother in view of a projected marriage; then he took another for a short time. He afterwards looked on all of this as foul and very sinful. See John T. Noonan, Jr., *Contraception* (Cambridge, MA: Harvard University Press, 1966), p. 125.

5. C.14; Carl Joseph von Hefele, *Histoire des conciles,* translated by Henri Leclercq, 1.1:230.

6. See Epist. 61 *Ad Pomponium,* in *Ante-Nicene Fathers* 5, edited by C. Coxe (New York: Scribners, 1903; Grand Rapids, MI: Eerdmans, 1957): 356-58.

7. For example, in the penitential ascribed to St. Bede the Venerable, c. 3, no. 1: "Adulescens si cum virgine peccaverit, annum I peniteat." F. W. H. Wasserschleben, *Die Bussordnungen der abendlandischen Kirche* (Graz, 1851), p. 221. Cf. Robert of Flamborough, *Liber poenitentialis,* edited by Francis Firth (Toronto: Pontifical Institute of Medieval Studies, 1971), pp. 231, 235-36, 243. This popular book of instructions for the confessor, composed about 1210, is based on sources that are much earlier.

8. See *Summa Contra Gentiles* 3.122, in *The Pocket Aquinas,* edited by Vernon J. Bourke (New York: Washington Square Press, 1960), pp. 219-22; *ST.* 2-2.154.2; *On Evil (De malo)* 15.1,2; Noonan, pp. 279-82. Earlier authors spoke sometimes in this connection about the importance of proper upbringing for the child; see Noonan, pp. 84, 127, 152. Other implications of St. Thomas's reasoning in these texts will be discussed near the end of this chapter (pp. 00-00).

9. See Anthony Kosnik *et al., Human Sexuality: New Directions in American Catholic Thought* (New York: Paulist Press, 1966), pp. 14, 24, 148-49. Cf. F. Van der Meer, *Augustine as Bishop,* translated by Brian Battershaw and G. R. Lamb (New York: Sheed and Ward, 1961), pp. 180-83.

10. See Robert of Flamborough, pp. 78-85, 197 with n. 52, 232-35, 298.

11. Cap. 50; Hefele-Leclercq 5.2:1372-73. Cf. C. Henry, "Affinity" and "Consanguinity," *New Catholic Encyclopedia* (1967) 1 and 4.

12. C. 9; Hefele-Leclercq 1.2:1036.

13. Regarding both of these attitudes, see Joseph E. Kerns, *The Theology of Marriage* (New York: Sheed and Ward, 1964), pp. 13-30.

14. See above, chapter 1, pp. 30-33.

15. See L. Godefroy, "Mariage: Le mariage au tempts des Pères," *Dictionnaire de théologie catholique* 9.2:2101-18.

16. See G. LeBras, "Mariage: La doctrine du mariage chez les théologiens et les canonistes depuis l'an mille," *Dict. de théol. cath.* 9.2:2196-219.

17. See ibid., cols. 2132-207; C. Donahue, "Pope Alexander III on the Formation of Marriage," *International Congress of Medieval Canon Law, Toronto, 21-25 August, 1972* (Vatican City, 1976: see also *Bulletin of Medieval Canon Law* n.s. 3 [1973]: xii; 5 [1975]: xii).

18. See LeBras, cols. 2138-197; Robert of Flamborough, pp. 64-66, 88. When in the thirteenth century canonists and theologians came to agree that marriage was formed by mutual consent externally expressed, it had already been firmly established in canon law that even after this consent had been expressed, provided the marriage was not consummated, either party might enter a religion of solemn vows and the other was then free to marry. See *ST.* suppl. 61.2-3; text from *Sent.* 4.17.1.3.2-3; also James A. Coriden, *The Indissolubility Added to Christian Marriage by Consummation* (Rome: Univ. Greg. extract, 1961).

19. St. Justin, *First Apology,* c. 29, in *Early Christian Fathers,* edited by C. C. Richardson (New York: Macmillan, 1970), p. 260; cf. Athenagoras, *Plea for the Christians* c. 33, in *Early Christian Fathers,* p. 337; also Kerns, p. 45.

20. See Noonan, pp. 46-49, 76-85.

21. See ibid., pp. 60-69, 77-85, 281-82.

22. See ibid., pp.95-98.

23. See *The Good of Marriage (De bono conjugali)* edited by R. J. Deferrari, esp. c. 6 (no. 6) and c. 24 (no. 32), in *The Fathers of the Church* 27:16-17, 47-49; Godefroy, cols. 2093-96, 2105-09.

24. *The Good of Marriage* c. 10 (no. 11), p. 24. Cf. Noonan, pp. 126-30.

25. *Confessions* 10.29-40. Some translations render *minus* here as, "so much the less." But surely in this context it means (as the comparative can often mean in Latin) "too little."

26. See *Christian Instruction (De doctrina christiana)*, translated by John J. Gavigan, 1.22-33, in *The Fathers of the Church* 2:41-54.

27. See Book 10, ch. 29-40.

28. See *The Good of Marriage* c. 3 (no. 3), pp. 12-13.

29. See ibid., c. 4 (no. 4), pp. 13-14.

30. See ibid., c. 3 (no. 3), pp. 12-13.

31. See Noonan, p. 150, n. 9.

32. See Venerable Bede, *Historia Ecclesiastica Gentis Anglorum* (Bede's Ecclesiastical History of the English Nation), Book 1, c. 27, answers 8 and 9, edited by Bertram Colgrave and R. A. B. Mynors (Oxford, Clarendon Press, 1969), pp. 94-103.

33. See Robert of Flamborough, pp. 236-39; Kerns, pp. 46-65; Noonan, pp. 197-98.

34. See Bede, pp. 88-93.

35. See Robert of Flamborough, pp. 97-98, 198, 236-39; *ST*. Suppl. 64.7 (*Sent*. 4.32.5.3).

36. "In only two ways do married people come together without any sin: for the sake of generating offspring and of rendering the *debitum*. Otherwise there is always sin involved, at least venial," or, "Otherwise there is always at least venial sin involved." *ST*. Suppl. 49.5c (*Sent*. 4.31.2.2). (Translations by the author.)

37. See *ST*. Suppl. 64.2 (*Sent*. 4.32.2.1).

38. See *ST*. 1.6.4; *On Truth* 21.4.

39. See *ST*. 2-2.25.1.4,5,7; *De caritate* 7.

40. See *ST*. 1-2.1.6.109.3.

41. St. Thomas finds that a Christian in the state of grace who has intercourse motivated by pleasure does not break this more fundamental orientation: "Although he does not actually refer the pleasure to God, he does not place his will's last end therein; otherwise he would seek it anywhere indifferently. Hence it does not follow that he enjoys a creature; but he uses a creature actually for his own sake, and himself habitually, though not actually, for God's sake." *ST*. Suppl. 49.6 ad 3 (*Sent*. 4.31.2.3). Aquinas is here using the terms "enjoy" and "use" in their Augustinian sense of "find ultimate satisfaction in" and "refer to a further end" (as they were used in the objection).

42. See *ST*. 1-2.34.1,2.

43. See *ST*. Suppl. 49.4 ad 3 (*Sent*. 4.31.2.1); *ST*. 1-2.34.1 ad 1. Cf. Noonan, pp. 292-94.

43a. See *ST*. 1.90.2.

44. See *ST*. 1-2.3.4; 4.2; 1-2.34.1,2; Noonan, *loc. cit.*

45. See *ST*. Suppl. 49.6 (*Sent*. 4.31.2.3).

46. *ST*. 49.5 ad 4 (*Sent*. 4.31.2.2); cf. Noonan. p. 242.

47. See above n. 41.

48. See Noonan, pp. 85-88.

49. See Noonan, pp. 90-95, 144: R. S.Callewaert, "Les penitentiels du Moyen Age et les pratiques anticonceptionelles," *Vie spirituelle* Suppl. 18 (1965): 353-54, 357, 364-65.

50. See Noonan, pp. 137, 144; Callewaert, p. 364.

51. See Noonan, pp. 222-27.

52. See Noonan, pp. 34-35, 101-02; A.-M. Dubarle, "La Bible et les Pères ont-ils parle de la contraception?" *Vie spirituelle* Suppl. 15 (1962):598.

53. See Noonan, p. 85; Callewaert, p. 354; Robert of Flamborough, p. 238.

54. See Noonan, p. 77.

55. See Dubarle, pp. 589-603; 608-10.

56. See Callewaert, pp. 344-46; Noonan, pp. 77-81, 93-101. Both of these authors find St. Jerome and St. John Chrysostom, for example, explicit enough in condemning contraception.

57. See Noonan, pp. 119-39; Dubarle, pp. 604-07; Callewaert, p. 346. Callewaert says that

for Augustine the kind of means used (rhythm or other) makes absolutely no difference.

58. See Noonan, p. 138 n.; Dubarle, pp. 607-08; Callewaert, pp. 346-47.

59. See A.-M. Dubarle, "La contraception chez saint Césaire d'Arles," *Vie spirituelle* Suppl. 16 (1963):515-19; Noonan, pp. 145-47; Callewaert, pp. 347-50.

60. See Noonan, pp. 148-99; Callewaert, pp. 350-66.

61. *Summa cont. Gent.* 3.122 in *Pocket Aquinas,* pp. 219-22. Cf. *ST.* 2-2.152.2; *On Evil* 15.1,2; Noonan, pp. 238-46.

62. See Noonan, pp. 279-81.

63. *ST.* Suppl. 49.1c (*Sent.* 4.31.1.1).

64. This is St. Thomas's notion of a mortal sin: one which is incompatible with charity; see *ST.* 2-2.24.12.

65. See Noonan, pp. 238-46. Noonan points out that Aquinas considered that an inversion of position between man and woman was also against nature and mortally sinful.

66. Tertullian as a Montanist declared that all such carnal acts *ultra iura naturae* were not mere sins but monstrosities; see *On Purity* c.4, in *Ancient Christian Writers* 28:62. Most authors in the early Church who speak of such things simply condemn the vice of "corrupting boys;" e.g., Didache 2.2, in *Early Christian Fathers,* p. 172. Medieval penitential books are more specific, while often preserving a prudent reticence about details; see, e.g., Robert of Flamborough, pp. 195-97, 229-31. In all of these sources such acts are considered very serious. Cf. Noonan, pp. 77, 223-27. Although one recent work (John Boswell, *Christianity, Social Tolerance, and Homosexuality* [Chicago: University of Chicago Press, 1980] argues that the Church really did not oppose homosexuality until the Middle Ages, the teaching of the early Church Fathers indicates to the contrary as evident from the sources cited above.

67. See Robert of Flamborough, pp. 196-97, 229, 242. The word *molles* (sing., *mollis*) found in the Latin Vulgate 1 Cor. 6:10 was thought to refer to this vice, which hence came to be called *mollities.*

68. See *ST.* 2-2.154.11,12.

69. See *ST.* 1-2.91.1, 2.93, 94; Etienne Gilson, *The Christian Philosophy of St. Thomas Aquinas,* translated by L. K. Shook (New York: Random House, 1956), pp. 264-67.

70. *Summa cont. Gent.* 3.122, in *Pocket Aquinas,* p. 219.

71. See Etienne Gilson, *The Christian Philosophy of St. Augustine,* translated by L. E. M. Lynch (New York: Random House, 1960), pp. 90-93, 130-31.

Chapter 3

The Development of Catholic Doctrine Concerning Sexual Morality 1300-1918

James F. Hitchcock, Ph.D.

The rise of Nominalist theology and philosophy in the fourteenth century tended to have a general effect of stressing the voluntary and indeed even arbitrary character of God's dealings with men, since rational principles were no longer deemed adequate to expound a natural law which was clear and forthright. The followers of the leading Schoolman of the century, William of Ockham, for example, tended to expound morality according to the Ten Commandments, stressing prohibitions over virtues or positive moral principles.[1] Thus, as might be expected, there was little tendency to revise traditional ideas about marriage in the light of changing customs, if such a change did in fact occur.

However, the dominance of the Nominalists should not be over-stressed. Realism, with its general belief in a rational natural law, continued strong in many universities. The leading realists of the previous century, especially St. Albert and St. Thomas, had diverged from the Augustinian tradition in certain respects. While they were far from identifying human practice with moral rightness, they were less inclined than the Nominalists to posit a moral law whose claim on people was largely authoritarian.

Humanism

The fourteenth and fifteenth centuries also saw the development of the movement known as Humanism, the flowering of the larger movement known as the Renaissance. For nearly five hundred years the exact nature of these movements, and their real significance, have been debated by historians and others. At a minimum it is safe to say that they represented an intense interest in the classical culture of the ancients, a largely literary preoccupation. However, an interest in Greek and Latin literature for its esthetic qualities was not likely in ignore content as well. To a degree not easy to determine, some Renaissance humanists imbibed pagan attitudes towards marriage, sexuality, and human behavior generally that were at odds with Christian teaching. The importation of classical pagan norms meant that, in some rather restricted circles, practices like adultery, divorce, and homosexuality had a respectability officially denied them by the Church. In some instances these new attitudes reached even into fairly high clerical circles.[2]

But the explicit effect of Humanist ideas on Catholic moral doctrine was almost non-existent. The Church's official theologians were the Scholastics, whether Realist or Nominalist. While some Humanists could perhaps be called theologians, they had no public status as such, nor were their ideas considered relevant to the Church's teaching mission. In addition, Humanism did not radically change existing beliefs. For example, perhaps the most daring of the Humanists was Lorenzo Valla. He actually proposed a kind of Christian Epicureanism, in which the highest good of man is pleasure. However, he pointed out that the ultimate pleasure is Heaven. In good Epicurean fashion, he urged that it is wise to forego lesser pleasures for the sake of greater ones. Thus Christians should lead chaste lives; the pursuit of bodily pleasure would be justifiable only to someone who did not believe in life after death.[3]

In Northern Europe, in the latter fifteenth century, there emerged a movement called Christian Humanism, founded by people who were to various degrees uncomfortable with the undigested paganism of the Italian Renaissance. In particular the Christian Humanists proposed the intense study of Scripture as the proper activity of the believing scholar.

The "prince of humanists" was Desiderius Erasmus, of Rotterdam, a monk who lived as a layman, a vowed religious who seems to have had grave doubts about the legitimacy of the life of celibacy and of the monastic vocation generally. Suspected of heresy in his own time, Erasmus has ever since been proposed as a kind of "liberal" in Church matters. However, his own treatise on marriage was highly traditional.[4] His friend Thomas More, a married man and father of a family, was also one of the greatest of the Christian Humanists. But More's faith did not depart from common Catholic teaching on any significant point, including marriage or sexuality.[5]

It was among the Scholastics who enjoyed quasi-official status that some developments took place. In general, the history of the Catholic doctrine of sexuality over the next five hundred years can be summarized fairly succinctly – sexual activity is intended for the procreation of children and may be legitimately engaged in only in marriage when the possibility of such procreation is present. Whatever divergence existed among theologians on the question concerned how conscious and explicit the motive of procreation had to be, whether there were lesser motives which had a validity of their own, and, if so, to what extent these justified sexual activity. During this long period no reputable theologian justified the direct thwarting of procreation, although a few permitted its avoidance in extreme cases.[6]

Theology of Marriage

A study of Catholic moral teaching during this very long period also necessarily focuses on the theology of marriage and its purposes. Not a great deal of attention was paid to activities like adultery, fornication, homosexuality, bestiality, or masturbation. In some cases (e.g., homosexuality), writers seem to have been deliberately reticent, as though dealing with subjects not really fit for open discussion. But beyond this, there was not much that needed to be said. Given the stated purposes of sexual activity, all of the above practices stood overwhelmingly condemned. Adultery, besides violating marital rights, either aimed to avoid offspring or produced offspring in situations where the proper spiritual nurture of the child would be impaired. Fornication did the same. Homosexuality or bestiality were profoundly contrary to nature, perversions of God's purpose for man. Masturbation wasted the seed intended for the begetting of children, and was additionally unnatural in its perversion of an act intended to involve male-female complimentarity. Permeating all these actions was lust, an inordinate seeking of selfish pleasure (of which extra-marital activity was considered an expression virtually by definition, since it involved no permanent commitment to the partner nor responsibility to children who might be born).[7] Indeed, it was the possibility of lust in marriage, and to what degree it could be accommodated, to which a good deal of moral theology addressed itself.

Motives for Intercourse

The possibility of three distinct but possibly interrelated motives for marital intercourse was recognized by theologians in the late medieval and early modern periods – procreation, avoidance of fornication, and pleasure. The first was beyond question legitimate. The other two were questionable but possibly valid as concessions.

Marriage as an alternative to fornication seemed to have the authority of St. Paul behind it, although this in itself, since it was in the nature of a concession, did not necessarily mean that no sin was involved. Although it was never a universally held opinion, some theologians in fact believed that all acts of intercourse involved at least venial sin.

In the fourteenth century Peter of Palude and St. Bernardine of Siena (the latter in some respects a rigorist) admitted the legitimacy of marital intercourse as an alternative to fornication, even when there was no possibility (as during pregnancy) of conceiving children.[8] In the fifteenth century this position was upheld by Martin LeMaistre, although he was not really part of the theological mainstream of his age.[9]

By the sixteenth century, however, this opinion had become the dominant one, taught by the most influential theologian of the early part of the century, Cajetan (Giacamo de Vio Gaetano), as well as

56

Dominic Soto and the catechisms both of the Council of Trent and of St. Peter Canisius. Sylvester Prierias, the papal theologian of the age, approved it cautiously.[10]

Marital intercourse solely for pleasure had generally been condemned, the main disagreement being whether it was a mortal or venial sin. Interestingly, this condemnation was perhaps motivated in part by a desire to recognize the dignity of women, who were not to be used simply as "sex objects." Thus Bernardine of Siena, in the fourteenth century, answered the hypothetical objection, "Why can I not use my wife as I see fit?" by replying, "She is not yours but God's."[11]

In the fifteenth century Martin LeMaistre admitted the possibility of pleasure as a motive, albeit cautiously. However, as already noted, he was rather out of the mainstream of theology and did not have great influence. In the sixteenth century the Scottish Catholic theologian John Major, a Scholastic who taught at Paris, also admitted both the avoidance of fornication and pleasure as legitimate motives, although he too was a somewhat eccentric figure. The LeMaistre-Major position had no patristic or medieval precedents, and it was rejected by Cajetan, Soto, and the other leading theologians of the sixteenth century.[12]

Questions of population, both negative and positive, sometimes entered the discussions, although not in a definitive way. Duns Scotus, for example, had enjoined a duty to procreate in order to populate heaven, but the Thomistic tradition explicitly rejected this, and it was always a minority view. Despite the disastrous reduction in European population caused by the Black Death in the mid-fourteenth century, no theologian urged the moral necessity of restoring numbers to society.[13] However, the general duty of propagating the human race was of course always taken as an obligation.

From fairly early times the duty of producing offspring was always seen as implying the duty of raising them, which included, especially, their proper spiritual formation. This tended to temper any notion that parents were obligated to produce as many children as possible. In the fourteenth century Peter of Palude had cautiously suggested that a couple might avoid conception because of dire poverty. In the sixteenth century this was upheld by Soto and condemned by Prierias.[14]

The Protestant Reformation

The Protestant Reformation of the sixteenth century had one major effect on sexual attitudes – it denied the primacy of celibacy over marriage and in general discouraged celibacy except in rare instances. The Christian vocation was then seen as almost inevitably including marriage.[15]

There was no radical change in sexual ethics as a result, however. Adultery, fornication, homosexuality, bestiality, and abortion remained condemned as before. So for the most part did divorce – Martin Luther, for example, was one of the European theologians who condemned Henry VIII's divorce from Catherine of Aragon, and his abhorrence of divorce was so intense that he once advised a German prince that bigamy was preferable.[16] If anything, the new centrality of marital life in Protestant thought might have reinforced a determination not to admit any forms of sexual pollution or anything which tended towards the undermining of marriage.

Curiously, in a somewhat roundabout way the Reformation may have induced something of a softening of Catholic teaching. Since the major Reformers like Luther and John Calvin espoused an Augustinian theory of justification, Augustinian theology fell under something of a cloud. As a result the Augustinian idea of the sex act as inherently sinful tended also to fall into neglect. St. Robert Bellarmine, one of the leading Jesuit theologians of the Counter-Reformation, was among those rejecting Augustine's idea that original sin is transmitted through the marital act itself.[17]

At least since Aquinas, some theologians had spoken of love and friendship as appropriate to marriage (not a self-evident proposition when the majority of marriages were arranged). The Council of Trent also spoke highly of marital love, although that theme was not touched on in the new Counter-Reformation catechisms. The Council made no connection between marital love and sexual intercourse.[18]

Jansenism

Especially in the French-speaking lands, the new movement called Jansenism arose in the early seventeenth century from a variety of causes – exposure to Calvinist theology, revival in reaction to late-medieval Scholasticism of a study of the original works of St. Augustine, and the desire of devout Catholics for a more rigorous and demanding faith than that which they often found being practiced around them. Jansenism to some extent developed in symbiotic relationship to the newly developing science of moral casuistry, which, while there were few radical departures from traditional teaching, did tend to a certain permissiveness in the practical application of those teachings.[19] Such laxity was especially associated with the Jesuits, and was wittily scored by Blaise Pascal in his *Provincial Letters*.

In general, Jansenistically inclined theologians, dominant in France until the nineteenth century, returned to the classical notion that the conscious purpose of procreation alone rendered the act of intercourse entirely sinless. (In practice it would seem that few if any acts were characterized by such purity of intention.) Although the genealogy is by no means clear, it is often said that Jansenist influences entered the Irish Church through the seminary at Maynooth founded at the end of the eighteenth century. In fact, certain Irish Franciscans were strong influences on Jansen himself at Louvain. Allegedly, Jansenist influences then entered the United States both through the French Sulpicians so influential in the early history of Catholic America and through the later Irish clergy.[20]

It is necessary, however, to be clear as to exactly what is meant by Jansenism. When Innocent XI condemned a number of "laxist" propositions in 1679, he did not include among them the notion that intercourse was permissible as an alternative to fornication. Neither, in condemning Jansenist propositions, did the popes of the age condemn their rigorist views of the question.[21] The heretical elements in Jansenism involved its theory of justification and attitudes towards Church authority, not its moral doctrines. What is often called Jansenism in morality is simply the survival of the ancient tradition of rigorism which the Church has had to moderate again and again throughout her history.

The Jesuit Thomas Sanchez (d. 1610) was probably the most important of the "laxist" theologians of the age and was among those attacked by Pascal. Sanchez taught that the motive for sexual intercourse was essentially irrelevant to its morality, although a motive of pleasure alone was probably a venial sin. Several other seventeenth-century authorities were prepared to justify the pleasure motive, provided it was not exclusive, a position strongly attacked especially by the theologians of Louvain, who described this idea as

59

"brutish."[22]

St. Francis DeSales was perhaps the leading "moderate" in seventeenth-century French Catholicism and wrote his very popular *Introduction to the Devout Life* at least in part for married people. Despite the importance of love in his general approach to spirituality, he did not depart from the traditional view of marriage as primarily for the sake of procreation.[23]

Prior to the seventeenth century, intercourse as a procreative act could be thwarted mainly in only two ways – when the partners knew that conception would not result (because of proven sterility or existing pregnancy) or by failing to complete the act. Most theologians permitted intercourse in the first instance, since the aim was not to thwart conception. *Coitus interruptus* was always forbidden by moralists, but some theologians allowed *amplexus reservatus.* Peter of Palude and a few lesser early-modern authorities were willing to permit it under certain circumstances, notably extreme poverty. The subject was largely ignored until the sixteenth century, when Prierias condemned Palude's position in strong terms. Prierias' position remained the dominant one.[24] Even those who justified *amplexus reservatus* did so only if the semen was not discharged after the withdrawal of the penis, their opinion being that the full act of intercourse had not taken place, thus its procreative purpose had not been deliberately thwarted.

Also condemned, although not much discussed, were kinds of sexual activity, like oral or anal intercourse, obviously intended to avoid procreation. During the Renaissance and Baroque ages, when boys were sometimes castrated to preserve their high-pitched singing voices, most theologians who noted the practice also condemned it, even though it went on, among other places, at the Vatican.[25]

The Seventeenth Century

The seventeenth century was, however, a kind of watershed in the development of marital practices, since historians note for the first time in the West, localized patterns of declining birth rates which appear to have been voluntary rather than the result of some natural catastrophe like disease or famine. The pattern is particularly noticeable, for example, among the Calvinist burghers of Geneva.[26] These early manifestations of what would in time become a universal Western phenomenon already showed certain distinctive characteristics of the spread of "family planning" later – its use first among the prosperous middle class interested in protecting and consolidating its economic position and thus guarding against the possibility of too many children, and the secularization of society. (Orthodox Calvinism was rapidly waning in seventeenth-century Geneva, and in the next century the militant skeptic Voltaire would describe that city, including its clergy, as remarkably enlightened and even skeptical in matters of religion.)[27]

What methods were employed to limit families are mostly unknown. *Coitus interruptus* seems most likely. Drugs and potions of various kinds had been known since ancient times, although they were of doubtful effectiveness and were universally condemned by theologians. Leather condoms are also known to have existed in ancient times, and there are occasional references to them later, but they seem to have been associated with recourse to prostitutes (as much to prevent disease as pregnancy) and were probably not used by married couples.[28]

Whatever the methods, there are discernible signs of deliberate limitation of family size from the mid-seventeenth century on. This was, as indicated, chiefly among the middle class, since the aristocracy often still regarded large families as a sign of affluent social position and could usually support them, and the lower classes were naturally slow in taking up new fashions. Among the poor, however, shocking neglect of infants, and sometimes actual infanticide, were fairly common.[29]

The first major theologian to write after the beginnings of these developments was St. Alphonsus Liguori, the most influential moralist of the next two centuries. In general Alphonsus espoused a moderate position. He rejected the Augustinian notion that marital intercourse is always a sin and permitted motives for intercourse other than procreation, provided that procreation was not excluded. Weighing the question of whether couples might refrain from the marital act in order not to produce more children than they could support, he cautiously argued against this as likely to give rise to fornication. Alphonsus' influence grew in the nineteenth century, and was a counterweight to the declining authority of the French Jansenist tradition. Alphonsus, like other theologians of the age, did not take specific account of changing social practices, if he was aware of them.[30]

61

The Nineteenth Century

The eighteenth century was one of the low points in the history of the Church in terms of substantial theology. The intellectual attacks of the Enlightenment and the political attacks of the French Revolution left the Church in a badly weakened and somewhat demoralized state by the end of the century. Partly in reaction to the often sterile intellectualism of the Enlightenment, the most vigorous religious movements of the age, like Pietism and Methodism, tended to be experiential and devotional rather than theological. This tended to be true of Catholicism as well, and the revival of Catholic life after 1800 was largely devoid of serious intellectual work. This in turn affected the education of priests and the general teaching of theology, so that in the early nineteenth century traditional answers as contained in old manuals were simply being repeated without much thought.[31]

Family Planning

In this atmosphere the practice of family planning was growing, in part made possible by the secularism fostered in the previous century (virtually all the Protestant churches still had a sexual morality not essentially different from that of the Catholic Church), in part by new scientific and technical discoveries. By the mid-point of the century contraception as being openly promoted in some places, notably England and the United States, although it was stll not a respectable subject of public discussion and remained illegal.[32]

As early as 1816 the Vatican was receiving inquiries from French priests in particular as to their obligations in the confessional in cases where a penitent confessed *coitus interruptus* or other deliberate thwarting of procreation. The traditional condemnation was repeated. However, leniency was advised in cases of women who, should they refuse their husbands the "marital debt" rather than cooperate in a sin, might risk a violent reaction.[33] (Glimpses of this kind into married life help explain, perhaps, why for so long theologians said so little about love in the context of intercourse and so much about lust. A "romantic" revolution was perhaps beginning to change some attitudes about male-female relationships, but for a long time to come casual, pragmatic, even brutal attitudes probably prevailed in the largest number of instances.)

The torpidity of Catholic theological life in 1800 left pastors and moralists unprepared for the sudden rise of a popular interest in limiting offspring. Paradoxically, this very torpor seems to have contributed to a situation in which the classical doctrines had not been much stressed, so that confessors who now inquired about their obligations often implied that the classical doctrine was new both to them and to their parishioners.

In 1842 a French bishop reported to the Vatican that the majority of young couples in his diocese sought to limit the size of their families, would not refrain from intercourse, and reacted negatively when advised otherwise in the confessional. The use of the sacrament of Penance had in fact fallen off for this reason, he said. The Sacred Penitentiary counselled caution in such cases, seemingly desirous that priests not inquire too closely into delicate and perhaps scandalous matters. (Alphonsus Liguori's position had been that confessors should not inquire about marital practices unless asked for advice by the penitent.) The Penitentiary also seemed to say that, where married couples were unaware of the classical doctrine, it was not necessary to disturb their consciences on the matter, and this opinion gained some currency in the French Church. What was being talked about was apparently mainly either *amplexus reservatus* or *coitus interruptus*.[34]

Pastoral Response

The pastoral response was kept clearly distinct from the doctrinal issue, however, and in 1851 Pope Pius IX condemned the proposition that "for decent reasons" the "practice of Onan" could be employed.[35] Since permissive practice seemed to call the doctrine into question, the Vatican then began to urge that confessors pay closer attention to the matter. As condoms came into common use, they were unequivocally condemned.[36] (However, the First Vatican Council did not concern itself with the issue.)

Beginning in the 1870's, the French hierarchy, apparently the national group most directly confronted by changing practice, began to speak out much more vigorously on the issue, sometimes alluding to France's declining birth rate. The first theological work specifically on the subject of contraception appeared in 1876, and its strictness was unequivocal.[37] In his 1880 encyclical on marriage, Leo XIII did not mention contraception but did reiterate that marriage could not be considered merely naturalistically, that it came under the judgment of the Church.[38] There was no longer any uncertainty as to the Church's stand on the question, although there was still a great deal of uncertainty as to how vigorous priests should be in pursuing a matter which was delicate and possibly scandalous. As knowledge of the Church's teaching spread along with the practice of contraception, and as society became less reticent about such matters, Catholic leaders became increasingly vigorous and outspoken in their statements. Theologians, especially the influential Belgian Jesuit Arthur Vermeersch, began to emphasize the confessor's obligation to inquire about practices which penitents were likely to conceal.[39] The subject was more and more treated in segments of the Catholic press. The first American contribution to the discussion – a strong reaffirmation of classical doctrine – was written by Monsignor John A. Ryan, the noted Catholic University moralist, and appeared in the *American Ecclesiastical Review* in 1916.[40]

Prior to the nineteenth century there was little understanding of infertility, although by empirical evidence a couple might know themselves to be sterile. Anything like "rhythm" was, however, impossible. After about 1870 abstinence during fertile periods was a scientific possibility. Some theologians condemned it. However, the Sacred Penitentiary and the major authorities agreed at least that those who engaged in the practice should not be disturbed in conscience, the opinion that remained in effect into the twentieth century.[41] There were ample precedents in earlier consensuses that, for example, it was permissible to have intercourse during pregnancy. During the nineteenth century a few theologians also began to speak of conjugal love within the context of sexual intercourse, the expression of which might be a legitimate motive for such intercourse.[42]

Summary

During the period 1300-1918, the development of Catholic doctrine with respect to sexual morality can be summarized as follows:

1. Sexual activity was always linked directly to the purpose of procreation.

2. Consequently, acts likely to undermine marital stability and the proper providing for offspring, e.g., adultery and fornication, were also condemned.

3. Acts obviously not intended for procreation, e.g., homosexuality, were also condemned. (Such acts were also condemned as being against nature.)

4. Acts within marriage obviously not intended for procreation, e.g., oral or genital intercourse, were condemned. (Like homosexuality and bestiality, for example, there was little said about these practices.)

5. While the Augustinian tradition held that acts of intercourse were at least venially sinful even within marriage, this position was never universally accepted and came to be increasingly denied as time went on.

6. While some theologians justified *amplexus reservatus* (the only practical method of contraception during most of this period), most condemned it as intended directly to thwart procreation.

7. A growing body of authorities held that other motives for contraception, e.g., the avoidance of fornication, were permissible provided procreation was not directly denied or thwarted.

8. A growing body of authorities was also willing to allow pleasure as a valid motive, provided it was not the sole motive.

9. So long as procreation was not deliberately thwarted, most authorities held that it was permissible to have intercourse when it was certain that no pregnancy would result, e.g., during infertile periods.

10. Although there was relatively slight disagreement as to what the Church's teaching was, there was a good deal of uncertainty, especially in the nineteenth century, as to what the appropriate pastoral response should be to those not living in accordance with that teaching.

Notes

1. Gordon Leff, *William of Ockham: The Metamorphosis of Scholatic Discourse* (Totowa, NJ: Rowman, 1975).

2. Charles E. Trinkaus, *In Our Image and Likeness* (Chicago: University of Chicago Press, 1970), 2 vols.

3. Ibid., 2: 273-78.

4. *Christiani Matrimonii Institutio* (1526), in *Opera Omnia* 5: 617.

5. For More's mature theological opinions see his *Dialogue Against Heresies* (1528).

6. For a summary of theological opinion see John T. Noonan, Jr., *Contraception: A History of Its Treatment by the Catholic Theologians and Canonists* (Cambridge, MA: Harvard University, 1965), pp. 249-51, 292, 304, 312-13.

7. Ibid., pp. 238, 247.

8. Peter de Palude, *De Sententiis* 4.31.2 and 4.31.3; Bernardine of Siena, *Seraphic Sermons* 19.3.

9. *Questiones Morales* (1940), II, "De Temperentia."

10. Prierias, *Summa Summarum Quae Sylvestrina Dicitur* (1540); Cajetan, *Summula Peccatorum* (1538); Soto, *Commentarium in Quartum Sententiarum* (1574); Canisius, *Catechismus Major* (modern edition, 1933).

11. *Seraphic Sermons,* 19.3.

12. Major, *In Quartum Setentiarum* (1519).

13. Noonan, pp. 275-76.

14. Palude, *De Sententiis* 4.31.3.2; Prierias, *Summa,* "De Debito Conjugali;" Soto, *De Sententiis* 4.32.1.1.

15. See, for example, William Lazareth, *Luther on the Christian Home* (Philadephia: Fortress Press, 1960).

16. Roland Bainton, *Here I Stand* (New York: Abingdon-Cokesbury, 1950), pp. 293-94.

17. *Controversiarum de Amissione Gratiae,* in *Opera Ormia,* IV.

18. Noonan, pp. 255-56, 322.

19. Jan Miel, *Pascal and Theology* (Baltimore: Johns Hopkins, 1969), pp. 108-47.

20. Edmond Preclin, *Les Luttes Politiques et Doctrinales aux XVIIe et XVIIIe Siecles* (Paris, 1955-56), 2 vols.

21. Noonan, p. 320.

22. Ibid., pp. 317-19, 326.

23. *Introduction to the Devout Life,* "The Married State."

24. Noonan, pp. 296-99, 336.

25. Ibid., pp. 336-39.

26. Orest and Patricia Ranum, eds., *Popular Attitudes Towards Birth Control in Pre-Industrial France and England* (New York, 1972); Edward Shorter, *The Making of the Modern Family* (New York: Basic Books, 1975); Peter Laslett, *Family Life and Illicit Love in Earlier Generations* (Cambridge: Cambridge University Press, 1977).

27. Peter Gay, *The Enlightenment: An Interpretation* (New York: Knopf, 1969), 2: 463-65.

28. Noonan, pp. 200-31, 387-476.

29. See note 26 above.

30. *Theologia Moralis* (1748).

31. Edgar Hocedez, S.J., *Histoire de la Theologie au XIX Siecle* (Brussels, 1947), 1: 67-69, 132.

32. Noonan, pp. 387-438.

33. Ibid, pp. 398-405.

34. Ibid., pp. 414-32.

35. *Decisiones Sanctae Sedis,* pp. 19-20.

36. Noonan, pp. 414-32.

37. Ibid.

38. *Arcanum Divinae Sapientiae.*

39. Noonan, pp. 419-32.

40. "Family Limitation," *American Ecclesiastical Review* 40 (1916): 684-96.

41. Noonan, pp. 439-42.

42. Ibid., pp. 491-92.

Part Two:
Contemporary Scientific and Philosophical Approaches to Human Sexuality and Personhood

Introduction

The brief historical overview in Part One of this volume looks primarily to the doctrinal teaching of the Church on human sexuality and personhood as it developed over the centuries. But doctrine can only be taught in the context of the scientific and philosophical understanding of any given era of human history. The following four chapters represent an overview of the *current* understanding of human sexuality and personhood from the perspective of a physiologist, a psychiatrist, a sociologist, and a philosopher.

James A. Monteleone, M.D., a professor of pediatrics and adolescent medicine at St. Louis University School of Medicine, reviews in a brief synthesis the physiological development of each person's sexuality. He notes that for the first two months of human existence there is no difference between the proto-genital systems of the male and female and describes current scientific knowledge about the differentiation process. He includes significant data on possible physiological roots of homosexuality and transsexualism. He concludes with his opinion of the three most significant areas of study on the genetic role in abnormal sexual behavior.

Rev. Michael R. Peterson, M.D., a priest of the Archdiocese of Washington, D.C., is President of the St. Luke Institute in Washington which provides treatment and rehabilitation for alcoholics and is also a clinical assistant professor of psychiatry at Georgetown University Medical School. His chapter on "Psychological Aspects of Human Sexual Behaviors" begins with a discussion of six aspects of human sexuality: sexual identity, gender identity, heterosexuality, homosexuality, heterosocial and homosocial behaviors, and dimorphism. He then reflects on the cognitive/affective component of human sexuality as its uniquely human component and analyzes the neural development and the complex psychological elements that influence sexual behaviors.

Paul Peachey, Ph.D., an associate professor of sociology at Catholic University of America, next presents a profound analysis, first of culture itself, and then of cultural influences on sexual behavior. He focuses on American attitudes in the current period of re-examination of sexual roles and stereotypes. While documenting the increased levels of sexual activity in contemporary America, he hesitates to speak of a sexual rebellion or revolution. Social differentiation has occurred, he notes, but has not yet been matched by personal individuation. He points to the messianic vision traceable to Jesus and the ancient Hebrew prophets as a source of the major values of the Western world.

The final chapter of this section, by Rev. Ambrose McNicholl, O.P., Ph.D., a professor of philosophy at the Universities of St. Thomas and the Lateran in Rome, reviews the actual trends of thought prevailing in current philosophy about the key notions of substance, person, and nature. Fr. McNicholl highlights the fact that the ontological awareness which originated in Greek philosphy can only be found faintly reflected in much contemporary philosophy. He describes the impact which that awareness has on anthropology, specifically on sexuality and marriage. In his concluding postscript he suggests that this awareness is not uniquely found in Greek or Roman philosophy but has a transcultural basis in the *humanum.*

These four chapters which synthesize massive areas of scientific and philosophical study will be followed in Part III by four chapters summarizing contemporary theological study and Church teaching.

Chapter 4

The Physiological
Aspects
of Sex

James A. Monteleone, M.D.

A number of terms* are used to describe the various phases of normal sexual development, either anatomic or psychological. The anatomic terms are: *(1) genetic or chromosomal sex,* referring to the sex chromosome arrangement, XY or XX; *(2) gonadal sex,* referring to the type of gonad present, testis or ovary; and *phenotypic sex,* referring to internal and external genital development, Müllerian or Wolffian structures, vagina or penis and scrotum. Phenotypic sex usually refers to the external development, how it appears to the observer, male or female. These terms are all used to describe the various components of anatomic sex. The terms used in describing normal psychological sexual development are: *(1) sex of rearing,* the sex assigned to the individual, male or female, including the name and appropriate dress; *(2) gender identity,* how the individual perceives himself or herself, which sex he or she identifies with; and *(3) gender role,* the public acknowledgment of that gender identity.

---

*See glossary of terms at end of chapter, p. 84.

In the normal individual these events take place in sequence. First, there is the establishment of genetic or chromosomal sex, by the presence or absence of a Y chromosome. This determines the gonadal sex, ovary or testis. If a testis is present, hormones are produced which determine phenotypic sex, development of both internal and external sex organs. At birth after viewing external phenotypic sex, a sex is assigned and the parents name the child; the child is dressed and taught appropriately. As the individual matures, he or she identifies with either the mother or father for gender identity and role.

There are a number of causes of abnormal phenotypic sexual development: *environmental insults,* influences which originate outside of the individual such as drugs and viruses; *chromosomal aberrations,* primarily of sex chromosomes, XXY, XYY, XO, etc., and also several autosomal aberrations. A number of recognizable birth defect syndromes have been associated with abnormal sex development. The mechanisms causing the defects is not known. *Single gene inheritance* resulting in inborn errors of the steroid hormones can result in the abnormal production of androgens (male hormones) which result in ambiguous genitalia in the genetic female; or the inability to produce normal male hormones can result in ambiguous genitalia in the genetic male. In the condition called testicular feminization, the genetic male produces normal male hormones, but the target cells are missing receptor proteins and cannot effectively use the hormone for masculinization. Disorders of sexual development in *Homo sapiens* are listed in Table I.

TABLE I

DISORDERS OF SEXUAL DEVELOPMENT

I. Errors of Genetic Sex
    A. Errors due to sporadic aberrations of X and Y chromosomes
        Turner syndrome
        Klinefelter syndrome (XXY, XXXY, XXXXY)
        Double fertilization chimera (XX-XY mosaic)

For a definition of each of these terms refer to a current genetic textbook such as: Max Levitan, *Textbook of Human Genetics* (2d ed.; New York: Oxford University Press, 1977).

Mixed gonadal dysgenesis
XYY Syndrome
XXX Syndrome
Deletion syndrome (X and Y)
B. Errors due to absence of X (YO, OO)
(To date none have been identified.)
II. Errors of Gonadal Sex
A. Familial true hermaphroditism
B. Sex reversal syndrome
XY female
XX male
C. Gonadal dysgenesis
Familial XX type
Familial XY type
Sporadic non-familial
III. Errors in Phenotypic Sex
A. Male pseudohermaphroditism
1. Defective testosterone synthesis (enzyme deficiencies)
2. Defective androgen action
5α-Reductase deficiency
Receptor disorders
Receptor positive resistance
3. Persistent Müllerian duct syndrome
4. Sporadic forms
Congenital gonadoblastoma
Chronic congenital renal disease
B. Female pseudohermaphroditism
1. Abnormal androgen production
Congenital adrenal hyperplasia
2. Environmental (maternal in origin)
C. Familial defects of Wolffian-Müllerian development
Rokitansky-Kuster-Hauser syndrome
Cystic fibrosis
IV. Errors in Gender Role Identification
A. Transsexual (Gender Dysphoria Syndrome)
B. Homosexual

Embryonic Differentiation

In every individual during the embryonic state, there is the potential for both male and female development. In the first two months of gestation, there is no differentiation in the genital system. At seven weeks gestation, the testis begin to function, if present, and precipitate changes for male development. The ovaries play no known role in phenotypic development until puberty. The effect of estrogen on gender role in humans is not known.

The embryonic differentiation of male and female genital ducts from Wolffian and Müllerian primordia (Figure I) begins at seven weeks gestation. In the indifferent stage, there is a bi-potential indifferent gonad, a Wolffian duct system, and Müllerian duct system. In the female, the indifferent gonad becomes an ovary, there is lysis or

DIFFERENTIATION OF MALE AND FEMALE GENITALIA

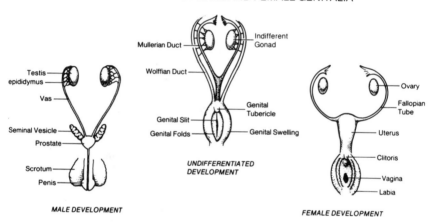

Figure I

destruction of the Wolffian duct system, and persistence of the Müllerian duct system which develops into fallopian tubes, uterus and upper vagina. In the male, the indifferent gonad becomes a testis, there is persistence of the Wolffian duct system, and lysis of the Müllerian duct system. The Wolffian duct becomes epididymis, vas deferens and seminal vesicles. Each embryo has both Wolffian and Müllerian ducts and depending on the presence or absence of a Y chromosome one of the two is selected. In external genital

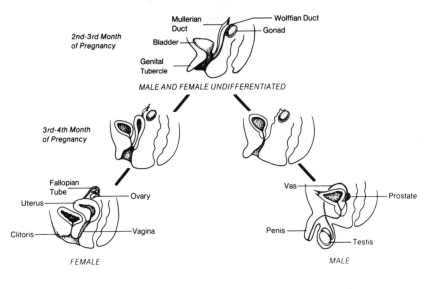

Figure II

development, there is just one system for both sexes (Figure II), the genital tubercle, labial scrotal swelling and urethral folds. Depending on the hormones present, either female or male genitalia will develop. In the female, the genital tubercle becomes the clitoris, labial scrotal swelling becomes the labia majora, and the urethral folds develop into the labia minor. In the male, the genital tubercle develops into the penis, the labial scrotal swelling becomes the scrotum, and the urogenital folds are incorporated into the penis.

Function of the Y Chromosome

The determining factor in precipitating changes resulting in maleness is the Y chromosome. It was first believed that the Y chromosome was inert and that maleness was carried on an autosome; that femaleness was determined by the presence of the XX chromosomal arrangement and that maleness was the X plus autosomal arrangement or that it was the ratio of X to autosomes. With perfection of chromosomal analysis techniques, this was disproved and it was decided that the Y chromosome determined maleness. The chromosome arrangement of XXY was a phenotypic male. Though this male had inadequate testis and was sterile, internal and external genitalia were clearly male, as was XXXY. This proved that XX was not responsible for femaleness nor was the ratio of autosomal to X responsible for maleness, since it was learned that individuals born with just one X chromosome (XO) were phenotypically females. The number of genes on the Y chromosome which are necessary for male determination is not known but it is clear that there must be more than one gene responsible, since partial loss of genetic material from the Y chromosome will result in incomplete male indifferentiation.[1]

In addition, the Y chromosome carries the determining gene for H-Y antigen. In 1955, Eichwald and Silmser showed that among inbred strains of mice, male to female skin grafts were rejected; male to male, female to female, and female to male grafts survived.[2] Since the only difference in these genetically identical mice was the Y chromosome, they attributed this phenomenon to a specific Y-linked cell surface protein they named histocompatability-Y antigen (H-Y antigen). Wachtel and co-workers found that H-Y antigen was also present in rats, guinea pigs, rabbits and humans and they developed an assay to measure its presence.[3] H-Y antigen has been demonstrated to be present as early as the 8-cell stage of embryogenesis. Studies in humans with 47, XYY chromosomal carrier types showed that a double dose of H-Y antigen was present in these individuals and supported the hypothesis that this gene was Y-linked. Studies in individuals with abnormally formed Y chromosomes have indicated that the location of the gene for H-Y antigen is in the pericentromeric region of the Y chromosome.[4] Wachtel and Ono and co-workers have studied individuals with the sex reversal syndrome, XX males and XX true hermaphrodites.[5] In all patients tested H-Y antigen was detected. They postulated that H-Y antigen had the function of, or was closely associated with, the induction of testis during the early embryonic state.

Jost's Experiments

In 1953, Jost studied rabbits during early embryogenesis (Figure III).[6] He removed the indifferent gonad in the very early embryo. All early castrated individuals developed phenotypically female. Jost concluded that maleness depended on a functioning testis in utero and

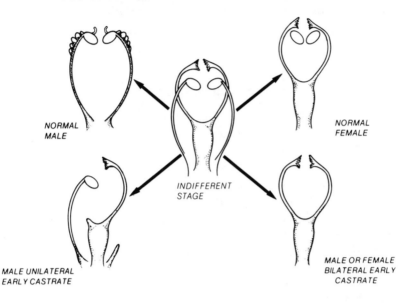

NORMAL
MALE

NORMAL
FEMALE

INDIFFERENT
STAGE

MALE UNILATERAL
EARLY CASTRATE

MALE OR FEMALE
BILATERAL EARLY
CASTRATE

Figure III

that each testis had a unilateral effect. This effect was not due to
androgen secreted by the testis, but was due to a substance which he
named "duct organizing substance" and which was later called
Müllerian regression factor (MRF) and more recently Anti-Müllerian
Hormone (AMH). He felt that androgen had an effect, but this effect
was greatest during later embryonic development and most affected
the external genitalia. He concluded that femaleness resulted from an
absence of a functioning testis. Jost postulated that normal embryonic
sexual development occurs in the following sequence. First, there is
the establishment of genetic sex arising from the Y chromosomal
constitution. This is translated into gonadal sex as the indifferent
gonad develops into a testis in the male and into an ovary in the female.
Gonadal sex is translated into phenotypic sex which is the direct result
of the gonad formed in the first and second steps. Three fetal
hormones are responsible for phenotypic sex. First is the Anti-
Müllerian hormone, which prevents the development of the uterus
and fallopian tubes. The testis then produces testosterone which
promotes virilization of the urogenital tract, stimulates the Wolffian

ducts to induce the development of epididymis, vas deferens and seminal vesicles, and is the prohormone for dihydrotestosterone. Dihydrotestosterone acts on the urogenital sinus to form the prostate and the genital tubercle and the genital swelling to form the male external genitalia.

Normal Sexual Differentiation

To summarize present understanding of normal phenotypic sexual development[7,8] (Figure IV) the following may be said: In the early embryo, the indifferent gonad is acted on by the Y chromosome. In the absence of the Y chromosome the gonad develops into an ovary with persistence of the Müllerian ducts, which develop into uterus and fallopian tubes; there is little change in external genitalia and a normal phenotypic female results. When present, the Y chromosome and H-Y antigen signal the indifferent gonad to develop into a testis. The sertoli cells of the testis produce Anti-Müllerian Hormone, which

FACTORS AFFECTING ANATOMIC SEXUAL DEVELOPMENT

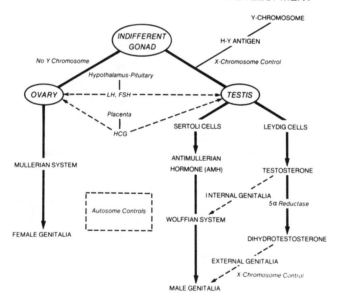

Figure IV

lysis the Müllerian system; the Leydig cells produce testosterone. Testosterone circulates in the blood stream bound to two proteins, testosterone-binding globulin and albumin. The protein-bound hormone is in equilibrium with the unbound hormone which comprises 1 to 3% of the total hormone present. Only the unbound hormone enters the cells. Inside the cell testosterone is converted to dihydrotestosterone by the enzyme 5α-reductase. The two hormones bind to androgen-receptor protein. The hormone-receptor complex is carried to the cell nucleus to interact with acceptor sites before effecting a biological response. The specific nature of the acceptor sites is unknown but the result of the interaction is the release by the nucleus of messenger RNA and proteins into the cytoplasm of the cell. What role estrogens have in augmenting and blocking androgen action at the cell level is not clear. Testosterone acts upon the Wolffian duct system to develop toward maleness; it is picked up by the target cells of the prostate, genital tubercle and other external genital structures where it is converted to dihydrotestosterone by the enzyme 5α-reductase. Dihydrotestosterone masculinizes the external genitalia. Other genes on the X chromosome and on autosomes that regulate H-Y antigen have been found. In addition the X chromosome carries the gene or genes responsible for the receptor proteins of testosterone and dihydrotestosterone. For normal testosterone production there are five enzymes necessary to convert early precursors to testosterone. The adrenals produce several androgens including androstenedione and dihydroepiandrosterone. The role of these hormones in normal sexual development is not clearly understood.

Gender Role

The factors which influence normal gender identity or gender role fall into three categories[9] (Figure V): *biological,* hormonal influences, both fetal and maternal and possibly postnatal which affect the psyche; *biopsychic,* non-mental stimuli from outside as well as within the individual which are outside of awareness; they have been likened to imprinting. To date there has been no direct evidence to prove the existence of these biopsychic forces; *environmental,* those forces originating outside of the individual which are conscious, such as reward, punishment, conflict, frustration and trauma.

The causes of abnormal gender role development such as

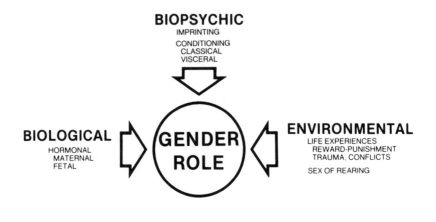

Figure V

homosexuality and transsexualism are not fully understood. Kallman studied 85 pairs of twins: 45 dizygotic, 40 monozygotic. Monozygotic twins originate from a single fertilized egg and have identical genetic make-up, whereas dizygotic twins would be equivalent to brothers and sisters.[10] The environmental influences were identical. He found that the concordance rate for overt homosexual behavior was 100% in monozygotic twins and was slightly over normal in the dizygotic. He suggested from this observation that genetic disposition was the basis for the development of homosexuality and that these factors interacted with environmental experiences. Rainer, and others, after a survey of a considerable number of one-egg pairs was able to find only seven who were not concordant for homosexuality.[11,12]

Margolese compared androsterone-etiocholanolone (testosterone metabolites) ratios in 10 healthy male homosexuals, 10 healthy male heterosexuals and 4 men who were not in good health.[13] In 7 of the homosexuals etiocholanolone production was greater than androsterone production; in one, androsterone was equal to etiocholanolone and in 2 of them androsterone was slightly greater than etiocholanolone. In all of the heterosexuals androsterone was greater than etiocholanolone. However, he found that in the 4 sick heterosexuals the ratio of etiocholanolone-androsterone was similar to that of the homosexuals. These data would suggest a specific hormone imbalance in male homosexuals.

Anke Ehrhardt studied the offspring of progesterone-treated women.[14] The female offspring were found to be more female, more satisfied with the traditional female role. The male offspring were less masculine. Kolodny found LH and estradiol levels in male homosexuals higher than in normal heterosexual males.[15] Kolodny found significantly lower testosterone levels in male homosexuals as compared to a matched group of heterosexuals.[16] Rohde found no difference in total testosterone levels but found decreased free plasma testosterone levels in homosexuals as compared with normal heterosexual males.[17] McGinley et al. reported 38 male pseudohermaphrodites with 5α-reductase deficiency and noted that a great majority of them at puberty or later changed gender roles successfully.[18] The authors concluded that environmental and sociocultural factors are not solely responsible for the formation of male gender role. Androgens make a strong and definite contribution.

In lower animals there is experimental evidence indicating that fetal androgen influences differential organization of specific control centers in the base of the brain, the hypothalamus, of the male and female. These centers control the cyclic function of the pituitary and in all probability the corresponding patterns of male or female behavior. The significance of these findings for human beings is speculative.[19] There are as yet no known human syndromes which can be ascribed to an error in the hormonal and sexual organization of the central nervous system.

The responsiveness of developing neural tissue to androgens and estrogens is determined by protein receptors within the brain.[20] The neonate has a potent blood-borne estrogen-binding protein, which appears to keep circulating estrogens originating in the mother from reaching estrogen receptors. It may have a protective function toward estrogen-sensitive tissues. Since this protein does not bind testosterone and is primarily an extracellular protein, the access of testosterone to the male brain is unhindered.

Although testosterone is the major secretory product of the testis involved in brain sexual differentiation, it does not seem to be testosterone which actually brings about sexual differentiation but rather a metabolite produced in some cases within the brain itself. The brain contains enzymes for producing the two major metabolites of testosterone, dihydrotestosterone and estradiol. In certain mammals the androgen pathway appears to be essential for sexual differentiation of masculine sexual behavior, whereas the estrogen pathway appears to be involved in masculinization of others. With respect to suppression of feminine characteristics, the estrogen pathway appears to be of primary importance in other mammalian species.

Harry Benjamin recently stated: "Transsexualism may be interpreted as a form of psychic intersexuality, the tendency of which varies. It appears to have more than one causation, a neuroendocrine etiology being perhaps the most frequent. So far there is no cure for it."[21]

In support of environmental influences, Bieber studied 106 male homosexual patients and found that they had a similar parental constellation: a hostile father and a close-binding, seductive mother who dominated and minimized her husband.[22] Many heterosexual men had a similar background. Homosexuals tend to be later children in the family. Geneticists cite this as proof of genetic propensity: old parents, therefore old genes. However, environmentalists cite this as evidence of an environmental cause: older siblings who baby and pick on the individual, and a mother who feels she is growing old and losing her husband's affection and clings to the child.

Gender identification is established very early in life. Case histories of adult transsexuals reveal that their cross-gender identification and behavior date back to childhood.[23] Parents of the affected children are able to clearly identify cross-gender behavior at age three years or younger. Studies to determine underlying causes of gender role abnormalities to date have not been conclusive; in fact, at times they seem contradictory. Investigators in this area agree that much is still to be learned, that the individual has little control over his condition and that efforts to treat these individuals have been unsuccessful.

"The future may see more efforts to solve the riddle of the etiology of gender role disturbances. How much can be psychological? How much may be genetic? How much neuro-endocrine? What would be the nature of a pre-disposition to transsexuality and how much of a role does it play in the final clinical picture? Can the imprinting phenomenon, as observed in animals, find a parallel in humans? And, to be personal once more, will I live long enough to see

82

the answers to any of these questions."[21]

A Personal Opinion

The most significant areas of study to date regarding the genetic role in abnormal sexual behavior fall into three areas. The twin studies conducted by Kallman and others, though they are rather old (1952), have stood the test of time with no reports to refute their conclusion to date. It would be nice if there were more recent studies to update these findings. These twin studies strongly suggest that the underlying influence on homosexual behavior is genetic.

A second important area of study has been the function of protein receptors in the brain. These receptors have been identified although their exact role in abnormal sexual behavior has only been speculated. Perhaps in transsexualism there is a parallel condition likened to testicular feminization in which these protein hormone receptors are altered or absent.

The third area, hormone-induced behavior modification, done in lower animals strongly suggests that homosexuality begins early in life, either *in utero* or shortly after birth, and is triggered by a hormone imbalance of estrogen or testosterone — an excess or absence of one or the other, or perhaps a relative change brought about by abnormal or altered hormone carrier proteins. These changes may be transient, leaving no traces other than in behavior which are permanent and persist in later life.

Blood hormone levels LH, testosterone, estrogen, etiocholanolone, and androsterone measured in adult homosexuals will be proven inconsequential, if this has not already been done. The data have been confusing and at times contradictory. A recent review relates these hormone changes to stress.[24]

References

1. Yunis, E. *et al., Human Genetics* 39:117 (1977).
2. Eichwald, E. J., Silmser, C. R., Wheeler, N., *Annals of the New York Academy of Science* 64:737 (1956).
3. Wachtel, S.S. *et al., Proceedings of the National Academy of Sciences (USA)* 71:1215 (1974).
4. Wachtel, S. S., *Science* 198:797 (1977).
5. Wachtel, S. S. *et al., New England Journal of Medicine* 295:750 (1976).
6. Jost, A., *Recent Progress in Hormone Research* 8:379 (1953).
7. Wilson, J. D., Griffin, J. E., George, F. W., *Biology of Reproduction* 22:7 (1980).
8. Griffin, J. E. and Wilson, J. D., *New England Journal of Medicine* 302:198 (1980).
9. Stoller, R. J., in *The Sexual Experience,* edited by Sadock, Kaplan, Freedman (Baltimore: Williams and Wilkins, 1976).

10. Kallmann, F. J., *The Journal of Nervous and Mental Disease* 115:283 (1952).

11. Rainer, J. D., Mesnikoff, A., Kolb, L. C., Carr, A., *Psychosomatic Medicine* 22:251 (1960).

Kolb, L. C., in *Current Psychiatric Therapies,* edited by J. Masserman (New York: Grune and Stratton, 1963), p. 131.

12. Davison, K., Brierley, H., Smith, C., *British Journal of Psychiatry* 118:675 (1971).

13. Margolese, M.S., *Hormones and Behavior* :151 (1970).

Margolese, M. S., and Janiger, O., *British Medical Journal* 3:207 (1973).

14. Ehrhardt, A. A., Annual Meeting of the American Academy of Child Psychiatry, Atlantic City, New Jersey, 1980.

15. Kolodny, R. C., Jacobs, L. S., Masters, W. H., Toro, G., Daughaday, W. H., *The Lancet,* July 1, 1972, p. 18.

16. Kolodny, R. C. *et al., New England Journal of Medicine* 285:1170 (1971).

17. Rohde, W., Stahl, F., Dorner, G., *Endokrinologie* 70:241 (1977).

18. Imperato-McGinley, J., Peterson, R. E., Gautier, T., Sturla, E., *New England Journal of Medicine* 300:1233 (1979).

19. McEwen, B., *Biology of Reproduction* 22:43 (1980).

20. Larsson, K., in *Endocrine Control of Sexual Behavior,* edited by C. Beyer (New York: Raven Press, 1979).

21. Benjamin, H., in *Transsexualism and Sex Reassignment,* edited by R. Green and J. Money (Baltimore: Johns Hopkins University Press, 1969).

22. Bieber, I. et al., *Homosexuality: A Psychoanalytic Study* (New York: Basic Books, 1962).

23. Bell, A. P., in *Human Sexuality,* edited by R. Green (Baltimore: Williams and Wilkins), p. 99.

24. Rose, R. M., in *Topics in Psychoendrocrinology,* edited by E. T. Sachan (New York: Grune and Stratton, 1975).

Glossary

Antigen:	Any of various sorts of material that stimulate an immune response.
Assay:	Analysis.
Autosomal:	Pertaining to any chromosome other than a sex chromosome.
Cytoplasm:	Substance of a cell outside of the nucleus.
Embryogenesis:	That phase of prenatal development involved in the establishment of the characteristic configuration of the embryonic body.
Epididymis:	The first, convoluted, portion of the excretory duct of the testis; develops from the Wolffian ducts.
Estradiol:	An estrogen, a metabolite of both estrogen and testosterone.
Etiology:	Causation: the cause of disease.
Gonad:	Sexual gland, testis or ovary.

Imprinting:	A particular kind of learning usually outside of consciousness characterized by its occurrence in early life, which determines subsequent behavior patterns.
Induction:	Production or causation; the influence exerted by an organizer gene.
Leydig cells:	Cells in the testis that produce the male hormone testosterone.
Lysis:	Destruction.
Metabolite:	A substance or compound produced by the chemical change or breakdown of one or more other compounds.
Müllerian Ducts:	Embryonic tubules which precede female internal sexual structures.
Neonate:	Newborn.
Neural:	Relating to the nervous system; as mentioned in this text, implies the brain.
Pericentromeric:	A position on a chromosome near the centromere or center.
Primordia:	Collection of cells in the embryo indicating the beginning of an organ or structure.
Prohormone:	A hormone precursor of a second hormone.
Sertoli Cells:	Cells in the testes to which the spermatids are attached, which also produce Anti-Müllerian Hormone (AMH).
Wolffian Ducts:	Embryonic tubules which precede male internal sexual structures.

Chapter 5

Psychological Aspects of Human Sexual Behaviors

The Reverend Michael R. Peterson, M.D.

Introduction

Since the recorded history of man in his various cultures, human sexual behaviors have always fascinated historians, lawmakers, tribal and national governments, prophets, religious leaders and theologians. Religious cults, puberty rituals, theological movements have all been interested in human sexual behaviors and have given differing explanations over those centuries for the causality of those behaviors.

Christian writings from earliest times, including various references in the Old Testament and New Testament, show a kind of preoccupation with sexual behaviors especially as they relate to ritual purity and the structure and functioning of the human family.

The biological understanding of human sexual behaviors and practices was, of course, unknown to our Christian writers prior to the nineteenth century and it is only at this time in our history that we are beginning to have a firmer understanding of the role of biological factors, psychological factors, and socio-cultural factors in determining these complex human behaviors that we label as human sexuality.

Despite this increase in knowledge and the seeming explosion of scientific information over the last thirty years, human sexual behaviors remain just as misunderstood and shrouded in mystery as centuries before for many Christian persons.

The purpose of this brief presentation of psychological aspects of human sexual behaviors is *not* to survey in any depth or detail the legions of scientific writings and research that have been produced over the past many years. Instead, this chapter will examine fundamental concepts needed to understand this major field of psychology and psychiatry. The chapter further will give the author's view of the directions of understanding, having in mind a rather eclectic model and approach to the vast scientific literature. The author would direct you to a number of updated reviews and fundamental textbooks in the literature that will give a broad overview of this delicate and sensitive subject matter.[1,2,3,4,5,6,7]

It is extremely important that the reader attempt if at all possible to set aside ingrained emotional reactions to the different subjects and seek to be open to these concepts, viewing them as biologically based and at this point not related in the development of the subject to any particular moral matrix or moral structure. In this way, the author is allowed to speculate more freely and to present some difficult questions which will be discussed in more detail by later authors and experts in moral theology in this book. After a disussion of six fundamental concepts, this chapter will reflect upon sexual behaviors.

Fundamental Concepts

It is the author's experience from wide lecturing and teaching in the area of human sexuality that much misunderstanding occurs because of major differences in understanding or defining concepts involved in human sexuality. For example, the word "homosexual" runs the gamut of understanding depending on past experiences of the person defining the word. In this brief section, the author will define and discuss six basic concepts to establish terminology and language.

(a) Sexual Identity or Genital Identity

Using the example of a young male child, sexual or genital identity is a process begun at that moment in time when the child makes the first cognitive correlation between the presence of a penis between his legs similar to his father's, brother's or peers', or the negative correlation of the absence of the male organ in the mother, sisters or peers. Most developmental psychologists believe that there is evidence of this first recognition of differences in genitals as early as the second year of life.

It is important to stop here for a moment and indicate the importance of seeng such cognitive correlations in a continuum or process of correlations and understanding. It is to state the obvious to say that the understanding of the male penis for the two-year- old child is quite different and rather unidimensional compared to that same child's understanding of the penis and its function and role in his masculinity and future when he reaches the age of twenty.

What has happened to that child as he grows and develops is that there is a cognitive change and neurological increase in functioning such that the young man is capable of understanding, correlating, and creatively using information so that he can look at complex problems and concepts and see them in a multidimensional manner as the brain develops and the cognitive functions increase. The author will refer to this basic developmental concept in neurology and psychology when talking about all development in sexuality in future pages.

(b) Gender Identity and Gender Role

Gender identity and assumption of gender role are slightly more complicated processes, one that is deeply affected by early childhood experiences and the culture in which the child finds himself. Simply put, they reside in the discovery that the penis and his sexual identity are tied to "maleness" or certain age-prescribed and social-prescribed roles that the young male child assumes as he develops. In previous centuries, the concept of the man being the "breadwinner" was a gender role as was the man's being the "priest"; however, one can see from these two examples how quickly such roles can change and what was "unthinkable" in previous ages now by virtue of culture and changing social roles may be a different reality.

The concept of gender identity also has a deep psychological dimension. "Maleness" or gender identity as a male could be thought of also as a "feeling state"; one develops an understanding and feeling about one's maleness which is rather ingrained early in childhood and is rather resistant to attempts to alter it by using psychological or chemical methods. The gender role, however, is more constantly changing and adapting to the age of the person and the changes in the society and culture.

Generally speaking, the sexual identity and gender identity of an individual are found to correspond with each other within the same individual. There is a very unusual form of clinical situation where the sexual identity and gender identity are 180° opposite each other; this is found in the gender dysphoria syndrome or in male and female transsexualism.[8] In this striking clinical entity, one finds, for example, from early age a child stating that he recognizes his male anatomy as being male, but that this is a "mistake," that his gender identity or "feeling" within himself is that of a girl or woman.

Such an unusual phenomenon, which historically has been with us in all centuries of recorded history, has always caught the eye of the culture and, most recently, the medical and psychiatric professions.[9] Here is an example wherein cognitive recognition is consonant with the anatomical evidence, but the "feeling" of maleness which we label as gender identity is absent, having been replaced by a feeling of gender identity with a person who does not have the correct anatomical equipment.

(c) Heterosexuality

Here is a concept that one rarely feels is necessary to define; instead correlations with "natural" or "normal" are usually made and it is assumed that the antecedents of such heterosexual behaviors are understood and obvious. It is interesting that most of the scientific literature is concerned with homosexual behaviors and other behaviors that are not "natural" and "normal," and little is still understood about the antecedents of heterosexual behaviors.

James McCary in his book, *Human Sexuality,* defines the concept of heterosexuality simply as: "sexual attraction to, or sexual activity with, members of the opposite sex."[10] Unfortunately, this definition gives little information or help to us as we attempt to look at causality and try to define homogeneous cohorts for scientific study. It is once again to state the obvious to say that there are a multitude of "sexual attractants" and many means by which "sexual activity" can be accomplished in the heterosexually oriented male or female. Perhaps one case history will be illustrative of the inadequacy of this definition:

A 52-year-old Caucasian physician made an appointment to see me as a psychiatrist. He was a Professor of Medicine at a prominent medical school and was married to another physician for thirty-one years, with six children, all of whom were married themselves.

Dr. T. had some sexual experimentation prior to puberty with older boys, but no homosexual contact since that time. He had intercourse with his wife in the first twenty years of their marriage on the average of three times per week, and he considered the sexual relations satisfying and felt his wife enjoyed their physical relationship also. The wife is orgasmic and has been so since early marriage. In the last eleven years of their marriage, they had become disinterested and intercourse was rare.

Dr. T. has recently become troubled by his attraction to a young, nineteen year old college student male, and had on one occasion engaged in fellatio with the young man to his mutual interest and satisfaction. His question and reason for coming to me: was he homosexual or heterosexual?

This, of course, is not an uncommon history that psychiatrists hear in their clinical practices. If one examines the case history carefully, a number of important pieces of information can be learned.

One should note the age of Dr. T. and be interested. To put it colloquially, "There may be snow on the roof, but there is still fire in the furnace." Although there is a physiological waning of the human sexual functioning with increasing age, sexual or erotic interest remains intact, and change in sexual functioning and activity is possible even at this age.

Second, one should note that the occupation of the person has little relevance to sexual functioning or interest, no matter what the age. There is some evidence that certain occupations may have higher or lower percentages of heterosexually or homosexually oriented persons; however, the usual stereotype of the florist as homosexually oriented and the football player as heterosexually oriented are simply not true.[11]

Third, it is mentioned that Dr. T. had some homosexual experimentaion prior to puberty. This is not unusual and according to the famous Kinsey study, 37 percent of the total male population surveyed reported at least incidental homosexual experience to the point of orgasm between adolescence and old age.[12] He found that 25 percent reported more than incidental homosexual experience or reactions for at least three years between the ages of 16 and 55 years;

18 percent reported at least as much homosexual as heterosexual behavior in their histories for at least three years between the ages of 16 and 66 years; 10 percent were more or less exclusively homosexual for a period of three years between the ages of 16 and 55 years; and finally, 4 percent of the males surveyed were exclusively homosexual throughout their lives after the onset of adolescence, and a further 4 percent were exclusively homosexual for at least three years between the ages of 16 and 55 years. This data is very impressive and has been reaffirmed in smaller study populations of males.[13]

Kinsey's figures clearly show that homosexual experimentation at different age levels among relatively heterosexually oriented males is not unusual; in fact, it would appear to be a rather common phenomenon, something our stereotypes and homophobic biases tend to ignore or not believe.

If we return to the definition of heterosexuality, one will note that at least two levels of concern are included: sexual *attraction* and sexual activity. That is, an exclusive focus on genital activity and the behaviors attached to their "sexual use or misuse" is not in keeping with the scientific information. The brain as the seat of sexual fantasies and source of erotic attraction may be equally important, if not of primary importance, when trying to understand heterosexual orientation. With the example of Dr. T. after long discussion with him, this patient disclosed that his fantasies for arousal and for maintaining an erection and intercourse with his wife were almost exclusively involved with young boys and young men. He was not capable of enriched fantasies involving young girls and women to serve as the erotic stimulus for his physiological functioning with his wife over those 31 years of marriage.

The question then arises: in making a decision about a patient's heterosexual or homosexual orientation, does the psychiatrist focus on the brain or the genitals? Does the time that one discusses this with a patient influence the decision of which category in which to place an individual? If one interviewed Dr. T. at age 53 when he was living with the nineteen-year-old college student and engaging in daily sexual, genital activity, would that help our decision-making process?

Dr. Kinsey and his colleagues attempted to look at the life histories of the individual persons they interviewed and see their sexual orientation on a continuum. Figure I shows the Kinsey Scale which rates heterosexual-homosexual behaviors taken at one point in

Figure I

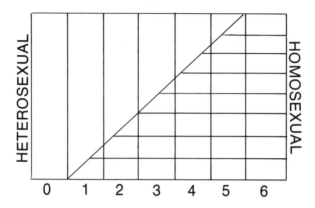

0. Individuals are rated as 0's if they make no physical responses which result in erotic arousal or orgasm, and make no psychic responses to individuals of their own sex. Their sociosexual contacts and responses are exclusively with individuals of the opposite sex.

1. Individuals are rated 1's if they have only incidental homosexual contacts which have involved physical or psychic response, or incidental psychic responses without physical contact. The great preponderance of their sociosexual experience and reactions is directed toward individuals of the opposite sex. Such homosexual experiences as these individuals have may occur only a single time or two, or at least infrequently in comparison to the amount of their heterosexual experience. Their homosexual experiences never involve as specific psychic reactions as they make to heterosexual stimuli. Sometimes the homosexual activities in which they engage may be inspired by curiosity, or may be more or less forced upon them by other individuals, perhaps when they are asleep or when they are drunk, or under some other peculiar circumstance.

2. Individuals are rated 2's if they have more than incidental homosexual experience, and/or if they respond rather definitely to homosexual stimuli. Their heterosexual experiences and/or reactions still surpass their homosexual experiences and/or reactions. These individuals may have only a small amount of homosexual experience or they may have a considerable amount of it, but in every case it is surpassed by the amount of heterosexual experience that they have within the same period of time. They usually recognize their quite specific arousal by homosexual stimuli, but their responses to the opposite sex are still stronger. A few of these individuals may even have all of their overt experience in the homosexual, but their psychic reactions to persons of the opposite sex indicate that they are still predominantly heterosexual. This latter situation is most often found among younger males who have not yet ventured to have actual intercourse with girls, while their orientation is definitely heterosexual. On the other hand, there are some males who should be rated as 2's because of their strong reactions to individuals of their own sex, even though they have never had overt relations with them.

3. Individuals who are rated 3's stand midway on the heterosexual-homosexual scale. They are about equally homosexual and heterosexual in their overt experience and/or their psychic reactions. In general, they accept and equally enjoy both types of contacts, and have no strong preferences for one or the other. Some persons are rated 3's, even though they may have a larger amount of experience of one sort, because they respond psychically to partners of both sexes, and it is only a matter of circumstances that brings them into more frequent contact with one of the sexes. Such a situation is not unusual among single males, for male contacts are often more available to them than female contacts. Married males, on the other hand, find it simpler to secure a sexual outlet through intercourse with their wives, even though some of them may be as interested in males as they are females.

4. Individuals are rated 4's if they have more overt activity and/or psychic reactions in the homosexual, while still maintaining a fair amount of heterosexual activity and/or responding rather definitely to heterosexual stimuli.

5. Individuals are rated 5's if they are almost entirely homosexual in their overt activities and/or reactions. They do have incidental experience with the opposite sex and sometimes react psychically to individuals of the opposite sex.

6. Individuals are rated 6's if they are exclusively homosexual, both in regard to their overt experience and in regard to their psychic reactions.

Kinsey Heterosexual-Homosexual Rating Scale. (Source: Kinsey, A. C., Pomeroy, W. B., & Martin, C.E. *Sexual behavior in the human male.* Philadelphia: Saunders, 1948. Reprinted with permission.)

the life of that person and rates them "0" for exclusive heterosexual contacts and "6" for exclusive homosexual contacts.

Although this method of rating sexual behaviors is inadequate in many ways, it does make one important point: the extremes of exclusive heterosexual activity or exclusive homosexual activity are not the "normals" from a statistical viewpoint; they represent just that, the minority or extremes. The "normals" from purely this viewpoint would be the Kinsey Scale #1 and Scale #5 if one looks at this from a purely statistical viewpoint and does not apply any moral judgment to the behaviors. This Kinsey Scale is a point of reference of all human sexuality textbooks and most research protocols, so the author felt it would be important for the reader to be informed about it. However, the faulty portion of the Scale is that it does not rate separately either the time at which the information is gathered nor does it help with clearly understanding the brain-vs.- genitals focus that was brought out in the section above.

(d) Homosexuality

The definition of homosexuality usually found, as in James McCary's textbook, is the opposite of heterosexuality: "sexual attraction to, or sexual activity with, members of one's own sex."[14]

The same inherent difficulties are encountered with this definition as with heterosexuality. A second clinical example may be helpful to see this inadequacy of definition and usefulness of the term:

> Mr. J. is a 32-year-old Caucasian male who came to see me as a psychiatrist immediately following his discharge from a Federal prison. He served eight consecutive years from age 24 in that prison and had multiple intermittent jail experiences between the ages of 16-24.

> In the pre-adolescent and adolescent stages of Mr. J.'s life, he experimented with peers in homosexual activity and had two successful incidents of heterosexual intercourse. He was with a New York City gang for a short time wherein homosexual activity was not uncommon.

> While in prison for the 8 years, Mr. J. had an exclusive, protected, caring homosexual relationship with his cellmate which included daily homosexual genital contact for those 8 years.

> His question to me: Am I a homosexual or could I pursue contact with the opposite sex? Can he change at this "late age?"

A similar series of interesting points can be made with reference to naming and using the heterosexual-homosexual categories. In exploring the brain or erotic fantasies of Mr. J., he admitted to homosexually as well as heterosexually oriented fantasies. He was able to maintain his erotic interests with his cellmate partner by using a mixture of both fantasies. However, he felt that the erotic fantasies were more intense when focused on female genitalia.

After a number of sessions of counseling, Mr. J. began drinking alcohol and dating young women while holding down a low-paying job. He married one young woman, age 18, and the marriage ended in divorce within one year. The sexual contact during the marriage was poor from both his and her perspective, although he was able to function in a rather mechanical manner. More important, the wife commented later on his lack of good social skills and ability to deal with peers without alcohol.

This clinical example helps us to see another dimension of human sexuality which is also not focused on genital activity and not on fantasies or erotic behavior: social skills related to pair-bonding (marriage) or related to courting.

The patient, Mr. J., had grave deficiencies in relation to his social skills in approaching women or men, in carrying on meaningful conversation or even approaching the issue of genital sexuality with either sex partner. These complex and important behaviors are learned from early infancy and are influenced greatly by the culture and by role models. Mr. J. came from a divorced family, was raised in foster homes, was physically abused as a child and teenager, and his only social skill was robbing banks, which he obviously did quite poorly.

(e) Heterosocial and Homosocial Behaviors

In clinical practice one sees many patients who have adequate sexual arousal patterns as well as the necessary behavioral repertoire to engage in the genital aspects of sex. However, these patients may be unable to engage in the type of social behavior necessary for meeting, dating, and relating to persons of the opposite sex or the same sex. This would be similar to the lack of socials skills we noted in our second clinical case study, Mr. J.

The social behaviors are very complex and are listed by different authors in various ways. Tollison and Adams divide components of heterosocial behavior into three elements: social behaviors necessary to initiate relationships with the opposite sex, social and interpersonal behaviors preceding sexual behavior, and behaviors required to maintain heterosocial relationships.[15]

For example, for the young male who is beginning to learn from role models and peers the methods of approaching the opposite sex, Tollison and Adams would list four skills as important for him to master:

1. Ability to ask open-ended questions
2. Art of the extended conversation
3. Conversation serving as an avenue for self-disclosure
4. Initiating relationships and appropriate eye contact.

Similar types of social skills would be required for the homosexually oriented male as he begins a lifestyle of initiating contacts and relationships with members of the same sex. The culture, however, here would dictate different surroundings and different kinds of approaches depending on the setting such as a bar, party, work or casual meeting.

The social skills and behaviors immediately preceding genital behavior would be of a different type and, again, this is a learned and culture-bound phenomenon. Self-disclosure of a different kind relating to sexual or genital preferences may be discussed or approached gingerly either verbally or tactilely. Reward for the behaviors in terms of sounds, or reinforcement with flattery might be involved here. Finally, ingratiating behaviors or flattery of a special kind in reference to performance may be important to continue the sexual pursuits.

These behaviors immediately preceding sexual or genital contacts may be extremely important and are quickly forgotten by the couple as they become "used to each other." It is in this area that a therapist can be most helpful in guiding the married couple in re-exploring new dimensions of these behaviors with the reward of increased sexual satisfaction and lack of the boredom with each other that is perceived in other areas of their married lives.

It is clearest to researchers in human sexuality that these kinds of behaviors related to sexuality are learned and are related to certain proscribed and prescribed cultural norms and values.[16] Without making specific reference to particular Roman Catholic cultures, it is again our clinical experience that certain normative values understood by many as being taught by the culture-bound Church (e.g., sexual intercourse is the "right" of the husband and "duty" of the wife) have led during this century to a great deal of marital dissatisfaction and unwillingness to be open and discuss these areas as if they were learned behaviors, like placing the fork on the left side of the plate. It would be inaccurate to state that this has been a "cause" for the increased divorce rate among Roman Catholic couples; however, it certainly has not been helpful in examining the marriage relationship as one where new learning can take place, and where old wounds and hurts can be healed, leading to an improved and happier marital state for the couple and their children.

(f) Dimorphism

In the past twenty years, a newer concept referred to as

"dimorphism" has emerged to help us understand sexual behaviors along the continuum of growth and development of the human person. John Money, one of the leading sexologists in the U.S. today, has defined it as: ". . . having two forms of manifestations, though of the same species, as in a juvenile and adult form, or a male and female form. Though usually used to refer to bodily form and appearance . . . the meaning of the term is extended by analogy to apply to sex differences in behavior and language."[17]

In the previous chapter Dr. Monteleone has described the dimorphic nature of the developing embryo; the potentiality of dual sets of parallel sexual organ systems — one female and one male — within every developing embryo until the sixth week of gestation at which time the addition of androgen and Müllerian Inhibiting Substance will enable the sexual anlage to develop as a male with the ultimate disintegration of the female anlage or cells.[18] In other words, programming for either genital organ systems is present from the moment of conception in the normal embryo and it requires a further "critical stimulus" to facilitate that differentiation in one direction either toward male genitalia or toward female genitalia.

A similar biological dimorphism occurs in the developing brain of the fetus. Apparently, with the addition of androgen and perhaps other hormone "messages," the male brain as it develops is programmed into a non-cyclic pattern in the hypothalamus; therefore, cyclic hormonal changes seen in the female brain particularly following puberty and leading to the ovulatory cycle and menses are suppressed or not favored in the programming of the male brain.[19] It is obvious that the brain must have the potentiality for either cyclic or non-cyclic hypothalamic functioning and, therefore, may be referred to as a dimorphic organ system capable of either "female or male" programming according to the endocrine stimulus, presumably given to it sometime after the sixth week of gestation.

It is very interesting to speculate that in the clinical phenomenon of transsexualism described earlier in this paper there is a "programming accident" of sorts. The "programming" of the genital ridge (embryonic tissue from which the gonads eventually develop) in the male-to-female transsexual moves in a normal fashion with normal male genitalia being produced; the "programming" of the dimorphic brain may occur in a fashion completely opposite that of the genital ridge, and behavioral programming occurs which ensures gender identity the opposite of sexual identity in the young, developing child. This is pure speculation on the part of this author. However, the discovery recently of the absence of the H-Y antigen (associated with the production of male genitalia) in phenotypically normal male transsexuals leads one again to look to prenatal influences and "errors in programming" rather than to the more facile psychological explanation of the complex behavior of the male-to-female transsexual in reference to etiology.[20] However, two other studies were unable to confirm this finding.[20a]

John Money and others have begun to use this concept of dimorphism in evaluating sex-specific behaviors after birth of the child. They are asking questions asked since early centuries: what are the unique behaviors of a woman, for example, which are biologically determined? psychologically determined? culturally determined?[21,22]

Sigmund Freund and his followers, particularly Carl Jung, had made observations about human behavior which clearly show a co-mingling of feminine and masculine traits in all persons. Although they treat these traits as dimorphic, they felt their etiologies were exclusively attributable to the early infancy and childhood experiences with the mother and father and siblings.

It is clear to this author that there is a kind of neural pathway programming which occurs early in the development of the fetal brain which serves as the template, analogous to multiple railroad tracks which lead the individual behaviorally in certain directions of behavior preferentiality.[23] This concept will be developed later in this chapter. It is mentioned here only to indicate that the age-old nature-vs.-nurture controversy is no longer given much credence by serious scientific scholars: there must be factors in the genetic, hormonal, psychological, social and cultural influences which all act on the person to produce the complex behaviors that we observe, whether in the area of sexuality specifically or in other behaviors of human persons.

Behaviors Comprising Human Sexuality

Sigmund Freud's reception in the Victorian period both by Protestant and Roman Catholic scholars was frigid. Freud dared to say that human sexuality had antecedents in early childhood experiences. He further perceived that behaviors involved with human sexuality were not all genital. It is this author's premise that the Christian church has had an exclusive focus on the genitals as comprising all of human sexuality, and it is only recently that we have witnessed an opening up of intellectual and academic concepts to allow for other behaviors to be labelled as sexual. One need only recall the Canon Law of marriage as well as the canonical prohibitions in religious life to see this preoccupation with genital sexuality, rather than an understanding of sexuality in a broader perspective.

It is helpful to this author to see human sexuality as comprising four major areas of behaviors and brain processes:

1. Erotic or cognitive/affective component
2. Heterosocial and homosocial component
3. Genital behaviors
4. Behaviors relating to family, child rearing, and nurturing.

The erotic or cognitive/affective component is a component of human sexuality which is uniquely human. It is our scientific inference that other animals, including primates, do not have active erotic fantasies since there is a presumption, whether correct or incorrect, that language is required for such an erotic component.[24] Human persons are able to initiate the human sexual response with only an erotic thought, whereas aural, olfactory, or physical stimuli are required for all other animals.

How this fantasy life comes into being with each person is certainly complicated and involves both nature and nurture components. However, it is possible, if one listens to John Money and Frank Beach with any credence, that there is some predisposition in the neural pathways which are encoded in some way *in utero* such that when a person is presented with a novel erotic scene, that person may have a predisposition to an intensified response with one scene but not another. Again, there is rampant speculation taking place with all of these theories of neural pathway predisposition, and they are only inferred from behaviors observed in man and other primates.

Clearly, two conditions must be present for erotic fantasies to develop at all: (1) age-specific neural development; and (2) conditioned learning, predominantly related to the onset of masturbatory activity.

With the monumental work of the developmental psychologist Jean Piaget, we have become aware of the delicate, yet stereotyped, manner by which children learn. For example, consider Piaget's famous experiment where he has two containers of differing heights and widths filled with the same volume of colored water. A child in the age range of six, when asked to tell which container has the most liquid, can only point to the tall, skinny container and say that that container has the most liquid, despite the fact that the child has poured an equal volume of colored liquid into both containers.[26] (See figure II) This is explained by the fact that the human brain continues to develop and grow after the birth of the child. At the age of six, the brain is capable of only certain operations and nothing can teach the child to skip ahead to more advanced operations. Intelligence is not the issue here, but rather the degree of maturation of the central nervous system, particularly the brain.

If this child were punished each time he or she did not get the correct answer, if would be a fruitless attempt to teach the child. For the child simply cannot conceptualize on that particular level. When

Figure II

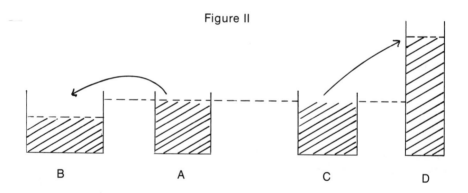

B   A   C   D

This is adapted from Piaget's experiment demonstrating periods of concrete operations.

The child is shown two containers (containers A and C above) and then asked if both contain the same amount of colored liquid. The child is capable at this stage of visually agreeing to the same volume of liquid in both containers A and C.

However, when the equal volumes are poured into two containers of differing size and width (containers B and D), the child can only visualize and conceptualize, at this stage in cognitive and neural development, that container D must have a larger volume of the liquid than container B.

the child reaches the age of ten to twelve, the correct mental operation may be accomplished without difficulty and the child can do over and over again similar experiments even if novel or new problems are presented to him.

In a similar fashion, the human brain cannot easily conceive of certain dimensions at early ages. For example, if Johnny sends a note to Susy in his third grade class asking to meet her behind the barn after school, and then appended, "I love you," to the end of the note, the mother confiscating the note would not be too worried. However, if the mother confiscated an identical note from Johnny and he was sixteen years old, she might have some room for worry. The meaning of the word "love" has a more multidimensional meaning to Johnny at sixteen than at eight; Johnny's brain has matured to a point where the multidimensions of love could be perceived in a new and novel fashion, and could be acted upon in a multitude of ways.

Knowledge of this phenomenon in terms of maturation of the brain with respect to concepts should be very important to the sexual educator as well as the religious educator.

Suppose Johnny is taught in the CCD class at age eight the simple concepts:

1. God is Father
2. God is love
3. Therefore, Father is love.

What if Johnny's father has been beating him brutally the entire eight years of his life? Johnny would not be able to make that multidimensional jump; instead he would toss out the window this "love notion" if it equated to father, or anyone like his father. When that same child is taught this concept at age sixteen, he has the neural mechanisms at this time to see father and love as concepts with multiple levels of meaning, and he is able to put in perspective the experiences with his own father and not generalize his father's behavior to all fathers' behaviors.

It is probable that the six-year-old child cannot conceptualize certain erotic fantasies; in fact, the child probably can only conceptualize a single function for his penis or his father's penis at this stage, no matter what pictures you would show him or what actual sexual activity he might witness. This might be likened to the elephant who saw his first naked man and was overhead to remark: "Can he actually breathe through that thing?"

It requires a certain stage of neural development before the visual material would have any impression on the child and before he or she could make any correlations with other persons, other parts of the anatomy, the use of the organ and its connection with conception, and its connection with love, etc.

Critical Periods

The concept of "critical periods" in physical and psychological development is an old one in biology, but one that is quite useful in understanding the rather stereotyped and normal development of sexual identity and gender identity/role in children and young adults.

In the previous chaper Dr. Monteleone indicated that there are at least two critical periods of development prior to the birth of the child: conception and the period extending from the sixth to the twelfth week of gestation (i.e., first trimester of gestation). Chromosomal errors at the moment of conception such as the XXY or XYY are thought to have rather important consequences on the later behavior of that child in terms of sexual functioning and sexual/gender identity. The second period mentioned by Dr. Monteleone is critical for the proper development of the female/male genitalia consonant with the chromosomal pattern programming.[27]

Such a concept of "critical periods" of development can be equally applied to the development of the human brain. As mentioned before, the human being is one of the only mammals born with a brain that requires at least twenty more years for complete and full myelination and neuronal maturation. This should be obvious to even the non-biologists for we nurture at least for 12-15 years all children and teach in graded levels in our schools. It is evident to us that in normal children at age six it would be most difficult, if not a biological impossibility, to teach that child elementary calculus. The brain is not at that period sufficiently developed to be able to synthesize, integrate, and apply simple principles which are required in elementary calculus.

Development of human sexual preferences, erotic interests and fantasies, human sexual social skills or heterosocial behaviors are no exceptions to this biological law of neurology and brain development. But are we able to this point to identify those critical periods after the birth of a child so as to be aware of the external or environmental components that would maximize or aid in the normal development of any child's erotic fantasies, heterosocial behaviors, and sex object choice? Unfortunately the answer is no . . . . at least in part. We are aware of important times for any child or young adult during which periods confusion reigns, and guidance is required, but beyond that little is known.

Perhaps it would be useful to consider another clinical example known to this author. The author would ask that you not make judgments on the behaviors described at this point; instead, attempt to view the different aspects of the behaviors as you would setting a table and judging someone who places the knife and spoon at the incorrect places on that table.

> J.T. is a 14-year-old male Caucasian teenager who attends a private school and was brought to my attention by the courts because of fire-setting behaviors in his neighborhood.

> J.T.'s father is a 36-year-old Irish Catholic contractor and married for 16 years to his wife, an Irish Catholic housewife, with six children. J.T. is the oldest child and his father has always held him up as an example to the other children, and his expectations of J.T. were quite high. He forced J.T. to participate in all sports activities against J.T.'s desires, but he tried hard in everything. He could be described as a loner with no close friends at school or in the neighborhood.

> Neither parents can accept that J.T. would set fires because he has never shown any other delinquent behaviors. When J.T. was last caught by the police near one of the small fires he set in a neighborhood home, he was noted to have semen on his pants and underwear.

It may appear strange that this clinical example would be chosen to explain concepts in development. However, J.T. represents an uncommon, but not rare, example of the type of sexual behavior problem we clinically see in our offices now and then. In order to understand the genesis of this type of behavior, it is important to understand, as described above, the critical periods of development of the brain, and the sexual, social and cultural place of the child in question and his family.

Another very important point is that the professional person who analyzes any situation like this tends to be rather opinionated. By that the author is implying that most people in the behavioral sciences are partial, wedded, or thoroughly indoctrinated in a single viewpoint of human sexual behavior and have personal feelings and specific moral views. A psychoanalyst will view the early years of interaction with the parents with greater weight than he or she would the prenatal programming or later teenage years. The behaviorist would virtually ignore the early years and focus on the behavior and its reconstruction into more acceptable behaviors. The more psychopharmacologically oriented psychiatrist may focus on endocrine disorders and possible pharmacologic agents which would be useful in altering such behaviors. It would be useful then to attempt to look at this clinical example, using all of the disciplines and seeing the contributions from each.

If one first focuses on the early family life of J.T., one finds that his father was rather distant from him. The father was the disciplinarian in the family. With J.T., not so with the younger children, he would tend to use corporal punishment for his misbehaviors rather liberally and usually in the context of his volatile temper. The father showed little physical affection for J.T. as he developed, but such affection was not unusual for the other five children in the family.

J.T. refers to his mother with great affection. She would serve as the protector of all the children. J.T. related many fights the parents would have, which all the children would witness, with respect to discipline and to expectations and goals that were not met by the children, especially J.T., and the disappointment in the father. The isolation that J.T. experienced from friends was in part due to his role as the eldest child and the physical work expected of him on the rural ranch house where chores were always to be done. He, in distinction from his other siblings, always prefered to play alone and had many imaginary friends when in his earliest years.

J.T.'s sexual behaviors were described by himself as not unusual for his age. He recalls his first connection with fires when he experienced orgasm lying quietly in front of the fireplace while his parents read and chatted nearby. It was a surprising and pleasurable experience, one that he was to repeat for many months, with and without his parents present. The discovery of masturbation at age twelve with ejaculation was not initially found to be as pleasurable from J.T.'s perspective until it was once again connected with warmth (hot water bottle). It was most intense when observing and experiencing the warmth of a fire.

Masturbation became a more frequent daily event, two to three times daily not being unusual by age thirteen, usually without benefit of a fire..J.T. had seen some magazines his father kept hidden in the bathroom closet which depicted explicit sexual acts, but found them less than interesting at that time. All masturbation was done in secrecy, but many times, because of the use of the fireplace, it was almost discovered. J.T. recalled one occasion when he believed his father actually witnessed the event totally when he was thirteen, but nothing was ever mentioned. The repeated recollection of the factor of his father discovering him in the act of masturbating actually increased his sexual excitement and orgasm.

J.T. began setting small fires in different areas of the ranch acreage allowing him both the excitement of possible discovery as well as the physical excitement of the stimulus of fire and masturbation. This progressed over a one-year period until his discovery and apprehension by the police at a fire at a neighboring house.

Although to this author's knowledge no study has been completed with relation to fire-setting, it could be safely stated that the family constellation and early childhood experiences of J.T. were certainly not unusual. It is also not unusual for a young male child to be introduced to orgasm through the physical closeness or stimulation of warm objects such as fires, poles, rugs, mattresses, etc. It is further not unusual that masturbation would begin at the age of nine to twelve; in fact, one could generalize and say that this would generally be the age at which many males begin this lifelong practice. Tollison and Adams summarize the data concerning masturbation stating:

> It is safe to say that most individuals have engaged in masturbation. Various studies have reported that 92-100 per cent of men and 58-85 per cent of women have masturbated at some point in their lives. It is also probably safe to assume that the vast majority of those individuals who masturbate do so without considering the effects of masturbation on the shaping and the strengthening of their "personal" pattern of sexual arousal.[28]

What is of particular interest to us is the exclusive interest in fires and sexual excitement that occurred in this young man. This is unusual. From a behaviorist's viewpoint, one could argue that he simply had pleasurable or positive reinforcement for the visual and tactile stimulus of the fire tied frequently and closely to pleasurable sexual satisfaction and orgasm.

If either the psychoanalyst's explanation of family dynamic and interaction early with J.T. or the behaviorist's explanation were absolutely correct and therefore applicable to any such like situation with any young male with the same constellation in the family and masturbatory experiences, our fire insurance rates would be higher each year than the cost of our homes. It would appear logical that other influences could be at play in this rather unusual form of sexual behavior.

It is important to point out that the treatment of this disorder of sexual behavior may be unrelated to the explanation of its etiology. This is another area of great confusion for persons not versed in the many schools of psychology and treatment of behavioral disorders. The efficacy of psychoanalysis as a treatment modality, aversive conditioning, short-term psychotherapy, milieu therapy, family therapy, psychotheological treatment, Rogerian therapy, or Adlerian therapy may be completely independent of the causes of the behaviors that those treatment modalities are treating. Psychoanalytic treatment of fire-setting may be more efficacious according to some persons in the field, but this does not validate the psychoanalyst's explanation of the etiology of the disorder.

Prenatal Programming

Let us first examine what possible role prenatal "programming" or neural preparedness could possibly play in dealing with this unusual behavior of fire-setting and erotic arousal. It would be stretching the data at this point to suggest that any kind of specific programming for attraction to fires could be involved in such complex human behavior. However, it would not be an extraordinary jump from the data at present to suggest that this young man was biologically or neurally prepared to respond to tactile stimulation (heat from fires) in preference to visual stimulation (the possible switch to the use of pornography offerred by his father's magazines) at that point in his development, a critical period in his environment where the possibility of masturbation beginning from a learning and endocrine viewpoint was reached in his life.

This may seem a little farfetched for everyone, so let us examine the area clearly explained by our behaviorist colleagues. It would appear from the research done that people must be biologically or neurally prepared for certain phobias, such as fear of snakes. Such a phobia is universal and occurs in a certain percentage of the population, reinforced with the first experience with a snake or a snake-like object. Ohman *et al.* showed that people are "prepared" to acquire fears of snakes, given an unpleasant experience with them, yet they are not "prepared" to develop fears of other objects such as faces or houses.[29]

In the light of his example, why is it that persons do not usually develop erotic attractions to grass and blankets but commonly develop erotic attractions to soft curvatures and angular features? So with J.T.; he could possibly have been neurally prepared for something to do with fires (heat, flames, intensity of heat, stimulation of fingers, etc.) that would make him preferentially choose that object for continued conditioning of the erotic sexual response through masturbation as opposed to a visual stimulus such as explicit pornographic scenes.

This author does not wish to make a great deal of this example except to suggest that there most likely is some type of preparedness related to prenatal programming of the dimorphic brain that could or does contribute to the later environmentally conditioned response. Certainly the repetitive use of masturbation for J.T. as the reinforcer of his behavior was the explanation for the clear repetition of the behavior despite dangers. Negative reinforcement of that behavior (e.g., punishing him when he was caught masturbating in front of the fire by the father) would not necessarily have a salutary effect on extinguishing the behavior; in fact, there is evidence that it could further contribute to the reinforcement of it and the repetition of the behavior made more likely.

It would be important here to examine a concept like "fault." Was the father at "fault" for not intervening at that moment in his son's life when he observed his masturbation? Was that the cause of his ultimate destructive behavior? Was the father at "fault" for not allowing his son to learn knitting instead of forcing him to play baseball? Should all parents avoid letting their children lie in front of fireplaces for fear of contributing to such unusual sexual practice? Should fireplaces be abolished from all homes in a mental health preventative measure? This may seem absurb to the reader, but such "logical conclusions" are reached each day by parents and societies in reference to other sexual behaviors and attempts to extinguish them.

Before leaving the clinical example of J.T., the readers would perhaps be interested in the two year follow-up of this very interesting young man. He was seen by the author for two years and included in a group of teenagers of his age group. The theory this author uses in treatment of this disorder is that the behavior will extinguish if not emphasized in psychotherapy, and the child should be given adequate social skills including heterosocial skills to learn to relate with age appropriate persons and to discuss the sexual issues in his life as well as other social issues which he had not had the opportunity to discuss or learn before. There have been no repeated episodes of fire-setting in nine years and J.T. is currently married and has two children of his own. Do you think the behavior will be repeated in his children?

Conclusions

As explained in the introduction to this paper, it was not our purpose to present a new and coherent description of the psychological processes involved in the development of sexual identity and gender identity/role for the human person. That would be an arrogant goal and one that would require far more time than allowed in this brief chapter.

Instead, it was the purpose of this paper to show that complex biological factors present during the development of the human person as a fetus and later as an actively maturing organism plus psychological elements of family dynamics, cultural surroundings, social condition, and life experiences in general all contribute to the ultimate product of the human person as a sexual person with complicated sexual behaviors.

It is the considerable experience of many committed Christian psychiatrists and psychologists that there is an ever widening gap between the sexual practices, and scientific explanation of those practices in human sexuality on the one hand, and the theological reflection of the Christian church including the Roman Catholic Church on the other. The fact that the authoritative teachers of the Roman Catholic Church would even request a conference to examine the complex issues in this area of human sexuality is a major step toward closing that gap.

The fact that this conference exists is further testament to this author personally of the movement of the Holy Spirit within Christ's Church. In His path the healing that is so necessary for those persons who experience and live within the teachings of the Church will be realized. At this moment in time, however, the gap in our understanding and the chasm between the biological sciences and theological sciences continue to cause, rather than heal, much human suffering.

Notes

1. Beach, Frank A. (ed.), *Human Sexuality in Four Perspectives* (Baltimore: The Johns Hopkins University Press, 1976).

2. Forleo, Romano and Pasini, Willy (eds.), *Medical Sexology* (Littleton, MA:, PSG Publishing Company, Inc., 1980).

3. Kolodny, Robert C., Masters, William H., and Johnson, Virginia E., *Textbook of Sexual Medicine* (Boston: Little, Brown and Company, 1979).

4. McCary, James Leslie, *Human Sexuality,* 2d ed., (New York: Van Nostrand Reinhold Company, 1973).

5. Money, John and Ehrhardt, A.A., *Man and Woman, Boy and Girl: The Differentiation and Dimorphism of Gender Identity from Conception to Maturity* (Baltimore: Johns Hopkins University Press, 1972).

6. Money, John, *Love and Love Sickness* (Baltimore: Johns Hopkins University Press, 1980).

7. Tollison, C. David and Adams, Henry E., *Sexual Disorders* (New York: Gardner Press, Inc., 1979).

8. Benjamin, Harry, M.D., *The Transsexual Phenomenon* (New York: The Julian Press, Inc., 1966).

9. Stoller, Robert J., M.D., *Sex and Gender* (New York: Science House, 1968).

10. McCary, *op. cit.*

11. Marmor, Judd (ed.), *Homosexual Behavior* (New York: Basic Books, Inc., 1980).

12. Kinsey, Alfred C., Pomeroy, Wardell B., and Martin, Clyde E., *Sexual Behavior in the Human Male* (Philadelphia, W. B. Saunders Company, 1948).

13. Weinberg, Martin S. and Williams, Colin J., *Male Homosexuals* (New York: Oxford University Press, 1974).

14. McCary, *op. cit.*

15. Tollison and Adams, *op. cit.*

16. Davison, Gerald C. and Neale, John M., *Abnormal Psychology,* 2d ed. (New York: John Wiley & Sons, Inc., 1978).

17. Money, *op. cit.,*

18. Monteleone, James A., M.D., chapter 4 in this volume.

19. Diamond, Milton, "Human Sexual Development: Biological Foundations for Social Development," in *Human Sexuality in Four Perspectives* edited by F. A. Beach (Baltimore: The Johns Hopkins University Press, 1976).

20. Spoljar, M., Eicher, W., Cleve, H., Murken, J.-D., and Stengel-Rutkowski, S., "The Current State of the Investigation of H-Y Antigen Expression in Patients with Transsexualism," *Human Genetics,* in press.

20a. Wachtel, Stephen S., personal communication.

21. Maccoby, Eleanor E. and Jacklin, Carol N., *The Psychology of Sex* (Stanford, CA: Stanford University Press, 1974).

22. Parsons, Jacquelynne E. (ed.), *The Psychobiology of Sex Differences and Sex Roles* (Washington: Hemisphere Publishing Corporation, 1980).

23. Whalen, Richard E., "Brain Mechanisms Controlling Sexual Behavior," in *Human Sexuality in Four Perspectives,* edited by F. A. Beach, (Baltimore, The Johns Hopkins University Press, 1976).

24. Beach, Frank A., "Cross-Species Comparisons and the Human Heritage," in *Human Sexuality in Four Perspectives,* edited by F. A. Beach, (Baltimore, The Johns Hopkins University Press, 1976).

25. Money, *op. cit.,*

26. Beard, Ruth M., *An Outline of Piaget's Developmental Psychology* (New York: Basic Books, Inc., 1969).

27. Monteleone, *op cit.*

28. Tollison and Adams, *op. cit.*

29. Ohman, A.,Erixon, G.,and Lofbeg, I. "Phobias and peparedness: Phobic versus neutral pictures as conditioned stimli for human autonomic responses," *Journal of Abnormal Psychology* 84:41-45, (1975).

Chapter 6

A "Sex Revolution" in American Culture?

Paul Peachey, Ph.D.

It is widely believed that since the early 1960s "a sexual revolution" has been underway in American society, and that "a new sexual morality" is in the making. Older institutional patterns and cultural norms ostensibly are yielding to freer, less inhibited and even unbridled expression of erotic impulses in society. Areas of behavior once strictly regulated by folkways, by moral code, and even by legal sanction, seem rather suddenly and painlessly abandoned to the vagaries of private or personal discretion. Deplored by some, heralded by others, the changes in any case seem inexorable.

Attitudinal, behavioral, and cultural data appear readily available to support "sexual revolution" and "new morality" verdicts. Separation and divorce rates continue to soar, as do the rates of "illegitimate" births and of abortions. Cohabitation without marriage for a variety of reasons is suddenly somehow accepted in the society. Sex roles in and out of marriage as well as the content of marriage are undergoing redefinition, sometimes for the better, sometimes for the worse. Both the printed and the image media treat sexual themes not only explicitly, but sometimes also in trivializing and exploiting ways. Finally the immense volume of academic publications on many themes pertaining to human sexuality suggests that something important is afoot. In a word, both opponents and proponents of these startlingly abrupt changes can with some justification describe them as "revolutionary."

Yet, as we shall show, there is good reason to resist, at least initially, any quick recourse to "revolutionary" terminology. The language of revolution quickly distorts the flow of cultural life. Thus, while older usages may fall into disuse, moral codes are recreated in the behaviors of new members entering societies. And if many persons manifest attitudes or behaviors as those just outlined, others are shaping their lives along "traditional" lines. "Decay" and "renewal" are commingled processes in societies. Generalizations about trends which fail to cope with the interpenetrations of the two processes can function as self-fulfilling prophecies on either side. Morever, on a deeper plane, a premature reach for the language of revolution betrays a lack of historical perspective. To be sure, particular societies, indeed civilizations, have collapsed in the past, and are likely to do so in the future. But it is also true that "decay" is a necessary corollary of growth and development. And when this perspective is brought to bear on the purported evidence of "a sexual revolution" at least the possibility of a rather different interpretation emerges.

This is not to deny that we are in the midst of a stormy passage or that a great deal of moral and hence social confusion and moral anarchy prevail. Many innocent people are caught in the cross fire of conflicting values. Persons at virtually all levels of leadership in society confront contradictory demands, entailing insoluble dilemmas. How can the needs of persons caught in difficult contexts be squared with the need for definitional and institutional integrity? Yet a serious examination of these very issues gives reason for pause before a rush to the barricades either to defend or to attack the "new sexual morality."

I. Problems of Cultural Analysis

It is the task of this paper to sift some of the evidence which bears on the purported sexual revolution, particularly with reference to the normative culture. What is the nature and scope of culture change regarding human sexuality? What is the likely import of the changes which can be identified for the future? Obviously only limited aspects of these questions can be treated in this brief compass. We shall comment primarily on the norms pertaining to primary sex behavior, to marriage, and to sex role and gender definitions. But measuring changes in the normative culture, as we shall see, is methodologically problematic for the social sciences. Consequently our treatment must be prefaced by a brief discussion of these methodological problems.

Paradoxically, in daily usage, the concept of culture presents little difficulty. In everyday terms, we "know" that ways of life vary from place to place and from country to country. We know also that the ways which are prevalent in a given society mold the conduct of the people within them. These ways, the "culture" of the given society, in some measure, then, "cause" specific behaviors or modes of conduct among its members. When we travel to another country, we anticipate that the behaviors we encounter may seem strange to us. These strange ways we try to some extent to understand, and within limits, to observe. Thus the time-honored proverb, "When in Rome, do as the Romans do."

Difficulties arise, however, when we seek to translate this everyday logic into the terms of empirical scientific investigation. Already the multiplicity of cultures poses problems, particularly today, when specific cultures increasingly interpenetrate one another. Moreover, societies generally embrace subcultures, and subcultures tend to increase in number as societies (cultures) increase in size. Finally, and most important, cultures themselves are highly complex phenomena. They embrace numerous traits, items, or elements. It is not clear whether "culture" is a "real" phenomenon, rather than merely a nominal category. If it is the former, we expect a culture to display a configurative integration of the elements comprising it, a kind of inner unity, a "Geist," a whole which is more than a sum of parts. If the latter, culture as a level of reality exists only in the mind of the observer as a mere summary concept which refers quickly to certain classes or categories of otherwise discrete phenomena. Correlations may indeed exist among some elements thus designated, but these must be ascertained empirically rather than assumed. Accordingly the investigator may be able to measure the effects of particular items of "culture" on specific behavior sequences or episodes, or certain interaction effects among several items, but the term "culture" itself is without empirical reference.

Here, for practical reasons, we shall take a mediating position, without embracing a particular general theory of culture, and thus also without proposing a basic solution. We shall assume that configurations of culture elements may operate as factors in human interaction. We shall follow Leslie White's (1980) assertion that "when things and events are considered in the context of their relation to the human organism, they constitute behavior; when they are considered not in terms of their relations to the human organism but in their relation to one another, they become culture by definition." Language illustrates the point. Conversation is behavior. But the language used in conversation may be analyzed for its structure apart from the persons who employ it. Language in the latter case is an instance of culture. But further, in preference to Tylor's (1865) classic omnibus definition of culture, White restricts the term to the sphere of "symbolling," to "a class of things and events dependent upon symbolling that are considered in a kind of extrahuman context." As the rules of syntax express the inner coherence of the signs which constitute the language, a given symbolic universe manifests some degree of inner coherence. That coherence permits an aggregate of individuals to function as a society. Abrupt disruptions of societies, whatever their source, can result in instability, confusion, and even conflict within the society, since moral blueprints will no longer correspond to the events or the exigencies which members of the collectivity face.

But there are further difficulties with the context of culture, difficulties which bear particularly on the discussion of changing sex roles, namely the dual nature of human existence *(homo duplex)*.[7] Human beings consist of both "nature" and of "spirit." Even apart from the question of the relationships between them, the latter term is problematic in its own right. Social scientists eschew the metaphysical dimensions of the term in favor of a sociocultural definition. Thus the social sciences have achieved the progressive substitution of sociocultural explanations for those stressing the determinative influence of physical nature.[46] Some scholars who work with an evolutionary conception of human development believe that in the human case cultural evolution has in effect supplanted biological evolution. Thus, as we shall see, sex roles and gender identities are viewed by social scientists as social phenomena, as culturally mediated learned behavior modes. Thus the nature vs. nurture debate, once so troublesome, has been regarded as surmounted.

Today, however, the old debate has reared its head with new and unprecedented vigor.[31,32] Thanks to important strides in many scientific fields, notably in biochemistry, genetics, primatology and ethology (stressing the force of biological, physiological, and genetic factors in human behavior), efforts are underway to develop scientific modes of explanation of human behavior which in time promise to dispense with sociological categories altogether.[57,14] From a rather different perspective, but with similar results, Skinner[38] rejects the "autonomous man" and the correlative concepts of culture still postulated by the social sciences in favor of "operant conditioning," a scenario in which the organism responds directly to rewards and penalties offered by the environment. Those sociobiologists most directly indebted to ethologists, such as Konrad Lorenz[25], have restated the case for the genetic base for drives such as aggression and male dominance. As a result, at a time when movements for sexual equality, buoyed by social scientific emphases on the sociocultural provenance of sexual inequality, attribute existing sex typing to the social system, renewed arguments and evidence are cited by others in favor of some degree of biological determinism.

An early composition of these differences is hardly in prospect. But here, too, there are mediating options. Phenomenological anthropologists have stressed the unique position and nature of the human animal in the biological kingdom – as such, of course, not a novel conception. What they have underscored, rather, is the anticipation of "spirit" in man's biological constitution.[24,3] With limited and unspecialized "instinctual" endowment, human beings are open to, and dependent upon, sociocultural completion. In effect, each component, the genetic-biological and the psycho-cultural, is realized through the other. In a similar vein, White[56] distinguishes four stages in the evolution of "minding": (1) simple reflex, where behavior is determined by intrinsic properties of both the organism and the thing reacted to; (2) conditioned reflex, where the response is elicited, not by properties intrinsic to the stimulus, but by meanings acquired in experience (e.g., the Pavlov dog experiment); (3) instrumental response, where the organism begins to control the environment, as when a chimpanzee uses a stick to reach a banana; and (4) the configuration of behavior involving nonintrinsic meanings, i.e., the uniquely human stage of "symbolling," the sphere of human culture. Each stage, White suggests, is carried forward into the next. By the same token, under certain conditions, regression is probable. Thus while organic drives are sublated, as it were, in moral personality, they remain as constitutive elements in human beings. Human beings advance from instinctive to learned and freely variable behavior while remaining biological organisms.

Finally, by way of prefatory remarks, note must be taken of the general crisis in modern culture. Traditionally culture served to integrate the systems of action of both individual and corporate actors into societies. But the growth of civilization has a curiously double effect on culture. On the one hand, the enlargement of the population aggregates who are effectively interdependent increases the scope and the power of certain core cultural values. The creation of the juridical, the economic, and the political structures which integrate 220 million Americans into a single "societal community"[35] entails a cultural development that is prodigious in scope and intensity. At the same time, however, such integration tends increasingly to relativize and to disintegrate the effective particular cultures within which these millions live out their particular lives. The result is a certain vertigo in modern life. A remote national community generates "terminal" norms — citizens can be sent to die at the frontiers of the community, according to norms thus virtually absolute in character – while norms which guide daily life become increasingly anarchical.

To summarize, culture is the system of symbolic meanings by which human beings realize and complete themselves as human beings. The symbols are man-*created* and *–creating*. As systems of symbols, cultures possess sufficient inner unity to secure the integration of human activities within their scope. Once constituted, that logic of unity, like the syntax of languages, displays both a structure and, as it were, a life of its own. Over time cultures grow, change, and decay, though in no necessary or inevitable sequence. Symbols, and the meanings they entail, flow intercursively as vehicles, as products, and as producers of interhuman reality of the species become human. Whether the stimuli received by the individual originate in the organism or in the environment external to the organism, definitions of, and responses to stimuli, are always culturally conditioned or culturally "scripted." Since cultural conditioning and molding begins from birth, the debate as to the relation

116

between organism drives and social learning foreseeably can never end. If, as it appears, all manifest behaviors pass through the prism of culture and therefore do not present themselves in raw culture-free terms, at the same time we can never assume that all contingencies are culture-anticipated or culture-tamed.

II. Culture and Human Sexuality

To what extent, then, and in what ways, are the manifestations of human sexuality culturally determined? To begin, several simple definitions will be necessary. First, the term "sex" (from L. *secare,* to divide) refers to the two divisions, male and female, by which organisms are distinguished with reference to their reproductive functions. Secondly, "gender identity" refers to the person's awareness and self-definition as either male or female. And third, sex role refers to the culturally determined set of behavior and attitudes considered appropriate for males and females. Finally, human sexuality refers to the quality or state of being sexual in the human instance. Included thus are both the direct biological and physiological sexual properties of human beings, and their definition and incorporation into the symbolic universe of human meaning and value – sexuality as humanly defined.[48,1]*

A full account of human sexuality requires the treatment of complex biological and physiological phenomena. These, of course, lie outside the scope of this paper. As in the above discussion on culture generally, the approach here to the "interface" of biology and culture in sexuality is that of philosophical anthropology. That is, one begins phenomenologically with human beings as culture-dependent and culture-producing. This means that while some biological and physiological processes involved in human sexual behavior are both analytically and operationally distinguishable, human sexual behavior always confronts us in culturally scripted or script-deviant form. This is not to ignore other situational determinants in behavior episodes, whether these flow from organismic drives or from environmental constraints.

---

*Cf. the statement published by a Committee of the American Medical Association: "Sex is understood to mean biological gender, but it also involves the self-image, or feelings of maleness and femaleness. It is both an appetite and the behavior which is oriented toward satisfaction of that appetite. What we call 'sex' has many meanings and shadings and is only part of the collective differences that mark an individual as male or female" (1972).

It is useful to distinguish between primary and secondary functions of sexuality in culture. Primary are the definitions pertaining directly to the regulation of sexual behavior and reproduction. Secondary are those definitions whereby gender characteristics or sex roles are implicated more broadly in the social structure. Traditionally the latter dominated the former. As we shall see, the attempt to free the primary from the "hegemony" of the secondary is an important element in the modern "sex revolution." For example, mate selection, the act by which new domestic groups are formed, was long subordinate to a family system which functioned as the basic unit of economic organization in the society. It also appears that sex as defined above, namely the divisions by which organisms are distinguished with reference to their reproductive functions, serves as the "primordial" division of labor from which further social differentiation evolved. By extension, "kinship" became "the prime organizing principle within each class until the rise of capitalism."[12] In some respects, as we shall see, the liberation of human sexuality from its secondary functions results in moral anarchy as it comes to be defined in purely autonomous terms – sex activity for its own sake.

Despite the rich lode of scientific findings available to us today on human sexuality, answers to basic questions, particularly on the relationship between the biological and the cultural spheres, still elude us. To be sure, much has been learned in recent years regarding genetic transmission and hormonal mechanisms. But despite important revisions meanwhile, the shadows of the nineteenth century giants – Darwin, Marx, and Freud – still hover over the discussion. Among these, Freud undoubtedly has had the greatest impact on our understanding of sexuality. In many respects that impact was doubtless positive. Yet his view that the sexual drive or libido is a biological constant, which must be coped with at all levels of individual, social, and cultural development[37] is an overstatement that has been revised meanwhile. Indirectly, however, arguments regarding the biological basis of behavior as advanced by ethologists[25] and sociobiologists today[57] have revived the case of those who seek direct biological roots for behaviors otherwise defined as social.

On the other hand, Friedrich Engels, continuing an inquiry begun by Marx, sought in a classic essay to link male dominance and sexual exclusiveness to the rise of private property, political rule, and class conflict.[9,19] That is, sex role differentiation originates *socially* rather than *biologically*. Marxists, of course, had other reasons for condemning the division of labor. Engels' thesis enjoys new popularity, thanks to numerous inquiries in recent years into the origins of human inequality. Yet there are two problems with this thesis. Given the prevalence of male dominance in a number of other species, where such dominance is not "historically" achieved, Engels appears to claim too much. Secondly, the claim is hardly more than a hypothesis, which at this stage of methodological development we are unable to prove or to disprove. Thus to argue the case for male dominance on biological grounds, or the case for sexual equality on archeological or historical grounds, appears equally dubious.

III. Sexuality in American Culture

What are the sexual modalities that are peculiar to American culture? Given the extraordinary diversity of American culture, indeed the multiplicity of American cultures, no single answer is possible. That diversity stems not only from the self-evident fact that with the constant infusion of new immigrants from many lands, the culture is highly pluralistic, but also from continuing differentiations generated by the society itself. Despite this basic diversity, however, certain general stereotypes prevail, particularly with regard to gender identity. Thus *masculinity* in American culture signifies aggression, dominance, strength, rationality, achievement – basically, goal-directed leadership. *Femininity,* on the other hand, signifies warmth, sympathy, tenderness, deference, devotion – basically expressive humanity. "For the most part, the private, familial domain is female, while the public, social one is male.[55]

In the assessment of these stereotypes, however, the agreement ends abruptly. There are population groups and strata in the United States where these respective conceptions of masculinity and femininity still largely prevail. In other milieux they are undergoing revision. Finally, in yet other circles they are totally repudiated and subjected to direct attack. Thus one critic writes: "The sexual division of labor – until recently, universal – need not, and in my opinion should not, survive in industrial society."[12] "Whatever the 'real' differences between the sexes may be," writes another, "we are not likely to know them until the sexes are treated differently, that is alike . . . ."[29]

With regard to primary sexuality, certain basic tendencies and motifs appear to transcend subcultural particularities. These appear to be linked to general tendencies and themes in the culture. Important here is the legacy of utilitarian thought and values which nurtures American individualism. The "pursuit of happiness" appears among our "inalienable" rights in our constitutional literature. Inalienable rights were formulated originally as a definition of the limits of government. Human fulfillment was to be realized in the acts of free men, rather than in acts of state. A path was thus hewn for free and responsible action. But by so much as well were the social restraints removed from egoistic and hedonistic pursuits. The frontier experience, where possibilities appeared unbounded, infused strongly individualistic, and hence self-centered, values into the culture. However creative these impulses may have been in the exploitation of the new continent, they have also been the source, or the occasion, for the proliferation of hedonistic values. The "counter-culture" of the 1960s, which at some points appeared as a reaffirmation of communal values in a society where individualism has run to excess, nonetheless spawned the new bumper sticker morality: "If it feels good, do it!"

As will be reemphasized below, such hedonism does not flourish in a vacuum. Instead it must be seen as a correlate of the continuing differentiation of the society and the culture. Insofar as a revolutionary change is underway toward erotic freedom, it appears thus as an extension of values already prevalent in the culture, and not as mere "breakdown" or the introduction of something alien and new. The manner in which differentiation processes generally abet the tendencies toward hedonism will be further explored in a moment. Meanwhile the probable association between male chauvinism and hedonism may be noted, though I am unaware of evidence that can be cited on the point. That is, where both male dominance and hedonism prevail in the culture, it is not hard to see how women came to be treated as "sex objects," along with a "double standard" of (im)morality.

Given its sources, American culture from the outset has been patriarchal, even though kinship in keeping with the nuclear family system has been reckoned bilaterally. Important aspects of the American experience have softened the patriarchal edge of the inherited old-world codes. In other respects, however, that experience appears to have intensified certain patriarchal traits. This can be seen particularly with reference to the frontier experience. Compared with the isolation of some wives and mothers in the nuclear family today, frontier women participated as equals in the drama and often the tragedy of frontier survival. This experience doubtless encouraged a certain openness and freedom in the relations of men and women in American society. On the other hand, the conquest of land, of nature, and sometimes of native Americans, undoubtedly fostered some of the chauvinistic and "macho" traits we associate with the American male today. It is precisely these traits which are glorified in the media and in some strands of ideology.[27,9a]

Similarly, the industrialization and urbanization of American society have had consequences in the development of the culture. Initially, in the rise of the factory system, whole families and later especially women and children were part of the factory labor force. But the hours were long and working conditions unhygienic. Eventually, as the separation of home and work was fully institutionalized, mothers and children were "liberated" from factory bondage, surely a victory for humanization. But with the culture still basically patriarchal, the adverse consequences of the separation of home and work would become evident only later.[11] A system which in the case of the married pair subordinates the identity and the status of the wife to that of the husband, and thus provides for her participation in the society only vicariously, rather than directly, appears inconsistent with the democratic and equalitarian values of the culture generally, not even to speak of the plight of the unmarried woman. Moreover the articulation of patriarchal monogamy with other institutional spheres, notably the economy, the polity, and public institutions generally (an instance of culture configuration), denies women the access which they need to achieve personal fulfillment in the human community. With broader experiences and involvements thus lacking, women frequently are not technically qualified for certain tasks and hence are not taken seriously by men as equals – a vicious cycle indeed! Yet we confront a serious dilemma. Possibilities for the full-time mothering of children in advanced industrial society represents, as far as it goes, an important achievement which can be replaced only at great cost.

Whatever the facts and merits of the case, it appears that the struggle for a redefinition of both gender identity and sex roles in our society will intensify in the years immediately ahead. Against the traditional assumptions, which until recent years were widely accepted, that masculinity and femininity as defined in our culture are biologically anchored, the reformers, as we have seen, attack them as essentially historical or sociocultural in origin and substance. Some even challenge the family system as a whole, given its association with traditional concepts of masculinity and femininity.

Transformation of the family system has been at the heart of the modernization process. Already more than a century ago, Henry Sumner Maine, the widely acclaimed English legal historian, described "the movement of the progressive societies" as a development in the course of which "the growth of individual obligation" follows "the gradual dissolution of family dependency." Moreover, "the individual is steadily substituted for the Family, as the unit of which civil laws take account."[30] Thus if Maine correctly identified the basic thrust of modernization, it is hardly surprising that the patriarchal conception would eventually be challenged. Anticipating the outcome of this development for the institutions of family and marriage, Emile Durkheim proposed, shortly before the turn of the century, that the occupational guilds would have to be revived to replace the solidary support for the individual in the modern society which the conjugal family could no longer provide. That is, Durkheim anticipated that a family unit based only on the romantic bond between the spouses could not provide a stable foundation for personal attachment in the modern world.[8]

In effect, the current challenge to male and female stereotyping in American society is but a phase of wider modernization processes. If increasing individuation is indeed the developmental destiny of human existence, then the encapsulation of the female in the family system, which was the model emergent in the mature industrial society, already appears anachronistic. Unless this broader framework of development is understood and recognized, the women's movement is likely to be seriously misperceived. As we shall see, however, this observation is not an apology for any particular feminist programs. Indeed, since both diagnosis and prognosis are as yet inadequate, there is still a stormy passage ahead. At this stage in history we cannot predict the eventual pattern of sex role differentiation in complex societies.

IV. Indicators of a Possible Sex Revolution

In the study of social interaction, analysts abstract three "systems" in interaction sequences: the actors as personality systems; the interactions of the actors (social system); and the culture, i.e., the expectations and rules that shape behavior. Though these three analytical systems are deeply interdependent, they nonetheless vary independently. As one ascends from personality through groups to culture, change is more gradual. Nonetheless, because the three components of action-systems vary independently, any may be a source of innovation. The force of personality variation is illustrated in the emergence of charismatic leaders or prophets, for example, a figure like Gandhi. The effect of the interaction process itself is seen in the case of a group of loitering youth, who decide quite suddenly on a summer night on a break-in. Finally the consequences of a change in rules is illustrated by the effect of civil rights legislation on segregated lunch counters. Typically, social action or social change are complex phenomena, and researchers frequently debate the question of the "causal" priority among them in specific instances.

Though the nature and the extent of the associations among the three systems can be determined only empirically, present methods permit only limited analysis. Changing behavior patterns may indicate changing institutional definitions, though not necessarily so. The normative culture consists not only of basic norms but also, though less explicitly, of the tolerable limits of deviation from those norms. Deviancy rates may fluctuate without direct or immediate modification of the norms themselves. Nonetheless, flaunted too long by deviant practices, the norms themselves lose their force. Thus it may be asked in the present instance: does the firmly documented increase in sex behaviors which deviate from traditional norms in American society represent basic institutional change, or only increasing deviation, and tolerance of deviation?

Take, for example, the rapid increase in the rate of cohabitation without marriage. The rate has climbed sharply over the past decade. Does this trend indicate that conjugal marriage as an institution is in jeopardy in society, that it is being supplanted by cohabitation without "benefit of clergy"? Does marriage remain as the "normal" pattern of cohabitation, while the change consists either of the willingness of individuals to experiment with other modes despite the "normal" definition, or increasing tolerance for such experimentation in society, or both?

FIGURE I

UNMARRIED COUPLES LIVING TOGETHER IN THE UNITED STATES: 1960-1978

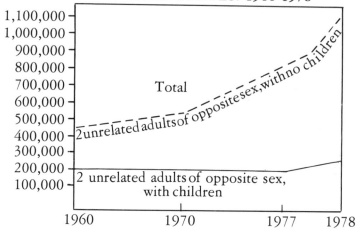

Source: Paul C. Glick and Arthur J. Norton, "Marrying, Divorcing, and Living Together in the U.S. Today," Population Bulletin 32, no. 5 (Washington, DC: Population Reference Bureau, Inc., 1977) and U.S. Bureau of the Census, unpublished Current Population Survey data for June, 1975.

Similarly, what is the significance of the relentless increase in the rates of divorce and separation among married couples? A chart from the U.S. National Center for Health Statistics (1979) shows that the rate of divorce in American society has not only increased steadily during the past century, but over the past decade the rate of increase has accelerated abruptly. If one reflects on the human and the social costs of this rate – about half as many divorces as marriages in a given year – only the language of "breakdown" or "revolution" appears adequate. Thus it has been suggested that monogamy survives in "serialized" form. At the same time, however, most divorced persons remarry eventually – in 1972 the Bureau of the Census estimated that

124

FIGURE II

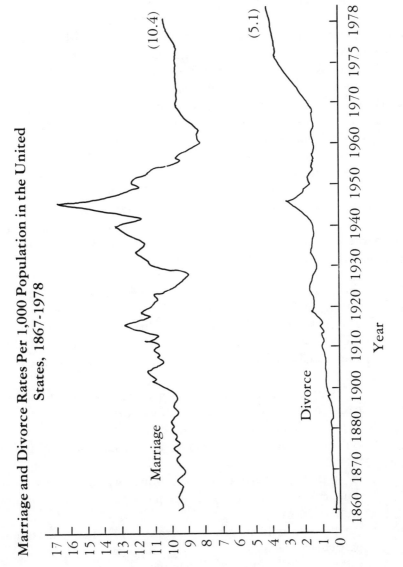

Marriage and Divorce Rates Per 1,000 Population in the United States, 1867-1978

(10.4)

(5.1)

Marriage

Divorce

Year

1860 1870 1880 1900 1910 1920 1930 1940 1950 1960 1970 1975 1978

Source: U.S. National Center for Health Statistics (March 1979).

125

four out of five persons do so[39] – thereby in effect indicating that marriage itself is highly esteemed. Thus some analysts argue that the high-divorce rate is tied to the increasing expectations of fulfillment which people bring to marriage rather than to the decline of the institution. Similarly it has been argued that, given the increasing impersonality of modern society, marriage is sought as the remaining structure which provides deep and abiding personal attachment.[35,17]

Beyond basic demographic statistics, however, there has been an explosion of studies in numerous disciplines on all aspects of human sexuality. Highly publicized studies such as those by Kinsey,[21,22] Masters and Johnson[28], Hite[15], themselves varied in nature, are but the tip of the iceberg. Moreover, to persons interested in the moral, the public, or the policy impact of social research, it appears clear that the freer investigation and reporting of sexual behavior contributes directly to the very changes which are under investigation. Greater permissiveness in the moral climate facilitates further clinical observation and analysis. Dissemination of the results further abets the permissive trend. Spanier summarizes the following list of documented trends from the research literature:[42]

1. An increase in the number of individuals having premarital coitus, particularly females.
2. An increase in the number of partners with whom an individual is likely to have premarital sexual relationships.
3. Individuals are having their first sexual relationships at earlier ages.
4. A lesser level of commitment is necessary before individuals become involved in sexual relationships.
5. A greater frequency of marital coitus.
6. A greater incidence of extramarital coitus, particularly among women.
7. A higher proportion of abortions are being given to unmarried women; a higher frequency of abortions among unmarried women.
8. An increase in the illegitimacy rate among unmarried women, particularly teenagers.
9. Increased utilization of family-planning services and contraceptives by females of all ages.
10. Widespread adoption of more effective methods of con-

traception by women of all ages, social-class levels, religions and races.

11. More open discussion of and exposure to sexuality in books, magazines, movies, and other media.

12. More liberal acceptance of alternative life-styles and alternate expressions of sexuality, such as homosexuality.

13. More freedom for females in initiating informal heterosexual social contacts and sexual relations.

14. A greater willingness to talk about sex, to tolerate different values and attitudes, and to accept sex, even in cases where another individual's standards may be different from one's own.

A similar, if less dramatic, explosion of literature on sex roles and gender can be reported, though results are more difficult to measure.[18] Here, as indicated above, the critical problem is the relationship between the biological and the sociocultural sources of sex role and gender distinctions. In a comprehensive summary of research findings published in 1974, Maccoby and Jacklin identified both unfounded beliefs about sex differences between boys and girls and others that are fairly well established. In a third category they placed open questions which included items on which the results are ambiguous or on which there is too little evidence.[27]

Unfounded beliefs concerning sex differences include these claims:

(a) That girls are more "social" than boys;

(b) That girls are more "suggestible" than boys;

(c) That girls have lower self-esteem;

(d) That girls are better at rote learning and simple repetitive tasks, boys at tasks that require higher-level cognitive processing and the inhibition of previously learned responses;

(e) That boys are more "analytic";

(f) That girls are more affected by heredity, boys by environment;

(g) That girls lack achievement motivation;

(h) That girls are auditory, boys visual.

Sex differences, on the other hand, that appear fairly well established include the following assertions:

(a) That girls have greater ability than boys;

(b) That boys excel in visual-spatial ability;

(c) That boys excel in mathematical ability;

(d) That males are more aggressive.

On the following items the verdict is still out, because findings are ambiguous or based on too little evidence, that is, differences between boys and girls cannot be regarded as either proven or disproven: tactile sensitivity; fear, timidity and anxiety; activity level; competitiveness; dominance; compliance; nurturance and "maternal" behavior.

While these statements are not misleading as they stand, the authors' qualifications and explanations need to be taken into account in any more detailed use of their findings. Thus "situation specific" differences may appear which on the surface appear to contradict various statements here cited. There are also individual differences related to personality factors. "In this vein, it is reasonable to believe that 'masculinity' and 'femininity' are essential self-defining attributes for some people but not for others."[27]

These findings, necessarily based as they are on phenotypical data, do not immediately resolve learned versus innate behavior issues. Nonetheless, they narrow the range of biologically determined traits which in American culture have been thought to distinguish the sexes. To that extent the findings compiled by Maccoby and Jacklin lend support to movements for sex-role and gender redefinitions in American society. At the same time, insofar as differences remain, particularly those going beyond the primary reproductive division of labor, the case of the sociobiologists gains plausibility. Thus efforts to reduce or even to extinguish sex-role differences in our society, but also the controversies associated with them, are likely to continue.

Finally, with regard to primary sex behavior, as the above summary compiled by Spanier[42] amply demonstrates, the volume of sexual activity in the society generally has greatly increased in recent years. It must be reemphasized, of course, that that is in part the product of increased research and greater freedom. In any case, we possess little directly comparable data from earlier times. And as historical records indicate, sex is a stream that recurrently rises above its banks. Whatever the quantitative balance, it is the "qualitative" transformations which they appear to manifest that are of first importance. Thanks to continuing social differentiation and technological advances, sex in American society has in recent decades become "autotelic",[44] an autonomous, self-validating end. Until then, primary sex labored, as it were, under a double bind. Pregnancy was a high risk, and with the family serving as the basic unit of economic ownership and production, illegitimacy was a threat to the social order. Sexual behavior was closely regulated. These functional realities anchored sexual behavior deeply in the wider moral fabric of the society.

Meanwhile the productive economy has been extracted from the family system, and the necessary link between the sex act and reproduction has been severed. Like most other human functions in complex societies, sex and sexuality have been drawn into the social differentiation process, thereby becoming, at least in some measure, autotelic and morally autonomous. Sex for its own sake, divorced from its moral and social matrix, is not new, as witness "the world's oldest profession." But prostitution always remained in some degree quarantined from sexuality otherwise. What appears to be new is the pursuit of erotic-affectional activity, without permanent interpersonal commitment, indeed, increasingly, notwithstanding other such commitment. Mutual consent obtaining, such behaviors are defined as private or personal, beyond the reach of the social code. An editor of a collection of papers concludes on the basis of his data that "today, recreational sex, whether inside or outside of marriage, is the rule rather than the exception."[42,55]

The movements for sexual equality and the emergence of autotelic sex profoundly impact the marriage institution and marital relationships. By definition, the married pair become a unity of interacting personalities, a solidary group such that the whole is more than the sum of the parts. Though initiated by way of voluntary contract, the old formula, "Till death do us part," symbolizes the mutation which renders the relationship a solidary one. Offspring extend the unit, and further manifest its solidary intent. Until in recent decades, at least in the American setting, the functional differentiation between the spouses resulted in "two-person careers,"[34] a pattern which illustrated, and frequently reinforced, the solidary nature of the unit. By the same token, today the two-career couple illustrates, and as well may reinforce, a definition of marriage, as a mere sum of two partners, a partnership to be disbanded when it no longer serves the two separate ends.

V. Sex Revolution: Decay and/or Growth?

To conclude, the redefinition of sex roles in American society today, along with the collision of stereotypes, values, and norms which it brings, whatever its gains, generates severe strains within the family system. Women are caught between conflicting expectations. Many desire marriage and motherhood, while feeling at the same time inwardly motivated and/or outwardly propelled toward the world of work or profession. Men at best face uncertainty in their comportment toward women; at worst, uncertainty regarding their own masculinity. Couples who had been socialized along conventional patriarchal lines find their marriages suddenly in flux as sex role redefinitions begin to work their way into their relationships.

All this, however, is only part, possibly the lesser part, of the changes that for some decades have been underway. In a society where all human functions are drawn into the differentiation process, thereby becoming both specialized and morally autonomous, sex activity likewise, as we have seen, has become increasingly "autotelic." The process which disengaged the family from the society, reducing it to a private sphere, likewise separated sex activity from the constraints of both reproduction and marriage. Where the revolution prevails, sex becomes amenable to pursuit for its own sake, and vulnerable to every sort of exploitation. Freed from archaic taboos and unwanted consequences, it is increasingly treated in amoral terms as well. The results are frequently appalling. The young suffer a surfeit of confusing signals. Increasing numbers of adults, as well, who apparently had accepted the responsibilities of marriage and family, are deflected from lives of purpose and commitment.

Doubtless, to many, perhaps to most people, these developments can only be described as revolutionary. Significantly, analysts who earlier discounted certain trends, especially mounting divorce rates, for the reasons indicated above, have begun to change their minds. Two leading Census Bureau demographers observe, "There seems little doubt that a basic transformation of the institution of marriage is underway."[33] With regard to this statement, Skolnick in a newly revised family textbook, writes, "Today . . . it is hard to find anyone who will disagree."[39]

Nonetheless, I shall risk repetition of the caution stated at the outset. The reasons are not merely the fact that culture tends to change more slowly than behavior, and that we cannot be certain as yet how fully changing behavior trends will modify the normative culture and institutions. There is also the fact that, given the sensational nature of many new phenomena, and the attention and documentation they receive, our perceptions may well be distorted. We know too little about the ways in which "conventional" norms not only persist, but are being renewed or reconstituted in succeeding generations. Thus as recently as 1978, a poll of students listed in "Who's Who Among American High School Students" reportedly found that "76 percent said they have not had sexual intercourse;" "62 percent said they abstain from sex because of their own moral standards," and "82 percent prefer a traditional marriage".[53] Behavior patterns and norms have indeed been "pluralized" in our society, but it is still far from clear what modal patterns will in the end prevail.

A third reason for caution is our lack of a clear base line against which degree or speed of change can be measured. One discovers quickly that while rates of behaviors may have increased, in some instances almost exponentially, the changes themselves frequently represent long-term trends. Where quantitative series data exist, one can compare changing statistical means, and then deviations from those means. Or one can employ moral norms in assessing the changes, though these, too, appear in some respects to be in flux. Such measures are certainly useful, and no doubt will continue to be employed. But these, too, hardly afford unambiguous verdicts.

A fourth, and for your purposes, the most important reason for uncertainty, remains to be introduced. It is grounded in the processes of differentiation which, as we have seen, have disengaged the economy from the family system, and sex from the hegemony of the economy and of procreative necessity. Pioneer social scientists early identified the division of labor as the critical mechanism in the transformations resulting in modernization.[41,43,7] The division of labor consists of the differentiation of a given activity, whether role or organization, into two or more roles or organizations which are functionally equivalent to the original unity, but which under changed conditions are more effective than the original undifferentiated unit.[40] Modernization has thus been defined as "the spread of roles which, functionally linked and organized in industrial settings, make their appearance in systems lacking an industrial infrastructure."[2] Differentiation thus entails a double movement: isolation of units and their (re)integration into a new configuration.

Differentiation, however, transforms not only specific operations, but cumulatively and more importantly, the entire sociocultural matrix as well. An urban sociologist accordingly defines "social differentiation . . . as variation in the normative structure among subgroups."[13] For the human beings comprising modernizing societies, and these are the focus of the present paper, "individuation" is the direct and inseparable reciprocal of "social differentiation." Thus the same writer defines individuation as "the probability that any two individuals will differ from each other in their controlling culture."[13] That is, once "multi-bonded" (Sorokin) communal entities (villages, clans, etc.) yield to specialized roles, organizationally integrated individuals become increasingly unique and differentiable from one another. Each becomes a unique combination of role affiliations.

Not only will the "controlling culture" for each individual differ; there is a subjective or psychological correlate as well. Here the preoccupation of social scientists with formal organization and bureaucracy as the implicit corollary of social differentiation has tended to eclipse the other side of the process. Organizations consist of, or are established in order to create, specialized functions or roles, distinct from the multibonded sociocultural matrices which integrate individuals in groups in traditional societies. The other dimension of the change, however, namely the emergence of autonomous persons, and the integrating functions of persons in the modern society, have been neglected, and as yet are poorly understood.[52]

On the subjective side, "individuation" has been defined as "a person's subjective mapping of the social world, in which self is differentiated, to a greater or lesser degree from the other social objects in the field."[58] "The act of freely making a commitment for which one assumes responsibility *individuates* the decision-maker" and thus separates him "from tribal ties to undifferentiated (safer) group action."[59] Differentiation thus involves both distance and interdependence between persons in collectivities, and the reorganization of personalities.

An important social psychological perspective in the analysis of modernization has been the emergence of impersonal human interaction in organizational societies. Strictly speaking, organizations and specialized groups consist of statuses/roles, not of persons. That

132

is, they include and integrate that aspect of persons which is susceptible to investment in the roles in question. As role incumbents, persons are implicated as means, not as ends (Kant). Against the backdrop of the vast role-based structure of modern society, Charles Horton Cooley cast up the profound metaphor of the "primary group".[6a] Eventually others spoke of "secondary" and even "tertiary" groups and/or relationships. Thus "if a primary relationship is one in which the individuals are known to each other in many role facets, and a secondary relationship implies a knowledge of the other individual only in a single role facet, then a tertiary relationship is one in which only the *roles* interact."[5] Modernization, of course, has meant the continued increase in the scope and volume of the secondary and the tertiary modes.

Our preoccupation with the "impersonal" nature of modern social systems has apparently eclipsed or distorted our perception of the profound personalism which emerges in the differentiation/ individual processes. In any case, we are lacking the profound models or paradigm of personalism in which *autonomy* and *accountability* are fully conjoined. Ralph Turner notes that people recognize "their real selves in feelings of an institutional nature," on the one hand, or "in the experience of impulse as an undisciplined desire" on the other. Today he detects a shift toward the impulse pole in the modal orientation of people in American society.[49] Similarly, Bertram Brown observed already in 1968 that "personal identity among the American young people is becoming far less a function of family or membership in traditional groups as church, community and occupation. It is rather shaped by self choice and action through assimilation of direct experience."[6] Correspondingly, the pursuit of "personal happiness" is seen by some as "an emerging ethic" precisely in the realm of family life and sexuality.[47]

A few analysts have argued persuasively that this reciprocal development of individuation and "defamilization" in the modernizing process is to be traced directly to the impact of the messianic Hebrew Christian prophetic tradition on the cultures into which that ferment was introduced.[54,36,52,51] This development is anticipated, e.g., in the profoundly personal imagery employed by Jesus, especially when placed alongside the tension between personal response and family bonds (Mt. 12:46-50). To this must be joined the Pauline conception that in the new order there is neither male nor female (Gal.

3:28). The claims of the above writers, it must be emphasized, are historical and phenomenological, not theological. That is, the writers here cited are identifying the historical consequences of certain conceptions, not their theological meaning or validity.

Much of modern individualism, to be sure, appears immediately indebted to "secular" sources – the Enlightenment, scientism, and the general rebellion of modern culture against the hegemony of "religion." In any case, it may be doubted whether individualism would have triumphed in the modern world without the reinforcement of the early market economy. Moreover, during much of the "Christendom" era, institutional Christianity opposed what today is called "religious liberty." Many modern intellectual movements, for their part, were "secular" or actively anticlerical. In the end, however, the argument of Salomon[36] and others deserves serious consideration — the major values of the Western world take their source in the messianic vision.

In a word, it appears that social *differentiation* has outstripped personal *individuation* in American society.[20] The consequences are both societal and personal. On the societal side, where responsible personal action is weak, the resulting malfunction invites inflated bureaucratic and even repressive public action. On the personal side, poor individuation results in self-centered orientation, in the evasion of opportunity and responsibility, and in premature concession in crisis. It also means that in the socialization of the young adequate ego models may be lacking. Conceptually, neither the social sciences nor the humanities, including religion, have been able to solve the crisis between "empirical" and "metaphysical" language in defining the person. Nowhere is the miscarriage of individuation processes more evident than in the crisis of sexuality. Older norms have collapsed more rapidly than new ones have grown. The real sexual revolution still lies in the future.

References

1. American Medical Association, Committee on Human Sexuality.
    1972 *Human Sexuality*. Chicago: AMA.
2. Apter, David
    1965 *The Politics of Modernization*. Chicago: University of Chicago Press.
3. Bemporad, Jack
    1978 "From biology to spirit: the artistry of human life." *Journal of Medicine and Philosophy* 3 (June: 74-87).

4. Berger, Peter
    1980 "How my mind has changed." *The Christian Century* XCVII (January 16): 43-45.
5. Berry, Brian J. L.
    1973 , *The Human Consequences of Urbanization.* New York: St. Martin's Press.
6. Brown, Bertram
    1968 *Mental Health and Social Change.* Washington, D.C.: HEW.
6a. Cooley, Charles Horton
    1962 Social Organization: The Study of the Larger Mind. New York: Schocken.
7. Durkheim, Emile
    1933 *The Division of Labor in Society.* Glencoe: Free Press.
8. Durkheim, Emile
    1921 "La Famille conjugale." *Revue Philosophique* 91, Paris.
9. Engels, Friedrich
    1895 *Der Ursprung der Familie, des Privateigenthums und des Staats.* Stuttgart: Verlag . . .Dietz.
9a. Friedman, Leslie
    1980 *Sex Role Stereotyping in Mass Media:* An Annotated Bibliography. New York: Garland.
10. Glehlen, Arnold
    1957 *Die Seele im technischen Zeitalter.* Hamburg: Rowholt.
11. Gordon, Michael
    1978 *The American Family: Past, Present, Future.* New York: Random House.
12. Gough, Kathleen
    1971 "The origin of the family." *Journal of Marriage and the Family* (November).
13. Greer, Scott
    1962 *The Emerging City.* New York: Macmillan.
14. Gregory, Michael S.*et al.,* eds.,
    1978 *Sociobiology and Human Nature.* San Francisco: Jossey-Bass.
15. Hite, Shere
    1976 *The Hite Report.* New York: Macmillan.
16. Homans, George
    1950 *The Human Group.* New York: Harcourt Brace.
17. Hunt, Morton
    1979 "The future of marriage." *Current Issues in Marriage and the Family.* Edited by J. Gipson Wells. New York: Macmillan. First printed in *Playboy,* 1971.
18. Hochschild, Arlie Russell
    1973 "A review of sex role research." *American Journal of Sociology* 78.
19. Horkheimer, Max
    1972 "Authority and the family." *Critical Theory: Selected Essays.* New York: Herder & Herder.
20. Janowitz, Morris
    1980 "Observations on the sociology of citizenship: Obligations and rights." *Social Forces* 59:1-24.
21. Kinsey, Alfred C., et al.
    1948 *Sexual Behavior in the Human Male.* Philadelphia: Saunders.
22. Kinsey, Alfred C.
    1953 *Sexual Behavior in the Human Female.* Philadelphia: Saunders.
23. Kohn, Melvin, and Carmi Schooler
    1973 "Occupational experience and psychological functioning: an assessment of reciprocal effects." *American Sociological Review* 38.
24. Landmann, Michael
    1974 *Philosophical Anthropology.* Philadelphia: Westminster Press.
25. Lorenz, Konrad
    1967 *On Aggression.* New York: Bantam Books.
26. McCormack, Thelma

1978 "Machismo in media research: a critical review of research in violence and pornography." *Social Problems* 25 (1978).

27. Maccoby, Eleanor Emmons, and Carol Nagy Jacklin
    1974 *The Psychology of Sex Differences.* Stanford, CA.: Stanford University.
28. Masters, Willam H., and Virginia E. Johnson
    1966 *Human Sexual Response.* Boston: Little, Brown & Co.
29. Millett, Kate
    1970 *Sexual Politics.* Garden City, NY: Doubleday.
30. Maine, Henry Sumner
    1861 *Ancient Law.* London: Murray.
31. Nelson, Stephen D.
    1974 Nature/nurture revisited I, II: A review of the biological bases of conflict."
        Journal of Conflict Resolution 18: 285-331.
32. Ibid.
    1975 19:734-61.
33. Norton, A. J., and Paul C. Glick
    1976 "Marital instability: Past, present and future."*Journal of Social Issues* 32:5-20.
34. Papenak, H.
    1973 "Men, women, and work: reflections on the two-person career." *Changing Women in a Changing World.* Edited by Joan Huber. Chicago: University of Chicago Press.
35. Parsons, Talcott
    1977 *The Evolution of Societies.* Englewood Cliffs: Prentice-Hall.
36. Salomon, Albert
    1949 "Prophets, priests and social scientists." *Commentary* 7.
37. Simon, William, and John Gagnon
    1969 "Psychosexual development." *Transaction* 6.
38. Skinner, B. F.
    1971 *Beyond Freedom and Dignity.* New York: Knopf.
39. Skolnick, Arlene
    1978 *The Intimate Environment.* Boston: Little, Brown & Co. 2d ed.
40. Smelser, Neil
    1959 *Social Change in the Industrial Revolution.* Chicago: University of Chicago Press.
41. Smith, Adam
    1776 *Of the Wealth of Nations.* London.
42. Spanier, Graham B.
    1979 *Human Sexuality in a Changing Society.* Minneapolis: Burgess Publishing Co.
43. Spencer, Herbert
    1874 *Principles of Sociology.* London.
44. Sprey, Jetse
    1969 "On the institutionalization of sexuality."*Journal of Marriage and the Family* (August).
45. Sprey, Jetse
    1974 "On the origin of sex roles." *Sourcebook in Marriage and the Family.* Edited by Marvin B. Sussman. New York: Houghton Mifflin.
46. Stanley, Manfred
    1968 "Nature, culture and scarcity: foreword to a theoretical synthesis." *American Sociological Review* 33: 855-69.
47. Sussman, Marvin B.
    1972 "Family, kinship, and bureaucracy." *The Human Meaning of Social Change.* Edited by Angus Campbell & Philip E. Converse. New York: Russell Sage Foundation.
48. Toby, Jackson
    1977 "Parsons' Theory of Societal Evolution." Introduction to *The Evolution of Societies.* By Talcott Parsons. Englewood Cliffs, N.J.: Prentice-Hall.

49. Turner, Ralph H.
    1976 "The real Self: from institution to impulse." *American Journal of Sociology* 81.
50.Tylor, E. B.
    1871 *A Primitive Theory of Culture*. London.
51. van Leeuwen, Arend
    1964 *Christianity in World History*. London: Edinburgh House Press.
52. von Oppen, Dietrich
    1969 *The Age of the Person*. Philadelphia: Fortress Press.
53. *Washington Post*
    1978 "Youth are shown strong on religion in pupil poll." December 15.
54. Weber, Max
    1927 *General Economic History*. London: Allen Unwin.
55. Weitz, Shirley
    1977 *Sex Roles*. New York: Oxford University Press.
56. White, Leslie A.
    1980 "Human Culture." *Encyclopedia Brittanica Macropedia* 8: 1951.
57. Wilson, Edmund O.
    1975 *Sociobiology: The New Synthesis*. Cambridge: Belknap Press.
58. Ziller, Robert C.
    1964"Individuation and socialization." *Human Relations* 17: 341-360.
59. Zimbardo, Philip
    1969 "The human choice: individuation, reason, and order versus deindividuation, impulse, and chaos." *Nebraska Symposium on Motivation*. Edited by W. J. Arnold and D. Levine. Lincoln: University of Nebraska Press.

Chapter 7

Person, Sex, Marriage and Actual Trends of Thought

The Reverend Ambrose McNicholl, O.P., S.T.D.

I am tempted to begin by asking you to try to imagine a world of sexless human beings, a world where there is no distinction of male and female in the human species; not a unisex world — such as some people seem to want nowadays — but simply a sexless world. There would be no human reproduction, no family life; human beings would not be complementary, as male and female now are, but self-sufficient. Would they then be open to each other as they now are, love one another, depend on one another, or rather oppose each other?[1]

Such questions may be idle but they are instructive. For one thing, they help one to realize how deeply sex enters into every aspect of human life; and they raise the problem of what exactly sexuality is. If one simply cannot imagine a sexless human being must one conclude that sexuality is essential to the human? Not perhaps in the way that body and soul, or intelligence and sense, are essential, but in somewhat the same way as social activities, or the capacity for social life, are essential. One thing does seem certain: that sexuality belongs to the social dimension of human life; that it lies at the root of the human need for fellowship and for social life. In this respect it is closely linked to rationality and to distinctive modes of human behaviour; at the same time it is no less clearly linked to the bodily function of reproduction. One of the many intriguing questions raised by sexuality is that of determining whether it should be considered primarily as connected with fellowship and love or with procreation. In any case, both of these aspects at least have to be taken into consideration.

I have been asked to deal with actual trends of thought, particularly philosophical ones, which influence our views on these topics. I propose to treat first the topic of the human person since that is the context in which sexuality finds its distinctively human meaning; then to propose some reflections on sexuality and the ways it is conceived today; finally to deal briefly with marriage as the context in which sexuality finds its adequate expression and full significance. The approach throughout is philosophical; the theological setting will be dealt with by other speakers in this seminar.

Before I come to deal with the topics mentioned I must draw attention to an all-pervasive mentality which influences contemporary thought about them; and here two factors seem pertinent to my theme.

Pervasive Mentality

The first factor is that referred to in the final document of Vatican II *(Gaudium et Spes,* n. 5) in the words: "And so mankind substitutes a dynamic and more evolutionary concept of nature for a static one." The mentality which is coming to prevail more and more, in the West at least, is aptly described as *dynamic and evolutionary.* There is an overall swing from a vision of the universe as formed of beings whose essential nature does not change, that are set in fixed relationships to one another so as to form an orderly universe where change is either generation/corruption or accidental, and where thought is seen as anchored to eternal and unchanging principles which are universally valid; to a quite different vision of the universe. This is now far more commonly viewed as marked intrinsically by change. The whole universe, and everything in it, is seen as constantly evolving, while matter is conceived in terms of energy. As a result, process is regarded as more basic than being, and thought is judged to be as much marked by historicity as the universe itself, and hence as dependent on axioms and categories that are no less subject to change than the experience from which they are drawn.

This dynamic and evolutionary outlook, due to such causes as: biology (discovery of the cell as the basic unit of life; genetic evolution), geology (evolution), theories about the origin and development of the universe, physical science (matter as equivalent to energy), conventionalism in mathematics, the growth of history as a strict science, philosophies of evolution and process, is in accord with the most striking phenomenon of our century: increasingly rapid change on the social, cultural and technological levels of existence.[2] It conditions people to view things and institutions, as well as systems of thought, as changing and hence as relative. It opposes the notions of substance and of natures that are essentially unchanging; it does not recognize principles that can claim to be absolute or universal.

The second, and perhaps even more significant, factor is the progressive loss of what may be called *ontological awareness.* This loss shows itself in, and is to a great extent caused by, a nominalism which is far more prevalent today than in the Middle Ages and which contends that "nature" is an empty word to which nothing corresponds in reality which is utterly and always individual. This outlook is fostered by the amazing success of technology and its characteristic modes of thought which, to use Heidegger's terms, are calculative as opposed to ontological,[3] and have been given maximum diffusion by systems of education aiming at producing scientists and by massive use of the ever more powerful and persuasive means of social communication.

The main assumption common to those who share this outlook is that physical and natural science is a privileged form of our knowledge of reality. This assumption can be said to lie at the basis of the technological civilization of the Western world. It maintains that knowledge, in order to have value, must be quantitative and exact, in principle available to all, and capable of being verified or controlled by anyone who uses the appropriate method. The older view, that to know reality means to penetrate, by intellect working in conjunction with sense, to the supposed essence of things, has been widely abandoned, at least from Kant onwards. It has been replaced by the conviction that to know means to describe as exactly as possible, by making use of mathematics, the quantitative structure of things as this is made known through observation sharpened and made precise by the use of instruments. This is the kind of knowledge that can be used for improving man's way of living and to extend his control over nature. The former qualitative and ontological mentality has thus been replaced by the quantitative and functional one. This assumption can be called scientism, although that term is usually reserved for the dogmatic assertion that science gives us the only kind of valid knowledge. It is part of the creed of the Positivist and above all of the Neo-Positivist school which, from about 1930 to 1940, expressly drew the conclusion that metaphysics is not only useless but meaningless.

Where there is little or no ontological awareness the notion of substance will be rejected, all the more so because it has been so consistently misunderstood; and this will entail the loss of a proper understanding of human personality. If personhood is conceived, not in terms of being and existing, but in terms of activities and relationships, it will inevitably follow that sexuality and marriage will be seen only in such a context. It is common experience that discussions often turn out to be fruitless or inconclusive; and the reason usually is, not that the arguments used are bad or miss the point, but that there is disagreement about fundamental assumptions which are not stated and of which the disputants may not even be conscious. I suggest that many, if not most, of the differences of opinion about sexuality and marriage must be traced to more basic differences, particularly with regard to what is meant by personhood and to underlying assumptions with regard to more fundamental notions, such as substance, nature and existence.

For that reason I propose first to deal with personhood; and here it seems best to begin with the notion of substance and then to reflect on what we mean by person and by human nature. To avoid repetition I will first of all try to organize some of the main trends of thought today on personhood by grouping them around these three basic themes; after that I hope to indicate the more important doctrinal aspects of those themes from the point of view of what we may agree to call the *philosophia perennis,* although in this case it would more accurately be called an updated Thomism.

I. Personhood

A. Main Trends of Thought Today[4]

1. Substance. The loss of the notion of substance accompanies, and is mostly the result of, the refusal to interpret reality first of all in terms of being. This refusal is characteristic of positivism in its many forms, but it is also present in philosophies and outlooks which affirm that *Becoming* is more basic than Being. This conviction lies behind the various forms of evolutionist philosophies, already in Hegel and Marx, and then in the thought of Bergson, Chardin, Whitehead and of those Naturalists who hold for emergent evolution (Lloyd Morgan, Alexander, Hobhouse, Sellars, Broad, etc.). It seems that the evolutionist outlook prevails among most scientists today; their common rejection of the notion of substance is also due to its being conceived on the model of those physical realities which can be directly observed and verified by the methods proper to the sciences.

2. Person. In recent philosophy, generally, the notion of subsistence, which presupposes those of being and substance, has been replaced by that of *activity* or of structures of activity, usually on the level of consciousness. This change is due mainly to the acquisition of what is called *subjectivity*. The Cartesian dualism of soul, conceived as a substance whose essence is thought, and body has led to that between the Self, conceived in terms of consciousness, and nature, and to the resulting stress on subjectivity as the basic characteristic of the person and indeed of substance where this notion is retained; for otherwise it would seem to follow that "consciousness must be seen as emerging from a source other than consciousness itself which possesses none of the attributes of consciousness, and may even appear as the very contrary of consciousness."[5] To define the Self or substance in terms of activity is to make them relational, to see them as constituted by a relation to what is not Self; and this may well be due to the fact that "a being can experience itself only through its relation to others; but to say that it can be a Self only on this condition is destructive of the foundation of Self"[6] because no finite activity can be its own self-sufficient foundation.

Phenomenology provides an instance of this kind of thinking in its most influential form. Husserl, having criticized Descartes for retaining the notion of substance,[7] and having correctly seized on intentionality as most characteristic of consciousness, had to identify thought and existence. Thought, for him, simply exists as thought; and since thought is always thought of something, it follows that to think of any thing is to *be* that thing. The main task of the philosopher will then be to uncover the eidetic structures of consciousness. This thoroughly relational notion of personhood is developed especially by Max Scheler. He saw the person as the dynamic centre of intentional psychic activities which link him to what is other than himself. The person is no longer defined in terms of being but of acts and relations; and it has been a constant temptation for those Personalists who lack what we have called ontological awareness to conceive personhood along similar lines.[8] Nevertheless, thinkers like Mounier, as also Marcel and Buber, have written with great sensitivity and insight about human relations and their importance for the full development of the person. Their reflections, together with those of many others who have dealt with this topic, must be incorporated into a Scholastic philosophy which is sadly deficient in this regard.

3. Nature. One may not identify substance and nature, for accidental realities have a nature of their own; and the same must be said of essence. When the traditional philosopher uses these words as applying to substances he does not refer to the basic characteristic of subsisting independently. Substance as essence is correlative to the act of existing; as nature it is conceived both as having a typical entitative structure which marks it off from other kinds of substances, and as being the radical immanent source of characteristic activities. To deny the reality of substance is to deny that of nature in this sense; and this denial is even more explicit in the existentialist mode of thought than in the phenomenological one.

A recent writer has pointed out that the Existentialists simply take for granted a number of unjustified assumptions, one of which is this: "that the Self is not a substance but a lived relation to that which situates it; that this relation is and only could be an internal relation (because only two substances could be externally related): and this in turn means that that which situates the Self – which shall be called the situating Other – enters into the very ontological constitution of the Self."[9] One might have to qualify that judgment if the assumption referred to essence rather than to substance; but it surely can be endorsed if taken to refer to nature. One may not take Sartre as representative of all Existentialists but it is he who carries the premisses of Husserl to their logical conclusion. If consciousness is always consciousness of something, he maintains, then consciousness cannot be a thing; it must be an *intentional activity* which exists only through its relation to what is other than itself. It has no nature or essence which could serve, for instance, as a foundation for morality or action. It reveals itself as actual choosing, for this is what existing means. Sartre does indeed speak of essence, as when he holds that existence precedes essence; but this "essence" turns out to be the very acts of choosing as transparently revealing themselves. The person is nothing more than the constantly renewed and free choice of self in the world insofar as it is a source of meaning.[10] Values, consequently, cannot be grounded in nature, much less in God; their only foundation is the free choice of Self conceived as a lived relation to the Other which situates it.[11]

The notion of nature has come under fire from a quite different quarter, from specialists in the relatively new "human" sciences of cultural anthropology, sociology, linguistics and kindred disciplines. These sciences have opened our eyes to the endless variety of individuals and of cultures and to the subjectivity and relativity of the world-views and systems of value that form the kernel of culture,[12] and which find expression in various forms of institutions, codes of law, political organization, art, religion, morality and so on. The sociology of knowledge seems to support the view that all these are to a great extent subjective constructs, and hence relative.[13] All this has led some to conclude that there is no such thing as human nature but an endless number of ways of being human, and that each culture presents its way of being human. Those who accept this conclusion would allow us at most to speak of certain inborn potentialities which are conditioned by acquired dispositions to actualize them in various ways.[14] This trend of thought carries on the tradition of those philosophers, such as Vico, Hamann, Herzen, Montesquieu, Moses Hess and Sorel, who call in question the validity of the concept of "man in general."[15]

Finally, and to return to our starting point in this brief outline, the Nominalists are always with us, especially under the guise of Empiricists, Positivists and Neo-Positivists, and Pragmatists. Thinkers in this tradition would generally agree, especially when they are under the influence of mathematics and logic, with B. Russell that, for symbolic logic, "a term is, in fact, possessed of all the properties commonly assigned to substances or substantives";[16] with the result that one should not distinguish the essential from the accidental or speak of substantial change.[17] In maintaining that substance and nature are logical constructs he has much in common with Ayer who holds that these notions are due to grammatical confusion.[18] Similar views are held by those Linguistic Analysts whose attention is centred more on language than on concepts or being, as though language afforded the only valid appoach to knowledge of reality. At least one of the Analysts, Strawson, defends, however, the validity of such concepts as person and individual and the need for what he calls descriptive metaphysics.[19]

To describe the overall effect of these trends of thought which eliminate or weaken the concepts of substance, person and nature, I am tempted to use H. Marcuse's phrase: one-dimensional thought.[20] These trends combine to confine thinking to the one dimension of concern with what is simply given or present to immediate experience or direct observation. On this factual level it is relationships and activities which seem to make up all that is real. The resulting relational notion of personhood is open to endless variations, and the norms for self-development will then be based either on purely personal choice or on the actual behaviour of a given socio-cultural group. The only way to meet this challenge, for the philosopher at least, is to justify the validity of the notions in question. Here I can only indicate what is meant by these terms within the Thomistic tradition, and then note how they provide a conceptual framework for an understanding of morality and of the role of sexuality.

B. The Ontological Approach

Although philosophers such as Bergson, Whitehead, N. Hartmann, Lavelle and Heidegger undoubtedly were gifted with ontological awareness, it is not quite the same kind as that preserved in the tradition reaching from Aristotle through Aquinas to the present day. Thinkers in this old but still vital tradition hold that reality cannot be fully or adequately understood unless it is considered from the most universal point of view, that is, insofar as it is being as such. Before anything is that or that particular kind of thing, and as such open to investigation by more specific ways of knowing, it is first and foremost a being, a reality, an existent thing. To study it under this most universal aspect is to be faced with principles which hold for all that is real.

Within this tradition Aquinas occupies a unique position for it was he who first intuited the sheer excellence of the act of existing and made this intuition the cornerstone of his ontology. Here I must simply state that, with him, I maintain that the *act* of existing *(esse ut actus)*, as distinct from the mere *fact* of existing, implies nothing else than perfection; that nothing is real or actual unless it exists or is related to the act of existing; that his act, as "the act of all acts, the perfection of all perfections,"[21] is the immanent principle in all things of whatever actuality, perfection and intelligibility they possess.[22] It is with the presupposition of this type of ontological awareness, as provoked by the abiding question so finely formulated by Heidegger: "Why in general does anything exist and not rather just nothing?"[23] that I set out the following considerations.

1. Substance. If one agrees that nothing is real unless it exists, the concept of "substance" expresses the basic characteristic of that which exists: a reality that is able to exist by and in itself and not just as a modification of some other thing. This does not exclude dependence on an extrinsic efficient cause as the source of existence; it does imply independence as not needing any other reality in which it would exist. The primary reference of substance is to this act of independent existence; it may also, and where finite beings are concerned it always does, imply a reference to various dependent kinds of being (accidents) which are not able to exist in themselves but only as modifications of a substance which shares its existence to them. "In and through substance a being has the capacity to be in itself, radically sufficient and complete in the integrity of its being. Substance, as it were, sets up the dividing boundary which distinguishes a being from others and gives it an identity – a selfhood."[24] As such it also allows a being to preserve its self-identity throughout all the changes which affect it. Since it is the substance which exists it is also the substance which changes while retaining its own identity; it is not, as Locke imagined, a static substratum which is unaffected by change on the level of accidents or which supports those accidents as a table supports books.

That which exists independently as a whole, and not as a part or mode of some other thing, is said to subsist; and the substance, in this respect, is called a supposit. This is always a complete and individual reality. It seems most likely, although not all who defend the traditional notion of substance would agree, that it is the act of existing that determines a substance to be a complete and total subject for that act. Since it is substance, as supposit, that exists, and since existence is the actuality of all actions, the supposit must also be regarded as the primary subject of activity and passivity. It is the supposit which acts, changes and endures while many of its accidental modes of being may come and go. Where living beings are concerned it is the supposit which lives, grows, matures, dies.

Through activity the supposit enters into relationship with other subsistent beings; it is linked to the other finite beings which compose our universe in a dynamic network of relationships based primarily on the activities by which they influence each other. If, however, substance connotes independent existence and activity is relational, it is clear that one may not identify substance and activity. Not only does activity presuppose substance as its source and support – a thing has to be in order to act – but if substance is conceived as relational in itself, and not only through its activity, it could no longer be seen as constitutive of selfhood in an independently existing being. What is relational does not exist in itself, for it implies that one thing (a subject) is related to another (a term) and hence depends for its existence on both. The substance, precisely because it is actuated by its own independent existence, is endowed with dynamic tendencies which lead to actions by which it both enters into relation with other beings and strives for that fulfillment to which it is oriented.

In short, we should conceive substance as "the integrating center of a being's activities, a center which is constantly pouring over into self-expression through its characteristic activities and at the same time constantly integrating or actively assimilating all that it receives from the action of other substances on it . . . Such a notion of substance as perduring principle of dynamic self-identity in an interacting system can go far in our day, it seems to me, toward making contact with the process philosophy tradition and assimilating much of its richness."[25] It also allows us to understand what is meant by the traditional notion of personhood.

2. Person. From the ontological point of view, which I take to be presupposed by other ones – psychological, moral, social, religious, etc. – the person is a supposit gifted with the powers of thinking and willing. Here I consider only the human person, and there is no need to repeat what Catholic philosophers have commonly taught on this subject. There may, however, be need to change the perspective from which they approach it, for this has frequently been too cosmological. By this I mean that the categories used to define personhood have been, in the past, drawn from the philosophy of nature, as though the paradigm of substantial being were the physical things which make up our material universe, rather in the way that the dialectical materialist sees matter as primordial and as rising progressively to higher grades or levels of reality.

The typically modern stress on subjectivity combines here with the insight into the excellence of the act of existing to correct any such perspective. If the person is "that which is most perfect in the whole of nature,"[26] and if the act of existing is the most perfect of all acts, we are invited, as Thomists at least, to conceive personhood in relation to that act. The paradigm of being, and of substance, will then be found in that reality which most fully allows the act of existing to share its perfection to it. The paradigm will be the most perfect type of being known to us; and, as far as our direct experience is concerned, this is what we call a person. Subjectivity stresses the fact that this supreme type of reality knows itself from within. Intelligent beings are self-conscious; and indeed it is their own spirituality which they first experience, for other beings are accessible to it primarily by thought which is formally spiritual and is experienced as such. The human person is that being who has knowledge, if only pre-conscious and perhaps preconceptual, of his being, who knows that he is a being, one that exists independently, that thinks and loves and knows that he thinks and loves and that he can freely dispose of his own actions.

I cannot improve on Fr. Clarke when from this perspective he writes: "For St. Thomas, the person is not a peculiar mode of being added on from the outside, so to speak, to what would be the normal non-personal mode of being. On the contrary, if being is allowed to be itself above a certain level of limitation, which disperses its act of presence into parts external to each other (matter), it naturally flowers out into the perfection of a person, i.e., its act of presence becomes luminous and transparent to itself, it becomes presence to and for itself (self-consciousness), and master of its own actions (freedom). Thus the fullness of being which is act of presence, is of its very nature personal, or self-possessing presence, and the nature of the person, on its side, is nothing else than to be an active self-possessing presence, present both to itself and to others – to the whole world, in fact, if its act of presence is intense enough . . . and since the act of existence is

148

the root of all perfection, being naturally turns into person wherever its restricting level of essence allows it to *be* intensely enough, transcending the dispersal of matter."[27]

The tradition stretching from Descartes to Husserl and Sartre has preserved the insight that in man consciousness and existence are closely related. Man's mode of being is indeed to be conscious of his act of existing and hence also of his thought and freedom. Insofar as he is called to think and to exercise his freedom he can be said to be an existent who must develop his inherent capacities; and this may be described as giving himself an essence if by this we mean a freely chosen way of being human, although I would prefer to use such terms as character or moral personality. If the general lines of this development are set and indicated by the fact that he is a human being, this does not imply any more determinism than is involved in the fact that he has not freely chosen to be a human being in the first place. It is his own free choice that decides in what particular and individual way he will be human; which means, as Sartre himself insists, that his freedom is not absolute for it is limited by his basic situation, that of being human and not some other kind of reality.

Owing to his faulty notion of substance, Descartes, while rightly seeing thought as man's most distinctive attribute, was led to identify it with thought; thought cannot indeed emerge from a substance first posited as a physical reality of a lower order of being. When the human substance, as person, is seen in relation to the act of existing, and this is grasped as the act of all acts, then the substance-person is seen as intrinsically intellectual by reason of the spiritual soul which, as embodied, formally constitutes man as man; while it is in and through consciousness that the person achieves fulfillment.[28] To see the self as constituted by consciousness is to see it in the light of a subject-object relationship, as primarily a relational kind of being, and thus to deny the primary characteristic of subsistence. The self has to be a subsistent being in order to be conscious and to be related to another reality; and this has first to be before it can become an object. "In this way, substance radically pre-determines the ontological conditions out of which the human conscious subject emerges as an individual conscious subject endowed with a capacity for conscious activity of a determinate kind to be exercised in intersubjectivity. One cannot dispense with these ontological conditions without destroying the foundation of the distinctive conditions of human subjectivity precisely as such."[29]

3. *Nature.* The concept "nature," although cosmological in origin, is used to signify another aspect of the one reality already conceived as substance and person.[30] If this reality is considered as a specific type of being which, as potential, limits the act of existing which makes it be, it is more properly called an essence; if this actualized essence is regarded as the intrinsic and radical source of characteristic activities it is known as nature. Activity is referred to the supposit as to the subject which acts; the type of activity depends on the nature of this supposit, and the nature is said to be that by and through which the supposit acts. Whereas the supposit signifies a subsistent and incommunicable whole, nature (as applied to substances) signifies a consistent and typical mode of being which is orientated towards determinate ways of acting which lead the supposit in the direction of self-fulfilment.

It is through the act of existing that the essence or nature is real. It is absurd to imagine an essence waiting for existence in some limbo of incomplete and non-actual beings, although it is rightly conceived as having its ultimate explanation as an idea in the divine mind.[31] Otherwise, and apart from the act of existing, it is simply nothing.[32] This does not mean that one has to agree with Sartre when he denies the existence of natures, or with Heisenberg who held that one cannot speak of a nature "in itself."[33] When the essence does exist it is real as the potential and limiting mode by which the fullness of existential act is confined to actualizing this specific type of reality rather than another; but then the essence is real only as a singular and concrete thing; and if it involves matter it is individualized through its particular material component. We can, by reason, conceive the essence or nature as abstract and as common to all individuals of the same species; but as it actually exists it is thoroughly individual. As nature it shares many features in common with other individuals of the same species;[34] but such features are realized in a different, a unique, way by each of those individuals. There are as many singular human natures as there are individuals.

Insofar as human nature signifies the mode of being common to all humans it is the source of an active tendency to fulfil the self through connatural activity. It ensures that the person is intrinsically orientated to a definite end and it inclines the person to act in such a way as to attain that end, that is, to complete and fulfil itself. The dynamic tendencies or inclinations inherent in nature indicate the appropriate way in which it can be brought to completion. In material beings other than man the way in which these active tendencies lead to action is determined by nature itself; such beings develop spontaneously along lines set by God as author of nature. The person, as intelligent, is conscious of these inclinations and is basically free to follow or to go against them; he or she is called to translate them into particular and definite ways of acting in order to fulfil the self. The actions in question are primarily immanent both as to their principle and their term, such actions as knowing, loving, choosing; such actions are at the root of the transient types of action which affect others. The immanent kind of action is however open or intentional; it is precisely by reason of intellect that man can "become all things," as Aristotle puts it,[35] and by will he can love all that he apprehends as good, that is, as completing and fulfilling him. It is here that we find the basis for what we call intersubjectivity, the freely chosen ways of relating to what is other than self and especially to other selves. The person is real only as intersubjectivity; if as substance it subsists as an independent whole, as intelligent it is a centre of perspectives open to others, and can fulfill itself only through relationship to them. Fulfilment is not egoism; it is attained through self-giving.

The cosmological tendency already mentioned seems to have led in the past to a too static and merely abstract view of human nature. The notion of nature is analogical; its meaning is not the same when used in reference to man as to inanimate beings, plants and animals. In these latter, their nature is fully determined in its structure and in ways of acting that have their source in it. Such beings act of necessity in determinate ways. In man, on the contrary, nature is to some extent flexible and plastic, in the sense that there are innumerable ways of being human through the exercise of free choice. What the person knows and loves, what he chooses and aims at, will result in a particular and unique way of being human; and it is in this context that one can agree with Sartre that the person gives itself an essence or nature. The person, as conscious and free, is the cause of that which most of all individualizes him and makes him unique. What human nature is, as common to all humans, can to a sufficient extent be known by reason and intuition; what it is in the concrete, in actually existing individuals where alone it is real, can be known only by experience and observation. It is here that the dimension of historicity has to be taken into account. The individual lives in the process of history; his ways of thinking, loving and acting are conditioned by historical circumstances and by social, cultural and economic factors as well as by subconscious influences of various kinds. One cannot hope to understand human nature adequately without the help of such sciences as history, biology, sociology, psychology and anthropology. If it is evident that there is an essential identity in nature between human beings, it is becoming every day more evident that the concrete and existential ways of being human are endlessly diversified.

If human nature, as abstractly conceived, i.e., with regard to its basic characteristics, does not change, as it is actually realized in existing individuals it is constantly changing, in regard to physical and biological features, in cultural traits, in intellectual activity, and in concrete ways of self-realization.[36] There is no change, however, unless there is something – the person-substance – which endures and preserves its self-hood throughout these changes. Change is meaningless where nothing is permanent and all is reduced to flux and process. In general, the changes can be along the lines indicated by human nature itself; then one can speak of development insofar as the succeeding stage realizes the possibilities inherent in the previous one. When this is the case there will be fulfilment, or at least progress towards the state of maximal well-being of which human nature is capable.

In traditional teaching on morality, which was set in the context of law, the concept of nature played a central role. If natures are seen as caused by God and ordained by Him to their due fulfilment, this ordination will reveal itself in the basic inclinations always found in those natures and can properly be regarded as a law of nature. Where the nature is intellectual the person will be conscious of this law and called to conform himself to it, i.e., to act in conformity with the basic inclinations which he finds in his nature, and so to fulfil himself. It is here that the notion of obligation arises in the consciousness of being called to perform, through free choice, the kind of action indicated by nature as leading, when it is not impeded, to fulfilment.[37] The person is free to follow this course or not; but the general lines of action, and the end to which they lead, do not depend on his choice; they are set by nature. Within these limits the person, as moral agent, is free to decide how, in each individual situation, to follow these inclinations in practice. The function of the precepts of natural law is to indicate how this is to be done.

To appreciate what natural law (in morality) is, as St. Thomas understands it,[38] one must consider the person under two aspects, as subject and object of moral rule. The person, as subject, is self-ruling, called to guide himself through directives which he forms in his mind as conscious of his basic inclinations and as freely choosing how to implement them. From this point of view, natural law, as conscious and free determination of ways of acting, can be simply described as ethical self-rule. The person is also object insofar as it is the self which is to be ruled; and here it is the aspect of nature which is stressed. This self, as nature, indicates through its basic inclinations, how it should be ruled. Here we deal not so much with law as with what St. Thomas calls natural right *(ius naturale),* the fundamental duties and corresponding rights which are grounded in human nature as such. To rule oneself in accordance with these natural tendencies is to conform to the law of nature. How the general precepts of this law are to be carried out in each individual case will depend on the free and responsible choice of the person. The general laws of morality will be personalized in each such personal decision, and this will depend on many individual factors, e.g., on how fulfilment is envisaged, how the basic inclinations are known and their implications realized, as well as on psychic, social and cultural influences.

Many moralists prefer now to set their teaching in the context of value rather than of law, partly in order to avoid the danger of legalism, but also because this seems to be the more human and more Christian approach. The gospel values are accepted through faith. If we rely on reason alone the values appear as those ideals or perfections which are conceived as integrating the complete fulfilment of personhood. These can well be represented as universal and absolute, as valid and desirable for all individuals in all conditions of time and space. Laws can then be seen as rational directives which indicate, in general terms, the ways in which these values are to be aimed at through fitting types of action. How these directives are to be followed in any given set of particular circumstances will depend on the conscientious decision of the person. If the value in question is, for example, justice, and the corresponding law tells me to give my neighbour what is due to him, it is up to me and to my conscience to decide what exactly I am to do in my particular circumstances. This approach fosters a truly personalistic ethics while at the same time it respects the dynamic trends inscribed in my nature.

Whether the approach to ethics is from the point of view of law or of value it may not, in either case, leave nature out of consideration nor see personhood merely in terms of inter-personal relations. To do so would be to make free decision the only basis and criterion of moral action. The moral act should be free; but if it is only free, without any regard for the basic promptings of human nature or for the nature of the total environment of the agent, it will be neither rational nor moral, for there would no longer be any objective ground for distinguishing good from evil.

A quotation from Fr. Nicolas may help to recall the leading theme of this section of my paper: "Before he is free, and in order to be so, man has a will which is *defined* by a natural tendency *(appetitus)* to goodness and happiness. And this same freedom is judged according to its conformity with the *inner law* of human nature. However 'intentional' knowledge and love may be, however 'relational' the person expressed in these activities, there is no intentionality or relation without a substantial being that truly exists in itself and is the subject of every activity, of every project, of every relation. There is no subjectivity without a subject, no subject that does not have a nature, nor can one conceive of a history unless there be a nature to be developed to the full, to be brought to its final fulfilment."[39]

What I have tried to do so far is to state, as clearly and briefly as possible, the immediate assumptions presupposed by the traditional approach to ethics and to a study of sexuality and marriage. The first thing is to be aware that they are assumptions – which it is the task of the philosopher to justify – and to be clear as to their precise meaning. If such a justification is not provided – by the metaphysician – the whole traditional treatment of moral questions will be conditional. Its conclusions will be accepted only on the following conditions: (a) if there is such a thing as human nature which is within certain limits unchanging, and (b) if we can know what it is, and (c) if the knowledge formulated by the traditional thinkers is correct; then we can speak of a specific and valid ethics. All this presupposes, moreover, the validity of the philosophical attitude called moderate realism which asserts the existence of extra-mental reality and of its intelligibility; and if values are invoked, it is assumed that they have been justified as objective and unchanging. These assumptions are readily granted by common sense, but it is also the common ways of understanding many of our basic notions – perhaps it would be better to say of misunderstanding them – that oblige the philosopher to attempt to indicate his assumptions and to clarify their meaning.

II. Sexuality

With regard to notions and attitudes relating to sexuality the influence of the mass media can hardly be exaggerated, especially in the consumer and permissive type of society in which we live.[40] They tend all too often to portray sex as a commodity to be bought and sold, as a biological means of procuring pleasure, and as the private concern of the individuals concerned. Where technological modes of thought prevail in society there is a mental climate which disposes people to accept such influences, since these modes of thought treat the human being as an object rather than as subject, if not simply as merely a more highly developed animal. Such an attitude is fostered by the many kinds of positivism and naturalism, especially when allied to materialism and atheism.

It is common for many psychologists and psychoanalysts to deal with sexuality only in the context of instinct, urge, desire or vital energy, and thereby to neglect its full human dimension.

The relational trends considered, although usually recognizing the personal and social dimensions of sexuality, tend to see it only in the context of the exercise of free choice without considering the exigencies of human nature.

One must also admit that the approach of traditional thinkers to the study of sexuality has in the past been, on the whole, too biological. This is understandable, given the elementary biology on which they had to rely and which was basically that of Aristotle, and the prevailing social and cultural patterns of thought and behaviour. Recent research in such sciences as biology, psychology and sociology, together with such movements as feminism and women's emancipation, have made it possible to view sexuality from more adequate and total perspectives. The aspect of procreation has been balanced and indeed overshadowed by that of partnership, with the result that marriage has come to be seen not just as a contract but as a covenant aiming at the personal fulfilment of the spouses.

Bearing in mind this background, I shall now try to indicate, again in summary fashion, how sexuality may be more adequately treated in the context of the philosophy of the person already outlined.

If human nature is real only in individuals, and if these are all different, it follows that human nature is different in each individual. Its basic features are common to all, but they are actually realized in individually differing ways. The person integrates all that belongs to it in the unity of the one subsisting whole; everything in it is actualized and made real by the one incommunicable act of existing; everything, including the body and all its functions, is personalized by this act. Every person has his or her way of being human.

The human soul, although specifically the same in all humans, is individually different in each person. One soul can be more perfect of its kind than another, for specifically the same form can be found in different beings according to different grades of perfection. [41] Signs of this difference are evident in the fact that some people are more intelligent than others, have greater willpower, more capacity for love as well as diverse talents. This difference shows also in the body. As St. Thomas sees it, bodily differences are due, in the first place, to difference of soul; the body is fashioned in view of the particular soul destined for it by God. [42] Difference in bodily constitution points therefore to difference of soul; [43] the more refined the body, the more refined is the soul. [44] Hence Aquinas can say that the substance of one soul is other than that of another by reason of the different ways in which souls are proportionate to their bodies. [45] Each human being is thus an individually different substance; each person is unique as this singular and non-repeatable substantial realization of manhood. [46] All this, needless to say, must be taken into account by the moralist when treating of the application of law, or the actualization of value, in individual instances.

If we accept these premises we must conclude that the difference of male and female is not bodily only; we will have to speak of the male soul and of the female soul, perhaps in such terms as animus and anima. Nothing could more clearly stress the extent of this difference or show more convincingly how radical it is. It will imply, and experience confirms this, that man and woman have different ways of knowing, loving, sensing, feeling and acting. Sexuality colours and permeates every human activity and relationship; and since everything in the human being is personalized, sexuality will be personalized and will affect the person on the level of intelligence, emotion and instinct. Like human nature itself, as it exists in the individual, it will be subject to variations due to heredity, environment, and occupation, as well as to historical, social and cultural context. Here one should bear in mind the distinction between male/female and masculine/feminine, for masculinity and femininity refer to traits and modes of behaviour which are mainly due to social and cultural causes. Yet, however great the variations, we are always dealing with the person and with the same type of being that we have called human nature.

As regards the reason for the difference between man and woman, there have been notable progress within the traditional trend of thought. St. Thomas, for the reasons mentioned a short time ago, seems to have held that it was primarily in view of procreation,[47] even if he also refers to family life and social relations.[48] But he also points out that there is a big difference between animal and human sexuality. Animal procreation is ordained to the preservation of the species, but human procreation is for the sake of the individual rather than of the species.[49] In other words, if nature is predicated analogically of animals and of man, this is also so in regard to sexuality which is not the same thing in both; in man it differs vastly from what it is in the animal despite the fact that in both there are some features in common. The finality of preserving the species is present also in human generation, but, precisely as human and personalized, this is ordained to the good of the person.

It is here, in sexuality as human, that we find the aspect of partnership. Sexuality contributes to personal fulfilment through the complementarity of male and female. Both male and female are, by themselves, incomplete as human beings. Each is so structured as to need the other and to find completion through affective union with those of the opposite sex. Sexuality inclines those of one sex to seek the companionship of those of the other and so to enrich each other; it opens human beings to a whole host of relationships based on love and mutual enrichment. As Bishop Mugavero puts it: "Sexuality is that aspect of personhood which makes us capable of entering into loving relationships with others."[50] Its purpose is to foster love and the mutual giving and receiving which love implies. As such it is personal and noble, a gift to be treasured and developed. Sexuality is, moreover, a means of communication between man and woman; sexual activity expresses the person and personal love for the partner; it is the language of self-giving and of personal commitment.

It is within this personal context that one must consider the biological and genital aspects of sexuality. To fail to do so would be to relapse into that cosmological outlook already referred to and which is

157

nurtured by those theories which portray man as nothing more than a highly developed animal. Since the person is one, and urged by nature to seek integral fulfilment through sexual union, the powerful forces and drives inherent in sexuality will have to be made to serve the total good of the person. This implies that the procreative urge must be fulfilled in the context of partnership founded on love. Both instincts should be under the free but rational control of the person and drawn into the unified stream of activity leading to personal completion. This is precisely the task of virtue – in this case, the virtue of chastity. The role of this virtue is primarily the positive one of so integrating sexuality into one's life as to be at the service of love and of the total well being of both partners as persons. To indulge in what we may call specifically sexual activities for their own sake alone, or for the pleasure that accompanies them, is to tear these activities out of their natural context, to depersonalize them, and to transform what is social into something merely selfish. They are meant to be used in order to give life and to draw persons closer together. Their morality is to be judged by the criterion of whether they serve these ends and so promote the total welfare of the persons concerned. It is value rather than pleasure that is a fitting goal for human intention and activity, and there is no human value greater than that of the person. To regard a person merely as an object that provides pleasure is to degrade that person and oneself.

By relating one person to another sexuality has an inbuilt social dimension, one that is still more evident when the union of the sexes leads to offspring. As relational it grounds many kinds of interpersonal relations. By leading to union and to offspring, and so to the family, it provides the basic social unit. Yet it seems that its primary role, as human, is that of enabling the person to reach fulfilment. The family does not, in the first place, exist for itself, nor for society, nor for the State; it exists for the person. Similarly the person does not exist just in order to procreate; the person is procreated in order to exist and to attain the fullness of existing as a person; and it is mainly through mutual communication and giving in knowledge and love that the person reaches towards such fullness.

If from these philosophical reflections we pass to theology, we will have to complete them by all that is implied in the basis of Christian anthropology: that the person is made to the image of God and called to grow in likeness to his Creator, in imitation of Christ and by the help of His grace, both as an individual and as a social being whose relations are meant to reflect those which bind the Three Divine Persons together and those which bind the Church to Christ as His spouse.[51]

III. Marriage

In connection with marriage and with sexuality in general, one more modern and all too common trend may be noted. It is that stressed by Archbishop Bernardin in his address to the recent Synod of Bishops in the name of the Episcopal Conference of the United States: "People no longer accept at face value the pronouncements of institutions or the rationales which they give for their policies or programs. People have become much more independent in their thinking. They want reasons for adopting a position, and they reserve the right to decide for themselves whether or not they will accept the reasons and embrace the position . . . Too many people look on our moral teaching as a laundry list of do's and don't based more on historical accident or institutional concern than a Gospel mandate. So they pick and choose what they want and reject the rest."[52] One way to meet this situation is, as he suggests, to offer proper and adequate motivation; and this, finally, cannot be other than commitment through love to the following of Christ.

Relying on reason alone, and insisting on the immense difference between animal and human generation, one can clearly see that the procreative union of man and woman is not intended by nature to be just momentary. Even in the animal world the female remains with her young until they can fend for themselves, and often the male stays with the same mate. Where children are concerned their support and education demand some form of stable union and of fidelity between the parents. It is not so clear, from reason alone, that such a union should always be permanent or exclusive or unbreakable, or that the family as we know it is the only – or the only natural – way to ensure the support and education of the children, although it undoubtedly is the most natural and efficacious way to favour the full psychic development of the offspring.

It is not easy, and it is to a great extent arbitrary, to decide what forms of union between man and woman should be included within the meaning of the word "marriage." We cannot, at any rate, restrict its meaning so as to apply only to Christian marriage, for there are many other ways of envisaging it. The union may not be, nor intended to be, procreative but entered into with the aim of seeking pleasure, mutual help and fulfilment; it may be based only on free agreement to stay together only for a time. When it is procreative, or intended as such, it can take various forms, many of which are culturally conditioned and may be socially acceptable or sanctioned by civil law, even though they do not meet the requirements of Christian marriage. Such unions may not be permanent or exclusive; they may be polygamous or progressive by stages, stages which may include sexual intercourse, as in some African cultures. It is even doubtful that one should reserve the term marriage for at least all unions recognized as marriages by civil law. As Rosemary Haughton points out: "We must not fail to take into sufficient account the social dimension of sexuality. We need, for one thing, to know what human group a person actually relates to, so that we may accurately consider the demands and pressures of that group on the individual and consequently on his or her ideas about marriage and about sex outside marriage. One's real 'society,' a *felt* one, is as I suggested often a great deal smaller than what we loosely call 'society.' "[53] All this creates ambiguity, but this very fact should make one chary about the use of such phrases as premarital or extramarital relations.

To admit many ways of conceiving marriage is not to grant that all of them comply fully with the exigencies of nature or the demands of personal love of spouses for each other and for their children. The totality of the love and self-giving expressed in sexual intercourse seem to call for a union that is permanent and exclusive; so too the task of caring for and educating the children. This kind of union, if not indicated as always obligatory, is surely intended by nature as most favourable for its purposes. A confirmation of this, and perhaps a valid ground for asserting that such a kind of union is of obligation, may be based on the meanings that are immanent in sexual acts and are independent of the intentions of the participants. In this connection, Rosemary Haughton refers to some phenomenologists who are quoted in the Kosnik volume as maintaining the fact of such intrinsic meaning.[54] This is a welcome development in the phenomenological school of thought, even if the presence of meaningful acts seems to be accepted by members of that school just as a fact or as due to the structure of subjectivity, without reference to the nature of the human person where it finds its explanation.

In this general context the Christian notion of marriage can be proposed as most fully in accord with the exigencies of human nature and of personal love. This notion is rejected by many; by others is regarded as just an ideal, one that makes too many demands to be realistic. For the Christian it is indeed an ideal but not just an ideal, for the Christian who enters into marriage is called to observe it. This will often require heroism of a kind that is made possible only through the aid of God's grace. The Christian calling, if taken seriously, does demand such heroism; and it may well be that today the heroic nature of that calling is more evident and more actual in the lives of those who are married than of those who are consecrated to celibacy and who, like myself, dare to write and speak about marriage.

Postscript

Behind the type of discussion carried on in this paper, particularly in its first section, looms the more fundamental problem of the role of reason, and of its cultural variations, in its task of clarifying and explaining revealed truths. This is a question for the theologian, although insofar as it involves reason it interests the philosopher also; for it is mainly through the use of reason that one may hope to understand reason.

To become aware of the importance for theology of the basic notions discussed in our first section one need only consider the following proposition: the second *Person* of the Blessed Trinity, *consubstantial* with the Father, assumed human *nature*.

From the fact that these truths have been stated as dogmas in these terms we must conclude that the use of such terms makes it possible to express those truths faithfully; in other words, that those philosophical notions *can* be used to express the mysteries of faith and to throw light on them. They have been so used in the long doctrinal development, and especially in the Councils, of the Church.

To understand the meaning of dogmatic formulas which make use of those notions one must know what meaning they had, for the bishops and theologians, at the time of the disputes and discussions preceding the dogmatic definitions. Moreover, these formulas can be changed if, owing to vicissitudes of language, the terms used no longer retain the original meaning, or if they are no longer apt to convey the revealed truths to modern minds. The new formula must, however, faithfully preserve the meaning of the substituted one.[55] It is also clear

161

that new aspects of the revealed mysteries can be formulated in appropriate language.

The pertinent question is: do those venerable formulas now *have* to be changed? If, as some writers assert,[56] the older notions and terminology are no longer apt, can the same revealed truths be expressed either by using quite different categories or by using the modern notions of person, nature, etc.? In that case, would there be just an enrichment in our understanding of the old truths, or would one have the formulation of new truths? Would the full meaning of the older formulas be preserved? The recent discussions on transignification, or transfinalization, as substitutes for transubstantiation, bring out the point at issue.

There is a wider dimension to such questions. The Western Catholic tradition has been content, until our century, to interpret revealed truth in terms of the Greco-Roman classical culture; indeed the Catholic Church, up to Vatican II, saw itself almost exclusively in the light of that Western context and spread this cultural version of itself even in non-Western countries.[57] Certainly this Western version is *one* way of interpreting and expressing Catholic thought and life; it cannot claim to be the *only* way. Vatican II has made it quite clear that the Church, and Revelation, transcend *all* cultures and are, in principle, truly universal; and that it is possible, at times necessary, to interpret divine Revelation in terms of different cultures and of present Christian experience.[58] In fact, one of the main difficulties, and challenges, that face the Church today is precisely this need for acculturation.

As a result it would appear to be less necessary now to insist on the use of terms and notions drawn from the Greco-Roman intellectual heritage of the West; and this might seem to lessen, or to deny, the force and value of the ontological considerations presented in this paper. Here, however, one surely has to make a distinction: the theologian may be free to dispense with the categories of Greek or Roman thought – insofar as they are nothing more than Greek or Roman. As such their availability is limited, however providential they may have been in the past. But the basic notions in question may turn out to be neither just Greek or Roman. Apart from the fact that they were given a new turn of meaning by Christian thinkers, they may well be quite simply fundamental *human* notions which were brought to light in the past by thinkers of the classical tradition and which remain

162

always valid and available.[59] In other words, they may be transcultural, even if the technical terms to express them may be lacking in any given language, and hence not only useful but necessary. This is not just a theological problem; like many others it is also, if not more radically, a philosophical one.

Notes

1. St. Gregory of Nyssa (*De Hominis Opificio* c. 17; *MG* 44.188B-192A) held that it is due to original sin that marriage, and the distinction of male and female, are needed to continue the human race. Without original sin humans would have been sexless and created by God in the way angels are given existence. It was because God foresaw the Fall that He created humans as male and female, thus providing for procreation in the way that animals fulfil this task. In this respect the Fall made humans similar to beasts. St. Thomas (*ST* la.98.2) firmly rejects this view, on the grounds that nature is not essentially changed by sin and that all the members of the body, before the Fall, would have served their specific purpose.

2. I have tried to indicate the main areas of change in an article, "A Century of Change," in *Aquinas* (Rome, 1975) 18:28-57.

3. Cf. *Holzwege* (Frankfurt, 1950), pp. 88, 100, 104; *Was ist Metaphysik* (ib., 1947), pp. 43-45; *Einführung in die Metaphysik* (Tübingen, 1953), pp. 33-50; 136, 137.

4. This outline is not mean to be exhaustive but rather to indicate some thinkers who exemplify the trend in question.

5. D. Connell, "Substance and Subject," in *Philosophical Studies* 26 (1977): 8.

6. Ibid., p. 11. This whole article deserves careful reading.

7. *Cartesianischer Meditationen und Pariser Vorträger* (The Hague, 1950), Med. 1, § 10; pp. 63-64.

8. Karol Wojtyla, in his book *The Acting Person* (trans. by A. Potocki; Dordrecht, 1979), tries to complete the Thomistic ontology of the person with insights derived from phenomenology, with special reference to Scheler.

9. W. Shearson, "The Common Assumptions of Existentialist Philosophy," *International Philosophical Quarterly* 15 (1975): 138.

10. Cf. *L'être et le néant* (Paris, 1943), pp. 17ff, 514-21, 539-43, 547, 655; *L'Existentialisme est un Humanisme* (Paris, 1946), pp. 22, 55, etc.

11. *L'Existentialisme est un Humanisme,* pp. 35-37, 71-72, 78-79.

12. Cf. B. Lonergan, *Doctrinal Pluralism* (Milwaukee, 1971), p. 4: culture is now taken to mean "a set of insights and values informing a common way of life;" cf. R. Williams, *The Long Revolution* (Pelican, 1965), pp. 57ff.

13. Cf. P. Berger and T. Luckmann, *The Social Construction of Reality* (New York, 1966).

14. Cf. J. Barzun, *Cleo and the Doctor: Psycho-History, Quanto-History, and History* (Chicago, 1974).

15. Cf. I. Berlin, *Against the Current. Essays in the History of Ideas* (London, 1977).

16. *The Principles of Mathematics* (Cambridge, 1903), n. 47; p 44.

17. Ibid., n. 143; p. 471.

18. *Language, Truth and Logic,* 2d ed. (London, 1946), p. 42.

19. *Individuals. An Essay in Descriptive Metaphysics* (London, 1959).

20. H. Marcuse, *One-Dimensional Man* (Boston, 1964).

21. *De Pot.* 7.2 ad 9; cf. *ST* la. 4.1 ad 3; 2 ad 3; 1a 2ae. 2.5 ad 2.

22. For an excellent and brief statement of this conviction, cf. W. Norris Clarke, "What is Most and Least Relevant in the Metaphysics of St. Thomas Today," *International Philosophical Quarterly* 15 (1975), especially pp. 415-417, 421-23. Commenting on the central part of Pope John Paul's address at the Angelicum (Nov. 17, 1979), I have tried to indicate the importance and some of the implications of this Thomistic "existentialism" in the article, "A Chant in Praise of What Is," *Angelicum* 57 (1980): 172-96.

23. "Warum ist überhaupt Seindes und nicht vielmehr Nichts?," *Was ist Metaphysik*

(Frankfurt, 1949), p. 38. The first chapter of *Einführung in die Metaphysik* is a series of reflections on this theme.

24. D. Connell, p. 10. For this author (p. 23, n. 2) "the best recent treatment, historical and speculative, of the metaphysics of substance is to be found in M-D. Philippe: *L'être. Recherche d'une philosophie première* (3 vols., Paris, 1972-4), vol. 1; 199-467".

25. W. N. Clarke, pp. 425, 426.

26. *ST.* 1a. 29. 3; cf. *C. Gent.* 3.112.

27. W. N. Clarke, pp. 424, 425.

28. Cf. Connell, pp. 20, 21.

29. Connell, p. 22.

30. For a fine exposition of the Thomistic concept of nature and of its many applications in philosophy and theology cf. M-J. Nicolas, "L'Idée de nature dans le pensée de saint Thomas d'Aquin," *Revue Thomiste* 74 (1974): 533-90.

31. Cf. *ST.* 1a. 15.1, 2; 44.3; *De Ver.* 3.2.

32. On this cf. J. Owens, *An Elementary Christian Metaphysics* (Milwaukee, 1963), c. 9, especially pp. 133-40.

33. Sartre, *L'Existentialisme est un humanisme,* p. 22; W. Heisenberg, *La nature dans la physique contemporaine* (Paris, 1962), pp. 18-19.

34. D. Walhout, in his article "Human Nature and Value Theory," in *The Thomist* 44 (1980): 282-83, lists fourteen characteristics which he regards as essential to man.

35. *On the Soul* III, c. 8; 431b. 21.

36. For a recent article on this topic cf. G. H. Marshall, "Human Nature Changes," *The New Scholasticism* 54 (1980): 168-81.

37. Cf. B. Miller, "Being and the Natural Law," *Archiv für Rechts und Sozial-Philosophie,* n.s. 2 (1963): 219-35.

38. For an extended treatment of this topic cf. J. M. Aubert," La libertè du chrétien face aux normes èthiques," *Atti del Congresso Internazionale: Tommaso d'Aquino nel suo settimo anniversario* (Napoli, 1977) 5: 28-49.

39. J. M. Nicolas, p. 589; my translation.

40. In chapter 2 of his *La rivoluzione sessuale* (Milano, 1974), F. Giardini treats of this and of the influence of literary works such as novels and plays.

41. cf. *De Ente et Essentia, c.* 5; cf. *ST.* 1a 2ae. 52.1.

42. *ST.* 1a. 76.5 ad 1; 91.3; cf. 42.6; 2a 2ae. 5.4 ad 3.

43. *ST.* 1a. 85.7c. and ad 3; *C. Gent.* 2.81; *De Pot.* 3.9 ad 7; 3.10; *Q. Disp. de Spir. Creat.* 9 ad 4.

44. *ST.* 1a. 25.7.

45. *C. Gent.* 2.81; *Q. Disp. de An. 3.*

46. Some of these texts are discussed by V. Marcos in his article, *"De Animarum Humanarum Inaequalitate,"* *Angelicum* 9 (1932): 449-68.

47. *ST.* 1a. 92.1.

48. Ibid. 92.2 and 3. On the development of the notion of sexuality cf. D. Georgen, *The Sexual Celibate* (London, 1976).

49. *ST.* 1a. 98.1.

50. Pastoral letter, "Sexuality — God's Gift," Brooklyn, 1976.

51. One puzzling text for the theologian is Mt. 22:30: "At the resurrection men and women do not marry; no, they are like the angels in heaven." After the resurrection bodies will be male and female, so presumably there will be sexual love and the intimacy which it entails, in however sublimated a form. One is tempted to ask whether then there will also be sexual intercourse; if so, it would evidently not be procreative but a sheer expression of love and a means of communication. If the act is good and holy it would not, on these grounds at least, be incompatible with the state of the blessed in heaven who would still be like the angels in not procreating; but again, the act would not be necessary in order to express love. The hypothesis of its endurance after death would at least favour the view that its finality is more unitive than procreative. On the other hand the text can be seen as indicating the eschatalogical sign-value of the state of celibacy embraced for the sake of the kingdom of heaven and as implying, therefore, that all the blessed will similarly be celibate.

52. Type-script, "The Need for a More Positive Theology of Sexuality," pp. 6-7.

53. Review of A. Kosnik and others, *Human Sexuality: New Directions in Catholic Thought,* in *Doctrine and Life* 29 (1978): 331.

54. Ibid., p. 338.

55. Cf. Declaration of the S. Congregation for the Doctrine of the Faith, *Mysterium Fidei* (June 24, 1973), especially § 5 (*A.A.S.* 65 [1973], pp. 402-04).

56. E.g., L. Dewart, *The Future of Belief* (New York, 1966); H. Küng, *On Being a Christian* (Munich, 1974), especially C, VII, 2.

57. Cf. K. Rahner, "Towards a Fundamental Theological Interpretation of Vatican II," *Theological Studies* 40 (1979): 716-27.

58. Cf. Vatican II, *Gaudium et Spes,* 42, 58; *Ad Gentes,* n. 22.

59. Cf. P. F. Strawson, *Individuals. An Essay in Descriptive Metaphysics* (London, University PB, 1964), p. 10: "There is a massive central core of human thinking which has no history — or none recorded in histories of thought; there are categories and concepts which, in their most fundamental character, change not at all . . . They are the commonplaces of the least refined thinking; yet they are the indispensable core of the conceptual equipment of the most sophisticated human beings."

Part Three
Contemporary Catholic Theology and Church Teaching on Human Sexuality and Personhood

Introduction

The moral theologians who have written the following four chapters have each adopted a particular approach to contemporary Catholic theology and Church teaching on human sexuality and personhood. Taken together, these four chapters offer an overview of the major theological concerns about human sexuality which have emerged in the Catholic Church in the twentieth century.

Father Francis X. Meehan, S.T.D., a professor of moral theology at St. Charles Seminary in Philadelphia, provides an opening overview. He cites the intrinsicism of the Catholic moral tradition which recognizes an inherent meaning in human sexual activity and the personalism which renders persons responsible for their own personal and interpersonal development. Fr. Meehan raises very effectively the difficult question of pastoral solutions to instances where following traditional sexual norms begets a conflict of values.

169

He finds, however, that the Church's essential teaching is socially prophetic, implies hope for the future, and builds a more organic human community through marriage and family commitments.

Father John C. Gallagher, C.S.B., S.T.D., a professor of theology at St. Joseph College of the University of Alberta in Edmonton, Canada, has sketched an overview of Catholic magisterial teaching on sexuality and marriage since the *Code of Canon Law* in 1918. His clear and carefully synthesized analysis reviews the development in the papal teaching of Popes Pius XI, Pius XII, and Paul VI, and also discusses the contributions of the Second Vatican Council, the Sacred Congregation for the Doctrine of the Faith, and the Roman Rota. He outlines the efforts to relate the procreative and unitive purposes of marriage and to present the teaching on contraception in a broader context of the nature of marriage rather than merely in a biologistic context. The three questions with which he ends are the essential core of current theological reflection on sexuality within the Church today.

Father Paul E. McKeever, S.T.D., dean of theology at St. John's University in Jamaica, New York, has captured in a brief chapter the single most critical controversy in Catholic moral theology about human sexuality. In a sympathetic and concise presentation he suggests that the methodology of proportionalism is not clearly ruled out by biblical moral teaching or by contemporary philosophical approaches to natural moral law. He questions the analytical soundness of this method of analysis of moral acts and identifies six serious objections. However, he also cites the rejoinders to these objections, thereby indicating that the current controversy is rooted in serious philosophical issues which are not easily resolved.

The closing chapter by Father Benedict M. Ashley, O.P., S.T.M., a professor of moral theology at the Aquinas Institute in Dubuque, Iowa, begins with the historic Church teaching on the inseparability of the procreative and unitive meanings of human sexuality. Father Ashley cites the objections which the contemporary secular culture raises to this teaching, and then reviews its biblical roots and the Church's continuing efforts to steer a middle course between libertinism and Manichaeism. He enumerates three major priorities in the Church's pastoral teaching on sexuality and seven major points of consensus among most Catholic theologians. Father Ashley concludes with a brief discussion of the problem Father McKeever presented, that of moral methodology as applied to situations of conflicting

170

values. While he rejects proportionalism, he does not base his own support, within a teleological framework, of certain basic exception-less moral norms uniquely on a Thomistic view of ethics or an essentialist view of human nature.

These four chapters reflect the creative tension in Catholic moral theology since the Second Vatican Council. The issues raised are not all thoroughly analyzed but they are competently and cogently presented.

Chapter 8

Contemporary Theological
Developments on
Sexuality

The Reverend Francis X. Meehan, S.T.D.

Introduction

Within the past two decades there has been much development in Catholic thought on sexuality. There has also been not a little criticism of our past. Most of us grew up in a Church in which there was "more than sufficient guilt in the room."[1] Michael Harrington in his *Fragments of a Century* satirized our past by noting the difference required for serious matter in the area of alcohol consumption as opposed to sexuality.[2] He noted with tongue in cheek and with some ethnic self-deprecation that the greater latitude given to alcohol might have signaled the measure of Irish dominance in the American Church.

This is not to throw out the baby with the bath water. The atmosphere of our youth also allowed some healthy restraint. Past teaching did contain the high ground of a constant and gifted instinct

173

for sexuality as a vehicle of loving self-donation in marriage. The task of the contemporary Church is to see that our reaction to the past is healthy and discerning, lest we replace the tyranny of a past superego with the no less tyrannical demands of a new libertinism. Harvey Cox was not the first to point out that the playboy phenomenon of the sixties was no less a manichaeanism than the early puritanism.[3] He wisely suggested at one point that a figleaf painted over genitals is one problem, but a figleaf placed over the face of the person's humanity signifies a demon worse than the first.

Not all has been sweet harmony in the past decade or more. Controversy has accompanied the before- and after-periods of Paul VI's issuance of *Humanae Vitae* as well as the 1977 publication of the Catholic Theological Society of America study, *Human Sexuality*.[4] Allow me to point out one danger from these controversies even as they continue today, namely, that they tend to absorb pastoral energies that could be better utilized elsewhere.

Paul Hanley Furfey in his inspired writings has so well taught us how issues of conventional and individual morality have managed to preoccupy the Church to the neglect of public, moral concerns which have cried out for more prophetic leadership.[5] Less than a few hours away right now there are priests and bishops, religious and lay persons undergoing imprisonment, danger, torture, even death. They struggle courageously over issues of faith and justice, freedom and food. It would be tragic if North American churches are seduced again into obsessions with the sexual that easily domesticize the Church, privatize her message, and divert her prophetic voice away from critical social judgments crucial to the moral and human well-being of the peoples of the world.[6] This is not to fall into the opposite trap of denying the Church any place in the sexual area. Anything so dense with issues of human growth and outwardness cannot help but have salvational implications which give entree to Church compassion, concern, and discernment. In fact, I will allude within these pages to some ways in which the social and the sexual are more closely related than sometimes appears.[7] With this sense of perspective let us take a brief bird's-eye view of several influential theological developments in sexual ethics.

Of all the developments in Catholic theologizing I would single out two which, I believe, underlie many of the others, namely, intrinsicism and personalism.

Intrinsicism

By the use of this word I am simply designating one important element in the Thomistic revival of this century. It can be described (negatively) as the effort to rid Catholic moral thought of nominalist influences.[8] The ethical insight of intrinsicism can be captured in one Latin phrase: *Prohibita quia mala.* This is, of course, the reverse of the ethical voluntarism of nominalism expressed as *"mala quia prohibita."* In other words, in re-finding Thomas, the intrinsicist thinker recognized that a sexual action such as adultery is evil not simply because of the extrinsic decree of God or Church, but because of something within the inner-worldly causality of adultery itself.[9]

Not long ago a phrase became popular: "If it does not hurt anyone, then it is ok." Obviously, we know that, as the phrase was used, it generally managed to cover a good deal of rationalizing and some unsavory behavior. But my point here is that the phrase captured theoretically an important insight in the intellectualist tradition of Catholic thought, namely, that ethical norms do not come out of the sky, that we name a behavior as evil precisely inasmuch as it is in some way hurtful to ourselves or to someone else. This in fact was one dimension — not the only one — of the renewal of Catholic natural law thinking in ethics.[10]

Personalism

The intrinsicism of our time was deeply connected to the rise of personalist thought. The twentieth century is not the first time-period in which people want to know the intrinsic reason for a sexual norm. John Dunne, however, gets at the special characteristic of our age by pointing out that there is an all-pervasive desire for personal appropriation. He recalls Whitehead's phrase, "the form of the forms of thought."[11] By this he means a form of thought so taken for granted that one can hardly name it. *Personal appropriation* includes resistance to any norm that has the slightest tinge of heteronomy, or of voluntarism. Putting it simply, our people ask in an accent rarely used before, if this or that sexual act really is going to hurt anyone? And here I do not mean merely the young people of the sixties, but even the giants of modern Catholic thought such as Jacques Maritain and Gabriel Marcel, and a Catholic value phenomenologist such as Dietrich Von Hildebrand. These men found intrinsic meaning to chastity, and intrinsic meaning to the norm reserving intercourse within marriage.[12]

Dietrich Von Hildebrand's and Herbert Dom's writings published between the two wars gave us one of the most significant and, in a sense, revolutionary developments in the Catholic theology of sexuality and marriage. They both recognized and developed in a thematic way what married people had for centuries known, namely, that sexual bodily action held within itself an intrinsic meaning other than the procreative, that it was not merely a means to an end, but that "the two partners grasp each other reciprocally in intimate love."[13]

For many of you this is a familiar history of how Vatican II finally incorporated this insight by refusing to endorse any explicit subordination of the end of marriage to procreation. Both Von Hildebrand's and Dom's insights ring all through the very carefully nuanced paragraphs of *Gaudium et Spes'* handling of marriage.[14]

This effort to get at the intrinsic meaning of sexual intercourse also yielded a new understanding of the meaning of sexual pleasure — now seen no longer as a form of extrinsic bait or reward for undergoing the burden of procreation, but a pleasure inherent in the loving self-donation itself. Rosemary Haughton has pointed out that the romantic tradition with its sense of playfulness and emphasis on personal love had contained seeds of such a theology. What might account for the long theological neglect of such a central human experience, unfortunately, could be that all the official theology stemmed largely from a celibate clergy who had little insight into the goodness of sexual play.[15]

So the personalist tradition finally joins sex with love, now not in an extrinsic Cartesian unity, which simply suggests that love ought to accompany sexual action, but as an embedded meaning of the bodily action itself. In an article written for the *New Catholic Encyclopedia* I tried to capture this insight by using the analogy of facial gestures.[16] Meanings are connected intrinsically to facial gestures regardless of the intentionality one might like to tack on. Similarly, then, in the issue of sexual intercourse itself we can garner from Church teaching something close to a proclamation that intrinsic to sexual action are the two meanings of love and life, the unitive and the procreative.[17]

An Intrinsic Ethic Due to the Unitive Meaning of Intercourse

Once one has grasped the idea that intercourse has its own meanings, then an intrinsic ethic simply asks that intercourse take place in a context where this inner meaning will be respected. Therefore, the norm that limits sexual intercourse to marriage is simply an outflow of the meaning of intercourse itself. The argument is simple; the following simply draws out the meaning of intercourse.

> By its very bodily intimacy sexual love has its way of crying out for exclusivity. And since the human person is historical, such a bodily being together implies a waking up in responsibility for one another tomorrow and tomorrow (fidelity). . . . Moreover, the human person is social, public, and ritual. Vowed love in public ritual brings a privately expressed love and fidelity into external proclamation. The love is as it were "named" into deepest reality. Finally, this lasting, exclusive public love shadows forth God's perduring love of His people "consummated" in the Incarnation, death, and resurrection of His Only Son. (Cf. *Gaudium et Spes,* no. 48).[18]

You can see, then, that the norm requiring the marriage context for sexual intercourse is not an extrinsic norm, but simply honors what intercourse is in itself. Intercourse is in itself a matrimonial act, since we do in fact understand matrimony as implying all the anthropological elements mentioned above, i.e., self-donating, perduring, tending to want to announce itself publicly, shadowing forth, etc.

Procreative Dimension Also As Intrinsic to Love

I have emphasized how Catholic moral theology has recognized the unitive dimension of intercourse. But the meaning of sex is also procreative. Sexuality implies by its very bodily phenomenon a human-life dimension. What is often not understood, and what I would like to emphasize here, is that life and love are really not two separate meanings but are inherently connected and mutually conditioned. For this reason *Humanae Vitae* is more than a teaching on birth control: it is an anthropological insight suggesting that love calls for life – indeed so much so that any lack of orientation toward life actually flaws the love.

This is not just an abstract idea. It has a certain common sense about it, a certain rooting in human experience. In other words, people notice that there is a tendency for love to become, as the French say, *"egoisme à deux."* That is, the love ceases to look outward; it becomes unhistorical. Authentic love seeks to involve itself in history, to become a new event. The child is the historical event, par excellence, and there is something about the overflow toward a child that allows the couple's love to grow stronger and richer.[19]

Von Hildebrand touches the same point when he says that procreation is the "superabundant" finality of intercourse. By using such a word he leaves place for the other *finality* of love-union. And he also casts openness to life as part and parcel of love-union. In human terms, if love is not overflowing (superabundant), then it tends to diminish, to "pull back," to become less risky, less abandoned, and less serious. Otherwise it risks becoming fixed, fixated, looking narcissistically inward at the self mirrored in the other.[20]

Theological Anthropology

As you can see, I am trying to bring out the intrinsic human dimensions of the sexual ethic. The Church teaching is more than an ethical teaching on contraception. It is a theological anthropology about the meaning of human love imaging forth the divine love.

That is why, I believe, it is fundamentally incorrect to say that we are dealing here merely with an issue of natural law – unless one were to qualify the term "natural law" with a host of theological insights regarding the relation of the human to Creation and Redemption.[21]

First of all, it goes beyond any mere physicalism and biologism. Procreation is respected not simply for the sake of respecting a physical process. When people speak about respecting the "integrity" or the "structure" of intercourse, I fear they unfortunately mislead people into thinking the teaching is all about physical processes. No, the teaching is about the meaning of love and life. The only reason the structure of the act assumes importance is because it is the vehicle not to mere biological life but to human life.

But the second and most important reason why we are beyond a "mere natural law" insight is, because we are touching on the life of the Trinity itself where love flows into life, where the Spirit issues forth as the eternal Love between the Father and the Son.[22] The Church's theology of human love is also guided by the meaning of God's marriage with His people in Jesus the Lord – a love that always issues forth in newborn children through baptism. In this sense the Church's

178

teaching touches upon an *economia* of salvation itself which is always a "missionary" *economia*.

This is a long way from physicalism. Unfortunately the teaching has reached our people's understanding as a physicalism, and worse, sometimes in terms still sounding suspicious about sexual pleasure.

The teaching is poorly served when we ourselves separate love and life, making them seem as two separate norms unrelated to each other. For example, in arguing against homosexual activity it is not enough to say something like, "The sexual activity may be loving but it is wrong because it violates the life-dimension." This misses the intrinsic connection. If it violates the life-dimension, then it is precisely to the point that it will be flawed in sustaining love. Nominalism has its subtle way of creeping in. We sometimes give the pastoral impression, because of some arbitrarily added requirement, that it is a sin to perform a loving action.

Donald Goergen missed the point of how a procreative dimension actually affects love when he quoted Norman Pittenger approvingly:

> "The wrongness in homosexuality is to be found in exactly the same place as the wrongness in heterosexuality – that is . . . insofar as the homosexual, like the heterosexual, fails to be a responsible person, . . . and lacks real respect for the one whom he loves . . ."[23]

What Pittenger and Goergen miss here is that the Church's conviction is not that homosexuality is wrong regardless of whether there are respect and love – that would be nominalist – but that the lack of life-orientation is such that ultimately respect and love will be eroded from within. Sometimes we argue against challenges to our sexual ethics in a way that does make it seem that we are sacrificing the needs of love to some extrinsic order of faculties.[24] Perhaps Basil Cardinal Hume said it well at the 1980 Synod when he spoke of his two contrasting dreams. In the first, the Church is a fortress; the stranger approaching is the enemy. In the other dream, the Church is a pilgrim limping along the road. He then noted that he sensed *Humanae Vitae* as right, "but alas we did not know how to speak to the people." This kind of speaking takes not the quick appeal to an abstract or authoritarian principle but in his words a "co-agonizing" with other pilgrims.[25]

Problems

I have spoken quicky and broadly about the great insight of the Church's sexual ethic, namely, her insight into the two hinged meanings of love and life and how they cohere together, and how this ethic even roots us into the central doctrines of Trinity and Incarnation. I am especially anxious in doing this to catch the intrinsicist mode of thought, or in John Dunne's terms, to catch the "form of the forms of thought." That is, I am trying to appropriate our sexual ethics into a synthesis that makes some intrinsic and personalistic sense. I wish to be clear that there should not be any illusion that this solves all problems. The broad terms we have used help to get across a major insight, but they do not necessarily provide an apologia against certain very real problems.

It would take us too far afield to deal with all the problems.[26] Allow me to pose only one as an illustrative example. It is one that comes up frequently in the literature as well as in pastoral practice. I will speak about it in less technical language than the rest of this paper, since it is a very human problem.

It concerns what is often termed today a "conflict-of-values" case, and I am confident that it is not unfamiliar to you. Let us take a case where contraception is the issue. The haunting pastoral question of recent years comes when the values of responsible procreation and unitive love seem to come into conflict with one another. For example, take a case where there is a serious danger to the mother's life and to the child's life, where there are already several children, where there have been serious but unsuccessful efforts to practice family planning, where there is fear of intercourse due to even the slightest possibility of conception, where the lack of intercourse is increasing the serious strain between the couples.

In regard to the case, some might say there can be no objective conflict of values.[27] They feel that, if one had correct teaching on temperature natural family planning and other methods, there just would be no danger. Perhaps they are right, but pastorally the ideal "givens" are very often just not all in place.

There is a particular form of solution to this case which is often given, under the name of "pastoral." For example, priests will say, "Church teaching is one thing, but there must be pastoral compassion." Others may say, *"Humanae Vitae* is an ideal, but we must expect people's slow growth toward the ideal." Others say something like, "Principles are one thing; but we must apply the principles pastorally."

My question is this: Are we merely involved here in an issue of principles vs. pastoral application? Or is the problem deeper? *Humanae Vitae* said that "each and every marriage act must remain open to the transmission of life."[28] In other words, the principle seems to have, contained within itself, the answer to every pastoral case. Some theologians do in fact seem to recognize that in some cases abstention seems to be the only pastoral solution available.[29] But if abstention is the only alternative, how do we keep the unitive value? And if intercourse does take place in a way that risks both the mother's life and the loss of the child, how do we keep the responsibility-value in the procreative effort?

My question then is this: Is the word *"pastoral"* being used to imply that sometimes an individual act of contraception would not be objectively wrong, provided we are keeping the general prophetic concern of the papal teaching intact? If this is the case, then are we not in violation of at least the literal words of the encyclical?

I raise this question because very often when I speak to priests who perceive themselves as very loyal to *Humanae Vitae,* I receive a paradoxical impression. While they are very critical of "those dissenting theologians," they themselves in certain, very desperate cases, seem to want the word "pastoral" to mean something less than "each and every act." Not only that, but it seems that by the time one finishes unraveling the case, they seem to feel that abstention would not be an ideal, nor would an intercourse that risked a dangerous procreation. Indeed, I have found in many cases that priests were happy to send couples to the more "liberal priest" who would be, as they put it, "less anxious or less scrupulous." In other words, sometimes I hear the word "pastoral" being used in a way that makes me wonder whether it does not mean the same thing that others mean when they say that "they agree with the general prophetic character of *Humanae Vitae* and its central teachings on the relation of love and life, but that they simply do not understand how it can be applied to each and every difficult situation (each and every act)."

Let me relate an anecdote that presses the point very sharply. A friend who has been a very strong defender of *Humanae Vitae* recently came home from a conference on moral theology. He recounted how one theologian felt that in certain cases where the woman would be unable to bring a pregnancy to term and would also be risking her life if she conceived, there could be a form of physical contraception. The theologian gave a rationale that, in this case, it was impossible to be open to procreation in any real sense of the word, so that the contraception was not really moral contraception since there was no action really being taken to close out an otherwise possible life. The priest to my utter surprise felt that this was a correct and pastoral application of *Humanae Vitae.*

I said to him that, if his interpretation is correct, it would be good to communicate it to the Catholic people. My point is, that what many see as "pastoral application," others see as precluded by the teaching — almost to the point that some ask if perhaps the word "pastoral" is being used as a form of evasion. In other words, some feel that the word *pastoral* is being used by priests and bishops to shield even themselves from the complications of conscience which would ensue, if they were to spell out the real significance of their convictions vis-à-vis the "each and every act" clause.

I have spoken of this problem in very human terms. Theologically it also bears upon the issue of what intrinsic evil really means when applied to sexual action. Some try to solve it on the level of what they call basic values, saying there are some basic values against which we can never act.[30] That is why there is often strong reaction to what is called the ontic evil approach.[31] One real problem is to find a way of systematically articulating our sexual teaching so that it is not seen as inconsistent with the kinds of exceptions traditionally allowed in the issues of life and death, such as self-defense. But since other papers are dealing with this, I will happily proceed to the final section of my paper, namely, the social dimension of our sexual teaching.

The Church's Sexual Teaching As Socially Prophetic

We have spoken of *Humanae Vitae* in the early section of this paper not in terms of the contraception issue alone, but as a broad synthesis which connects human love and human life. Amid the present controversies within the Church, what should not be missed is the extraordinary and, in a sense, surprising convergence of opinion regarding this general synthesis.

Many sense that the teaching is prophetic not only in that it goes against sexual trends today, but in that it announces a different vision

182

of the social community, and even of socio-economic structures. Let me merely hint at these interesting ideas by briefly touching on three illustrations: the issues of population, of hope for the future, and of a more organic community.[32]

Contraception, World Hunger, and Population

In the face of world hunger, there have been tendencies among Americans and other developed nations to make "population" the central problem. And the impulse to solve the problem becomes, typically, ruled by the technologic mind-set. Americans seem unaware that the real explosion is not population but the consumption explosion of the developed nations.[33] Paul VI hit the point sharply at the World Food Conference in 1974, saying, "It is inadmissible that those who have control of the wealth and resources of mankind should try to resolve the problem of hunger by forbidding the poor to be born."[34]

My point here is that the Church seemed to have an early insight into a very real population mechanism, namely, that population-decrease comes most effectively through economic development, and that there is something ecologically inhuman and unbalanced in a government's forcefully entering the sanctuary of the family, when economic justice and more organic development are left unattended.[35] The real point is, that this insight of the Church's is not unconnected with her conviction regarding the respect for both the life and love dimensions of human sexuality. In other words, instead of reading the Church's population-analysis as merely an overflow of her sexual "hang-up," I am suggesting that there is an ecology built into our sexual ethic that connects the organic demands of being open to life in intercourse with the organic ways of solving world-hunger issues.[36] Let us proceed more deeply, then, into the connections between the social and the sexual by a second example.

The Church's Sexual Ethic: A Prophecy Against Manichaeanism

There is something in the social order that interacts with individual morality.[37] One cannot separate one's feeling about sex from one's feeling about history and humanity.

Take, for example, the rather strong cultural impetus toward sterilization today. In a very insightful article, Midge Dexter touches

183

on the connection between the social and the sexual. She says:

> Look at the willfully childless couple in their early '30's . . . Both
> are suffering from a soul-killing lack of responsibility for the
> future and for someone and something beyond self that . . . is
> making their lives feel meaningless to them.[38]

Her thought is running deeper than the issue of judging an individual's motives for responsible parenthood. The concern is for a social trend, a lack of self-transcendence, a lack of care for the future. She finds a real lack of hope in the world, a deep distrust in the world's goodness, ultimately "the profoundest kind of self-hatred."

The Church's teaching is not merely a repetition of what she once had to insist upon against the Manichaeans, that procreation is good because matter is not evil.[39] She *is* saying that, but her insistence that sexuality remain in a procreative context is also proclaiming that the world is a place to hope in, that our love and our selves are worth reproducing.

The Church Against Narcissism

A similar thought is provoked by Christopher Lasch by his insights into contemporary narcissism.[40] He persuasively argues that narcissism is not only an individual pathology, but the underlying structure of our age.[41] One of his many insights is the way in which easier sex ends up trivializing not only sex, but relationships themselves. He extends an insight popularized by Rollo May – how too much erotica will spell the end of that healthy human passion which we call eros.[42] Lasch makes a key connection for our purposes here, saying that "when sex is for the couples alone, the relationship can be terminated at pleasure." This leads to a "wary avoidance of emotional commitments."[43] And then comes a central insight. He says that the inability to take an interest in anything after one's own death makes intimacy more elusive than ever.

Enter once again the prophetic instinct of Church teaching. She insists that sex is so untrivial that it must take place only in a situation of permanency with a procreative possibility.[44] The Church says relationships are not to be "cool." The Church implicitly requires a passionate love for the other person, and ultimately for the child who will exist even beyond our death. Correct sex looks for a future. It is no accident that sexual libertinism accompanies social apathy; no accident that the loss of hope in avoiding the bomb should foster sexual mores that escape into the "cabaret" of temporary liaisons.[45]

Against an Individualist Notion of Sin

It was this social sense which Rosemary Haughton felt the CTSA study most deeply missed.[46] Her point has to do with how we are easily absorbed into the deformed cultural milieu that Lasch and Midge Dexter are analyzing. She sees that the authors are caught up in an effort to rid us of the notion that sexual sins are something we can "slip into." In one way, of course, they are correct. We have all struggled pastorally to nurture in people a sense of sin that occurs on the intentional level, not on an accidental level. But she is saying that "sin is precisely 'something one can slip into.'" She adds that "Christ did not die to improve my moral posture, but to save me from sin, a sin which is in my bones and flesh and in my every inclination, vitiating my best efforts, spoiling my most precious relationships." One recognizes here a sense of sin that includes theological insights on "the sin of the world," and how it affects every aspect of human experience. And just as sin, so also redemption affects all material reality. She is speaking here of deep cultural deformations and the need for healing by the Incarnation at all levels.

In other words, I am saying that the Church's instinct for keeping the sexual in marriage goes more deeply than we had possibly dreamed. It is in the end a prophetic insistence against certain cultural deformations of sexuality which carry their effects into social realities such as hunger, the threat of the bomb, and a world worth being passionate about, a world whose future is worth caring about.

The Church's Sexual Teaching: A Prophecy for Community

We have seen how the Church's sexual teaching awakens an impetus to solve hunger issues at levels other than the technological, and how it symbolizes a Christian hope in ourselves and in a future as against a Manichaean despair of human history. Now let us see how the Church's insistence on reserving intercourse for marriage is more than a sexual concern. It touches the roots of community.

In a consumer society it is difficult to stop the dynamism that turns people into property. We end up "consuming" experiences and relationships, and then discarding them. There is little permanence. The early sociologists foresaw that the competitive nature of capitalism would lead to what they called the *"Gesellschaft"* society. By this they meant a society where "everybody is by himself and isolated."[47] In an earlier article I argued that a view of intercourse that demanded permanency slants us toward a less competitive, more sharing community. This is more than a sociological concern; it is one that goes to the roots of the New Testament ethic.[48]

If anything was important in the New Testament it was the communion *(koinonia)*, where people shared goods and an enduring, forgiving love.[49] At its depth a sexual ethic requiring permanent marriage is a proclamation about the importance of forgiveness and enduring love. It is a way of seeing a permanent, human relationship as shadowing forth the enduring love of Jesus on the Cross. This has enormous implications for a society where so many are left without much human experience of God's permanently caring love. It is no accident that in a society where there is so much transience, there will also develop a form of sex that is transient. The Church's concern asks for a family rooting of sexuality. And a family rooting can be at least one step toward a more organic community. And a more organic community has salvational meaning, in that it can become a sacrament by which we experience Jesus' perduring love of us.

Pastoral Implication: "Integral" Solicitude

We have been exploring how the Church's sexual ethic carries a form of social prophecy. For pastors of souls this yields a new dimension to their role of "watching over" *(episcopos)* the flock. Let me name it an "integral" solicitude. By this I mean that our watchfulness regarding correct sexual teaching touches into the deeper layers of social values symbolized by the sexual teachings. Take for example the three points we have mentioned, namely, world population, sterilization, and transience in community.

First, in regard to hunger and population, I am thinking of how Indira Gandhi's forced sterility program may have had some roots in the austerity programs imposed upon India through the International Monetary Fund.[50] An integral solicitude in this case, even for Americans, would include an effort not only to safeguard the Church's sexual teaching but to attempt to look at the economic mechanisms of American economic decisions on India. The temptation to forced birth control is not unconnected with our economic policies.

Second, take the solicitude required in the issue of sterilization.

Few other issues have provoked such anxiety among bishops. There have been questions sent to Rome and commentaries on Rome's reply. But if sterilization as a social trend has something to do with people sensing the worth of bringing a child into the world, we must be equally exercised over the issues that influence their subconscious fears. A bishop rightfully speaks against sterilization, but a bishop also rightfully addresses those matters that cause people to want to be sterilized because of their distrust in the world's future. So, the bishop who speaks against sterilization, if he wishes to be integral, will also speak against companies producing the weaponry that works its sterility at subconscious levels (not to mention the very literal sterilization being visited on people through our radioactive wastes). I do not intend here just a general fervorino encouraging Bishops to be vigilant on social issues. Rather, I am suggesting that there is direct and inherent interaction between sexual practices and social practices. The anti-child atmosphere is a phenomenon not at all unrelated to the chauvinistic narcissism embedded in nationalism, racism, and class-ism. It is intrinsically connected with whether sex is seen as an escape, whether the world is a place to be escaped from – a place definitely not to risk having a child in. The Church's effort to restore a healthy eros includes a judgment against those elements in the milieu that breed passionlessness and an escape from feeling.[51]

In regard to community, our solicitude against transitory sex includes a care about the very wellsprings of community in the life of the Church itself. For example, a priest may exhibit perfect loyalty to the Holy See in sexual teachings, but may be a sign of contradiction in the distant and bureaucratic way he administers the parish community. He ends curiously ratifying at one level what he preaches against at another level. The bishop's burden is here almost too heavy to mention. Perhaps we could even provoke a self-examination about how we ourselves, bishops and theologians, actually live community. Perhaps we actually live a form of *gesellschaft* – not only in our personal lives, but even in the way our structures of diocese and parish have evolved over the years. The prophetic teaching that demands a stable marriage before intercourse will be all the more congruent coming out of a Church of more permanent human relationships where people can sense the meaning of Church as real community.

Today we know better than yesterday how the milieu can subvert the best of our teaching. The pure water of healthy sexual teaching is a gift of God's Spirit to His people. But if the plumbing structure of social relations within and without the household become rusty, our best efforts are wasted. Water becomes contaminated at every juncture.

So we return where we began. The Church's vision of love and life in human sexuality is based on the intrinsic good of the human community of persons. It is ultimately a public issue. To be unintegral in our concern is to regress to an individualistic morality.[52] This allows our voice to be privatized. To be privatized is to be domesticized, to be subtle supporters of the status quo. Many feel that this is what happened in Germany. While National Socialism rose to power, too may in the Church had their heads turned inward. Sex is not only a metaphor for social living, it is also a symbol. A symbol is like a sacrament in that it also contains reality. Integral solicitude attempts to deal with both the *sign* and the *res,* the social reality of both sin and its individual symbol of unchastity, and the social reality of salvation and its individual sacrament of married sexuality.

Notes

1. The phrase is taken from a theme and title of an article by Eugene Kennedy, "Insufficient Guilt in the Room," *America,* March 27, 1976, pp. 244-51. For general bibliography one could cite innumerable sources. For all its problems the CTSA study did have an excellent bibliography: *Human Sexuality* (New York: Paulist, 1977), pp. 275-91; See also Andre Guindon, *The Sexual Language* (University of Ottawa Press, 1976), pp. 441-76.

2. Harrington's work is more concerned with social issues and his own evolution of thought, *Fragments of a Century* (New York: E. P. Dutton, 1973).

3. Harvey Cox, *The Secular City* (New York: Macmillan, 1966); see especially pp. 167-89.

4. The bibliography recounting the reaction to *Humanae Vitae* is of course immense. Richard McCormick's *Moral Notes* in *Theological Studies* are an excellent source. For the dialogue after the CTSA study see, for example, Stuhlmueller, *The Bible Today,* December, 1977; George Montague, *America,* October 29, 1977; my own article, *America,* October 15, 1977; James McHugh, *St. Anthony Messenger,* 1977; Daniel McGuire, *CTSA Proceedings 33,* (1978); Dennis Doherty, ed., *Dimensions of Human Sexuality* (New York: Doubleday, 1979).

5. See especially his work, *The Morality Gap* (New York: Macmillan, 1968); also *The Respectable Murderers* (St. Louis: Herder and Herder, 1966).

6. It is disturbing sometimes to sense the gap in perceptions of theological issues in North America from those in Latin America. Hugo Assmann once said the greatest discrepancy is not between preconciliar traditionalists and postconciliar reformists, but "the really profound discrepancy . . . is that which exists between intrachurch reformers, nourished on North Atlantic progressivisms, and Christians impelled by and committed to the fundamental challenges of the liberation process." See Philip E. Berryman, "Latin American Liberation Theology," *Theological Studies,* September, 1973, p. 379.

7. I touched on this issue in a panel talk to the Catholic Biblical Association, San Francisco, 1978, published in *Catholic Mind,* December, 1978.

8. See Louis Vereecke, *Studia Moralia 1* (Academia Alfonsiana, 1962), especially pp. 90-95.

9. For Thomas' reasoning, see for example, II-II. 154.2 Also Herbert McCabe, *What Is Ethics All About* (New York: Corpus, 1969).

10. There has been revived a clear distinction between "natural" in the sense of what the human has in common with the animal world, and *natura ut ratio.* See McCormick, *Theological Studies,* December 1967, p. 766. And also Monden, *Sin, Liberty and Law* (New York: Sheed and Ward), p. 89. See especially Pere DeFinance, *Essai sur L'Agir Humain,* as cited in Johann, *America,* April 10, 1965, p. 487.

11. *A Search for God in Time and Memory* (Notre Dame: University of Notre Dame Press, 1977), pp. 33-34.

12. See, for example, Gabriel Marcel, *Creative Fidelity* (New York: Farrar, Strauss and Co., 1964), pp. 147-74. See Von Hildebrand's *In Defense of Purity* (New York: Sheed and Ward, 1945). (The German edition came out in 1928.)

13. See John Noonan, *Contraception* (Cambridge, Mass.: Harvard University Press, 1965), pp. 495-500, for a very clear review of this development, and p. 497 for this citation of Doms'.

14. See especially nos. 48 and 49 where the unitive dimension of sexuality is richly developed.

15. See Rosemary Haughton, "Toward a Christian Theology of Sexuality," *Doctrine and Life,* June-July, 1978. See also *The Mystery of Sexuality* (New York: Paulist Press, 1972). This author, I believe, is one of the most insightful Catholic thinkers in the field today.

16. I was trying in the article to deepen an image first given me by Herbert McCabe, when he wrote against Joseph Fletcher in *Commonweal,* January 14, 1966. He used there the image of *currency* as a form of intersubjective meaning that is really objective in the sense of being built in and independent of whatever subjective wish the person would like to give to his money.

17. *Gaudium et Spes,* nos. 48 to 52. Also see *To Live in Christ Jesus,* 14-19.

18. "Sexual Morality" in the *New Catholic Encyclopedia* 17. Also, Bishop Mugavero's pastoral, "Sexuality – God's Gift" sees sex as an objective language. This little pamphlet is an excellent form of pastoral language.

19. Some efforts at phenomenologizing have taken place in order to analyze what the personal and attitudinal repercussions of contraception are. See, for example, an early article by Paul Quay, "Contraception and Conjugal Love," *Theological Studies* 22 (1961). See also E. Paci, "Per una Fenomenologia dell'Eros," *Facets of Eros,* edited by Smith-English (The Hague, 1972).

20. See Abel Jeanniere, *Anthropology of Sex* (New York: Harper and Row, 1967).

21. The problem of natural law's relation to revelation is a dense historical and systematic issue. For some moral insights see Monden, pp. 95-96. James Gustafson is helpful here. See especially his *Protestant and Roman Catholic Ethics* (Chicago: University of Chicago Press), pp. 111-126.

22. See Häring, *The Law of Christ* (3 vols.; Westminster, Md.: Newman Press, 1961-66) III: 328-29; see also William May, *The Nature and Meaning of Chastity* (Chicago: Franciscan Herald Press), p. 39.

23. *The Sexual Celibate* (New York: Seabury, 1975), p. 190. Despite what I felt were serious flaws in key sections of Goergen's work, much insight was offered.

24. Many have criticized the language of the Congregation of the Faith's *Declaration on Certain Questions Concerning Sexual Ethics.*

25. See *Origins* 10. 18:275-76.

26. The CTSA study, no matter how strong one's feelings of disagreement with certain sections, did in fact seem to surface a good number of theological issues.

27. There is an oft-cited Scholastic teaching that the perplexed conscience is merely a subjective phenomenon, that there cannot be objective conflicts of values. Interesting insights into the social justice dimension of this problem are given by David Hollenbach, *Claims in Conflict* (New York: Paulist, 1979), especially pp. 161-166. It would be interesting to see if there is room for parallel study in the sexual field.

28. Archbishop Quinn touched upon this point in his talk at the Synod. I had not read his talk until typing these notes. But since reading it, I am hopeful that the effort here is a small step in implementing his call for dialogue between theologians and bishops. See *Origins* 10.17:163-167.

29. See, for example, the commentary by William May on the July 3, 1980 statement of the American Bishops on Tubal Ligation in *Hospital Progress* 61.9 (September, 1980).

30. See the approach of Germain Grisez in *Abortion: The Myths, the Realities, and the Arguments* (New York: Corpus, 1970) and *Contraception and the Natural Law* (Milwaukee: Bruce, 1964).

31. A great amount of literature has already dealt with this issue. See McCormick, "Moral Notes," *Theological Studies*, March, 1980 and March, 1979; Also two collections: McCormick-Ramsey, eds., *Doing Evil to Achieve Good* (Chicago: Loyola University Press); and McCormick-Curran, eds., *Readings in Moral Theology* (New York: Paulist, 1979). My own fear is that the issue is beginning to be emotionally loaded with forms of code words that do not do justice to the complexities. If one wishes to react to his opponent captiously, one can then always reduce his point to absurdity. I have the feeling that we are in grips of a controversy not unlike the *De Auxiliis* controversy. Someone will have to soon demand that no more anathemas are to be cast about.

32. For a similar movement from the sexual to the social, see William Everett, "Between Augustine and Hildebrand," *CTSA Proceedings* 33 (1978):77-83.

33. See *Bread for the World* (New York: Paulist, 1975), pp. 27-38; also James McGinnis, *Bread and Justice,* which is implicitly about this point throughout.

34. Paul VI, World Food Conference, 1974.

35. See for example Barry Commoner's article in Bread for the World's booklet, *The Challenge of World Hunger,* 25a to 30a. Also Peter Henriot, "Global Population in Perspective . . ." *Theological Studies* 35 (1974):48-70; also "Vatican Delegation's Intervention at U.N. Conference on Population," *Catholic Mind,* May 1975.

36. The more organic solution to world hunger was perhaps not far from the surface in church teaching. *Humanae Vitae* is fairly explicit; see no. 23.

37. Marxist literature is accustomed to this sort of analysis. For example, Marcuse's *Eros and Civilization* was widely read in the sixties. Sociocultural analyses, I am told, have become more accepted in our time; witness the recent popularity of Lasch's *Culture of Narcissism.*

38. Originally a lecture at the Harvard Club and now published in *Catholic Mind,* September, 1980, pp. 15-23.

39. See Noonan, pp. 108-126.

40. Christopher Lasch, *The Culture of Narcissism* (New York: Warner Books, 1979), especially pp. 320-350.

41. *Ibid.,* pp. 87-88.

42. Rollo May, *Love and Will* (New York: Dell, 1969), pp. 13-36; 121-152.

43. Lasch, pp. 320, 328.

44. The Church thus asks that sex keep its passion. It is noteworthy that Thomas Aquinas insisted chastity not only avoid the excess of sensuality, but also the defect: II, II, 151.3.

45. The image of the "Cabaret" comes from the musical show. Just as the show depicted the cabaret as the place of escape from responsibility, so the Church could unwittingly be drawn into the cabaret by becoming involved in only the individualistic dimensions of moral judgment.

46. See Rosemary Haughton, "Toward a Christian Theology of Sexuality," *Doctrine and Life,* June-July 1978, pp. 332-35.

47. See Gregory Baum, *Religion and Alienation* (New York: Paulist, 1975), pp. 44-47.

48. *Catholic Mind,* December, 1978, pp. 47-50.

49. Rudolph Schnackenburg, *The Moral Teaching of the New Testament* (St. Louis: Herder and Herder, 1965), pp. 177-84; 323-28.

50. See Jeremiah Nova, "In Defense of the Third World," *America,* January 21, 1978, p. 35.

51. I have tried to say a word about the pastoral apostolate of the milieu in "Living Sacramentally," *Emmanuel,* September, 1978, pp. 433-38. See also Häring, *The Law of Christ* I:79-80. Victor Schurr was a German pastoral theologian who first gave this insight to me in his lectures and notes at the Academia Alfonsiana from 1963 to 1965.

52. Hannah Arendt has pointed out that to exclude people from the public realm is to begin the process of corruption.

Chapter 9

Magisterial Teaching From 1918 to the Present

The Reverend John Gallagher, C.S.B., S.T.D.

The Code of Canon Law

This paper traces the teaching of the Roman Catholic magisterium from 1918 to the present. It was in the year 1918 that the modern Code of Canon Law came into force. The code contains certain theological statements about marriage. One such statement concerns the ends of marriage. Paragraph One of Canon 1013 states: "The primary end of marriage is the procreation and education of children; its secondary end is mutual help and the allaying of concupiscence."

In view of the subsequent controversy it is well to look closely at what the code actually says. There is a widespread impression that the code says that the mutual love of spouses is only a secondary end of marriage. In fact, however, the code does not speak of the mutual love of spouses as an end of marriage in either way, as a secondary end or as a primary end.

This raises an interesting point. An end is the object of an act of will. One can, no doubt, have as one's purpose in marriage a growth in love. Love then can be said to be an end of marriage. However, it is an end in a special way. The love in question is itself an act of will responding to those further ends and goods which are the objects of love – namely, the persons who are loved and their welfare. Love is in this case an end which is a response to a more ultimate good or end. For this reason some thinkers who hold that love is central to Christian marriage may not wish to express that centrality by calling love an end of marriage.

The code does not give mere biological generation as the principal end of marriage. That end is procreation and education. Canon 1113 explains this. It states: "Parents are bound by a most serious obligation to provide to the best of their power for the religious and moral as well as for the physical and civil education of their children, and also to provide for their temporal welfare." The code sees marriage as an institution whose principal end is the total human good of the next generation.

What is the authority of the code's theological teaching about marriage? By including certain theological principles in the code the Church was not interested primarily in settling theological disputes. She was interested primarily in providing some theological background for law. For this purpose she adopted certain theological principles commonly accepted in the Church at the time. Some of these principles had already been taught authoritatively by popes and councils. Some had not. The inclusion of a theological principle in the code need not mean that the principle was being taught with new authority.

Casti Connubii

On December 31, 1930, Pope Pius XI published the encyclical, *Casti Connubii,* on Christian marriage. To some extent this encyclical was a response to the Lambeth Conference of 1930, at which for the first time the Church of England withdrew its official objections to artificial contraception. *Casti Connubii* does not limit itself to the problem of artificial contraception, however. It covers a wide range of topics concerning which the modern world either rejects or ignores the traditional teaching of the Catholic Church.

This encyclical seems to presuppose what one might call an organic notion of marriage. Some "reformers" would like to get rid of the institution of marriage or at least radically restructure it. Such efforts are suspect to those who have an organic notion of social institutions. A medical doctor does not begin with an abstract idea of what a rationally constructed human body should be, and then proceed to tear apart the human body and put it together along more rational lines. The human body exists and functions before any physician studies it. Analogously, marriage exists and functions before any theorist studies it. Marriage draws upon and channels certain human energies and instincts, it fulfills certain needs, and it embodies certain principles learned by trial and error, long before it is studied theoretically. In the organic view, the reformer of marriage should not try to destroy the existing institution and rebuild a substitute according to some abstract and partial view of what is needed and what is possible. The reformer of marriage, like the physician, should be humble, learning from the existing thing and respecting the requirements which flow from its nature.

Casti Connubii does not explicitly adopt this organic view, but it seems to imply it. Paragraph 6 states: "The nature of matrimony is entirely independent of the free will of man, so that if one has once contracted matrimony he is thereby subject to its divinely made laws and properties."[1] Paragraphs 49 and 50 argue that matrimony was instituted by God who is the author of nature. The argument seems to be that it was in creating the nature of things that God created marriage. Marriage is not something arbitrarily set up by God but an institution which arises because of the nature of human beings. The encyclical draws from this, that because matrimony is created by God it has laws which human beings should obey, laws which they cannot change. The point is elaborated in Paragraph 95, which contains a quotation from Pope Leo XIII.

> It is a divinely appointed law that whatsoever things are constituted by God, the author of nature, these we find the most useful and salutary, the more they remain in their natural state, unimpaired and unchanged; inasmuch as God, the Creator of all things, intimately knows what is suited to the constitution and the preservation of each, and by his will and mind has so ordained all things that each may duly achieve its purpose. But if the boldness and wickedness of men change and disturb this order of things, so

providentially disposed, then indeed things so wonderfully ordained will begin to be injurious, or will cease to be beneficial, either because, in the change, they have lost their power to benefit, or because God Himself is thus pleased to draw down chastisement on the pride and presumption of men.

Of special interest to our purpose is Pius's discussion of the ends of marriage. He quotes Canon 1013. "The primary end of marriage is the procreation and the education of children."[2] Elsewhere he reemphasizes the primacy of procreation. "Thus, amongst the blessings of marriage, the child holds first place."[3] The child is destined not only for a noble and dignified life in this world but also for eternal life. The sublime end of matrimony is to bring forth children who will become members of Christ and who will enjoy eternal life with God.[4]

Among the secondary ends of marriage Pius XI includes the two mentioned by canon law, mutual aid and the quieting of concupiscence. To these he adds a third, the cultivation of mutual love.[5]

It is clear that Pius does not consider these unitive aspects (mutual love, mutual aid) to have only minor importance. Concerning the union of spouses he speaks of "the generous surrender of his own person made to another for the whole span of life."[6] Furthermore:

> By matrimony, therefore, the minds of the contracting parties are joined and knit together more intimately than are their bodies, and that not by any passing affection of sense or heart, but by a deliberate and firm act of the will.[7]

The mutual love of spouses motivates them to help each other. Pius expands the scope of this traditional category, mutual help.

> This outward expression of love in the home demands not only mutual help but must go further; must have as its primary purpose that man and wife help each other day by day in forming and perfecting themselves in the interior life, so that through their partnership in life they may advance ever more and more in virtue, and above all that they may grow in true love toward God and their neighbor.[8]

There is some reason to believe that Pius XI was not completely satisfied with calling these unitive elements merely secondary ends of matrimony. Of the love between husband and wife he says that it "pervades all the duties of married life and holds pride of place in

194

Christian marriage."[9] Of the mutual help of spouses he says:

> This mutual inward moulding of husband and wife, this determined effort to perfect each other, can in a very real sense, as the Roman Catechism teaches, be said to be the chief reason and purpose of matrimony, provided matrimony be looked at not in the restricted sense as instituted for the proper conception and education of the child, but more widely as the blending of life as a whole and the mutual interchange and sharing thereof.[10]

It seems that Pius XI is insisting on two points which, in the theology of the day, were not easily expressed in one simple formula. The first point is that marriage has an essential orientation to children. The second point is that the mutual love and aid between spouses has an importance which is not adequately expressed by calling them secondary ends of marriage. To add a second primary end to marriage presents its own difficulties, however, as we shall see in discussing a later document. Pius XI resorts to the vague formula of two primacies according to two different points of view.

On sexual relations outside of marriage, the encyclical restates the Church's traditional teaching as follows:

> Nor must we omit to remark, in fine, that since the twofold duty entrusted to parents for the good of their children is of such high dignity and of such great importance, every lawful use of the faculty given by God for the procreation of new life is the right and the privilege of the marriage state alone, by the law of God and of nature, and must be confined absolutely within the sacred limits of that state.[11]

The order of the argument here is worth noting. Pius does not base his rejection of fornication and adultery only on an analysis of biological sexuality. His basis is the nature and end of the institution of marriage. That sex should be properly oriented toward procreation is a truth seen in the context of the orientation of marriage toward procreation.

In Paragraphs 53 to 59, Pius XI condemns artificial contraception as gravely sinful, and instructs confessors to hold to this teaching. Some writers have complained that here Pius resorts to biologistic reasoning. Biologistic reasoning in moral matters begins by discovering in a physical faculty an orientation toward some goal, and then makes that orientation into a moral principle. In sexual ethics, the biologistic approach sees that the sexual organs and sexual responses

195

are so constituted as to produce offspring, and concludes that therefore the production of offspring is the proper good of sex, and that any use of sex for any other purpose is immoral. Biologistic reasoning in ethics is open to serious objections.

Does Pius XI actually resort to a biologistic approach in condemning artificial contraception? Certain passages could suggest that he does. He states that artificial contraception is "intrinsically against nature," and that, "since, therefore, the conjugal act is destined primarily by nature for the begetting of children, those who in exercising it deliberately frustrate its natural power and purpose sin against nature and commit a deed which is shameful and intrinsically vicious."[12] In the context of the whole encyclical, however, it seems that what is "according to nature" is to be determined not by considering the physical aspect by itself but by looking at the nature and purpose of matrimony.

Paragraph 59 states that one partner in a marriage has a duty to try to convince the other not to use artificial contraceptives. However, one is not bound to refuse to have sexual intercourse with a spouse who insists on using contraceptives. The same paragraph states that spouses may have sexual intercourse when for natural reasons either of time or defect conception cannot occur. Intercourse at such times may be for such ends as mutual aid or the cultivation of mutual love, and one is free to pursue such secondary ends so long as they are subordinated to the primary end and so long as the intrinsic nature of the act is preserved. Pius thus rejects the rigourist opinion of some earlier theologians who allowed sexual intercourse only for the purpose of procreation and only when procreation is possible. In 1930 the researches of Ogino and of Knaus into periodic infertility had not yet led to widespread use of periodic continence as a way to prevent pregnancy. It is not clear, then, that in *Casti Connubii* Pius XI is thinking of periodic continence as a long-term strategy for avoiding pregnancy.

As the encyclical situates the meaning of sex in the context of marriage, so it briefly situates marriage in the context of society as a whole. The stability of matrimony is a fruitful source of habits of integrity and guards the well-being of the nation.[13] "The prosperity of the state and the temporal happiness of its citizens cannot remain safe and sound where the foundations on which they are established, which is the moral order, is weakened, and where the very fountainhead from which the state draws its life, namely wedlock and the family, is obstructed by the vices of its citizens."[14]

Herbert Doms and the Meaning of Marriage

The 1930's saw a lively controversy in the Catholic Church regarding the position expressed in the code of Canon Law regarding the primary and secondary ends of marriage. In 1935 Herbert Doms, a German diocesan priest, published a book[15] which appeared in 1939 in an English translation as *The Meaning of Marriage.*[16] Doms objected that Canon Law seemed to say that the meaning of marriage comes only from what is called its primary end, the procreation and education of children. Doms does not deny that marriage has this end, but he insists that it has a meaning in itself apart from this end.

> The constitution of marriage, the union of two persons, does not consist in their subservience to a purpose outside themselves for which they marry. It consists in the constant vital ordination of husband and wife to each other until they become one. If this is so, there can no longer be sufficient reason, from this standpoint, for speaking of procreation as the primary purpose (in the sense in which St. Thomas used the phrase) and for dividing off the other purposes as secondary . . . perhaps it would be best if in the future we gave up using such terms as "primary" and "secondary" in speaking of the purpose of marriage.[17]

Doms distinguishes the meaning of marriage from the ends of marriage. The meaning of marriage and of sexual activity within marriage consists in the actual realization of the unity of the two persons. Besides this meaning there are two ends of marriage. The personal end is the mutual completion and perfection of the spouses on every level. The specific end (i.e., that which gives marriage its distinctive nature) is the child. These two ends are equally primary, and one is not subordinate to the other.

The Roman Rota, 1944

The views of Doms stirred up considerable reactions. They failed, however, to convince Rome on the central point. A decree of the Holy Office on April 1, 1944,[18] stated that the procreation and education of children is to be considered the primary end of marriage and no other ends are to be considered as equally principal ends. Other ends are to be considered secondary and subordinate to the one primary end. In this decree, and in a "sentence" of the Holy Roman Rota earlier in the same year,[19] Doms is not named, but it is clear that his position is being rejected.

The sentence of the Rota appeals to a principle which can be found in St. Thomas, that the end specifies a reality. Applied to activity it means that the end determines the nature of the activity. If your end is to remove a brain tumor this requires one type of activity. If your end is to pass an examination in mathematics this requires a different type of activity.

One activity may serve two ends at the same time. You may run home from work both as a means to keep fit and as a means to get home. Doms claimed that marriage has two ends, both equally primary, and one is not subordinate to the other. In the view of the Rota this would mean that in marriage there are two distinct aspects, the marriage as directed toward the mutual completion and perfection of the spouses, and the marriage as directed toward the child; these two aspects would be only accidentally, not essentially, united. If they had no essential relation to each other there would be no theological reason for keeping them together. If someone wanted to have one without the other, there would be no reason not to do so. This is a consequence which the Rota would not accept.

In summary, the Rota seems to have rejected the notion that marriage has two primary ends, because this would destroy the essential relationship between the ends and leave the way open for allowing marriage with no procreative orientation. It is noteworthy that the acceptance by many Catholic theologians of two primary ends of marriage has been followed, a few years later, by the acceptance of deliberately childless marriages.

One may ask: what is wrong with deliberately childless marriages? The 1944 sentence of the Rota did not discuss this question, because Doms and his followers had not denied that marriage has procreation and education of children as an essential end.

If the two ends of marriage are not independent, how are they united? The Rota states that the secondary end is subordinate to the primary end. That is, the mutual help and perfecting of spouses is ordered to the procreation and education of children. This raises a question. May spouses pursue these secondary ends not only insofar as they are ordered to procreation but also for other reasons? Surely they may; in fact, to develop one's love for one's spouse and to help one's spouse *only* as ordered to procreation seems to offend against the very meaning of the love of one's spouse. However, if one can pursue these unitive ends not merely as subordinate to procreation, do they not thereby become primary ends? Here the Rota's explanation of the relation between the unitive and the procreative aspects of marriage left room for controversy.

Pope Pius XII

When Pope Pius XII enters the discussion he expresses concern that the secondary end be shown to be very important.[20] On the other hand he holds firmly to the notion of primary and secondary ends as expressed in canon law. He states also that the secondary end is subordinate to the primary end. The unitive aspects are placed by the will of nature and of the creator at the service of the offspring.[21]

In the address to the midwives Pius XII repeats the Church's rejection of artificial contraception, and adds that this moral teaching is valid for all time, a law which is natural and divine. Why is artificial contraception wrong? In some passages Pius XII seems to argue biologistically, from the nature of the physical sexual faculty considered in itself.[22] Elsewhere he seems to argue from the nature of marriage.[23] Further study is needed to show whether these two approaches can be fitted together.

Pius XII dealt with a number of practical moral questions concerning sex and marriage. In the address to the midwives he discussed periodic continence. There he first repeats the teaching of Pius XI that spouses may engage in sexual intercourse when the wife cannot conceive. May a couple restrict the marital act to only infertile periods in order to avoid conception? Pius XII replies that married couples who engage in sexual intercourse have a general duty to provide for the conservation of the human race. However, he says, "serious reasons, often put forward on medical, eugenic, economic and social grounds, can exempt from that obligatory service, even for a considerable period of time, even for the entire duration of the marriage."[24]

Pius XII rejected the use of artificial insemination.[25] He considers three situations. In the first the mother is not married. In this case the use of artificial insemination offends against the requirement that procreation take place within marriage. In the second situation the mother is married but the semen is from a man other than her husband. This is immoral because only the husband and wife have rights over the body of the other for purposes of generating new life. The bond of origin created by physical paternity creates a duty to protect and educate the child, but this cannot take place properly in this second type of situation. In the third type of situation the semen is from the husband of the woman. Artificial insemination is wrong even in this case because marriage and the marital act are not merely organic functions for the transmission of seed. The marital act is a personal act which expresses the mutual giving of spouses. This makes it the proper context for conception. Here, interestingly, Pius XII appeals explicitly to an aspect of the sexual act which is beyond the merely physical. Finally, according to Pius XII, artificial means may be used to facilitate conception after natural intercourse.

Pius XII rejects experiments in *in vitro* fertilization as immoral and absolutely illicit.[26] His reasons for rejecting artificial insemination using semen from the husband would rule out *in vitro* fertilization.

In an address on September 12, 1958 Pius discusses some moral issues related to genetics.[27] When genetic factors are likely to cause a couple to produce defective offspring, a prenuptial examination to discover the likelihood of such a result is licit. If the likelihood of defective offspring is great, authorities may even make such examinations obligatory. For genetic reasons one may advise a couple not to marry but one may not forbid them to marry. "Marriage is one of the fundamental human rights, the use of which may not be prevented." If the discovery of the genetic difficulty comes after marriage one may advise the couple not to have children but one may not forbid them to have children.

Vatican II

The Second Vatican Council dealt with marriage and the family in *The Constitution on the Church in the Modern World (Gaudium et Spes)*, sections 46-52. There were differences of opinion among the Council Fathers concerning earlier drafts of this document. One group wanted the document to follow closely the formulations of canon law and of papal documents on such crucial matters as the ends of marriage. Another group wanted to depart quite sharply from such formulations. Some wanted to open for discussion the question of artificial contraception. Pope John XXIII set up a commission to study the question. Pope Paul VI instructed the council not to pronounce on the question. He himself would pronounce on it after studying the report of the commission.

The treatment of marriage in *Gaudium et Spes* contains much from earlier papal statements, but the council gives its own particular emphasis to the material. Central to its discussion of marriage and family is what it calls "married love" or "spousal love." As a matter of human will, this love is much more than physical desire, but it includes physical expression. It is distinct from other types of friendship in that it is expressed and perfected through the physical marital act which both signifies and promotes the mutual self-giving of the spouses.[28] This spousal love wells up from the fountain of divine love, and is structured on the model of Christ's love for the Church. This spousal love is caught up in the divine love and can lead the spouses to God.

Spousal love leads to mutual help and service.

> Thus a man and a woman, who by the marriage covenant of conjugal love "are no longer two, but one flesh" (Mt. 19, 6), render mutual help and service to each other through an intimate union of their persons and of their actions. Through this union they experience the meaning of their oneness and attain to it with growing perfection day by day. As a mutual gift of two persons, this intimate union, as well as the good of the children, imposes total fidelity on the spouses and argues for an unbreakable oneness between them.[29]

The council expresses clearly the orientation of marriage toward children.

> By their very nature, the institution of marriage itself and conjugal love are ordained for the procreation of children, and find in them their ultimate crown.[30]

Clearly the Council Fathers are arguing not from a narrowly biological basis. It is the nature of marriage itself and of conjugal love to be oriented toward procreation.

Although it does not state whether or not artificial contraception is licit, the Constitution does discuss the problem. It stresses that parents are to procreate responsibly, taking account of their own welfare and that of their children. They are to consider the material and the spiritual condition of the times, the interests of the family group, of temporal society and of the Church. In some situations there will be a conflict between different factors. There may be strong reasons to limit the number of children. At the same time sexual abstinence can create problems. It may, for example, make it difficult to maintain the faithful exercise of love and the full intimacy of spousal life. The judgment about whether to have children is to be made by the parents, but it is not to be made arbitrarily. Moral duty involves not motive only, but the observance of objective standards. These standards, in the area of sexual behaviour, are those which "based on the nature of the human person and his acts, preserve the full sense of mutual self-giving and human procreation in the context of true love."[31] Parents are to reject abortion. They are to have an informed conscience, one conformed to the divine law and submissive to the teaching of the Church which interprets divine law.

Possibly the most controversial points about the treatment of marriage and the family in *Gaudium et Spes* concern what the document does not say. In at least one case an omission was a triumph for one point of view at the council. This case is the omission in the document of the old terminology of primary and secondary ends of marriage and the omission of any explanation of mutual help of spouses as merely subordinate to the procreation and education of children.

The conciliar text on marriage and the family left several questions unanswered. The problem of artificial contraception was, of course, deliberately left unresolved. Another question concerns whether there is an intrinsic relationship between the unitive and procreative ends of marriage. If there is no such instrinsic relationship then the way is open, as we have seen, to allow a type of marriage which is deliberately not oriented toward children.

The Papal Commission, 1966

In June, 1966, the papal commission on birth control reported to Pope Paul VI. Four documents eventually came to light. One was the "Theological Report of the Papal Commission on Birth Control." This document, which has since become known as "the majority report," was signed by nineteen of the theologians and by a number of the other experts on the commission. It represents the view of a substantial majority of those on the commission. A second document, "Pastoral Approaches," is in agreement with the majority report. They both advocate a change in the Church's official teaching in order to allow artificial contraception in some cases. A third document, the so-called "minority report," was signed by four theologians on the commission who disagreed with the majority report and who advised that no change be made in the Church's teaching. A fourth document is a working paper by some of the theologians who advocated change in the Church's teaching. It defends their position against arguments in the third document.[32]

The position of the first document, the majority report, can be summarized in six points. First, although it would allow artificial contraception in some cases, yet it insists that sex and marriage are properly oriented toward the procreation and education of children. The union of spouses is not to be separated from the procreative finality of marriage. Conjugal love and fecundity are in no way opposed, but complement each other. The community of life of spouses provides the proper framework for the procreation and education of children.

Second, the majority report approaches the problem from the point of view of the totality of the marriage. It wishes to take its moral direction not from a consideration of the sexual act or faculty by itself but from a consideration of what is good for the marriage as a whole. This allows the majority report to allow artificial contraception in certain cases while insisting on the procreative orientation of all sexual acts. In other words, the majority report does not fall into the trap of separating two independent ends for marriage and then justify artificial contraception as a pursuit of one end while excluding the other. It insists that if artificial contraception is used it must respect the procreative finality of marriage. How can it do so? The union of spouses, their mutual help, their love and their life together all have a procreative orientation. That is, they exist not only for their own sake, but for the sake of children. Therefore, if artificial contraception in a particular situation helps the union of the couple it indirectly serves the procreative end of marriage. Furthermore, if artificial contraception helps parents to provide for the proper care of already existing children it serves the procreative end of marriage.

Third, the majority report is somewhat situationist in approach. It does not see artificial contraception as intrinsically morally evil. (It does refer to a physical evil which is present in artificial contraception.) To decide what is morally good in a particular case one must consider the different values involved and try to harmonize them as well as possible. The majority report advocates this situationist approach in the case of artificial contraception, but this need not mean that it would suggest such an approach in all areas of ethics. Its outright and apparently universal rejection of abortion suggests that it does not adopt a situationist approach to that question.

Fourth, the authors of the majority report believe that they are being faithful to tradition. They hold that the values which the Church in the past protected by a universal exclusion of artificial contraception can now best be protected by allowing it in certain cases. They seem to be distinguishing two levels of moral norms. On one level are basic values which are seen to endure from century to century. Concerning contraception, one such value, apparently, is the orientation of marriage to children. On another level are the more specific rules by which such values are applied in particular times and situations. As conditions and available information change, so the Church's teaching on this second level may change.

Fifth, the majority report condemns any contraceptive mentality. It states that couples should be willing to raise a family with full acceptance of the various human and Christian responsibilities that are involved. The marriage as a whole should be procreative.

Sixth, the majority report stresses education. It expects couples to make their own judgment about what is best in their particular situation. To do so properly, they need a profound knowledge and appreciation of the values involved. There is an obvious danger of conforming not to Gospel values but to popular opinion and pressure.

The minority report argues at some length against various positions in the majority report. Clearly, however, for the four authors of the minority report the questions of tradition and authority are crucial. They maintain that the question of artificial contraception cannot be solved by reason alone. They seem to believe that reasons put forward by either side cannot settle the matter. The matter is to be settled then by tradition and authority. The Catholic Church has traditionally rejected each and every act of artificial contraception as gravely wrong. The Church could not have erred on so important a matter.

The minority report denies that the traditional teaching of the Catholic Church against contraception was based on a biologistic argument. It states that the traditional teaching does not appeal to some general principle that man must use all physical faculties in accord with the biological orientation of the faculty. Artificial contraception is wrong not because it goes against the biological orientation of simply any faculty, but because it goes against the orientation of the generative faculty. The generative faculty is concerned with the generation of new life, and life is not under man's dominion. By analogy, just as human life once constituted *in facto esse* is inviolate, so is the process inviolate in which the human life is *in fieri*.

Humanae Vitae

In August, 1968, more than two years after receiving the commission reports, Pope Paul VI published the encyclical letter *On Human Life (Humanae Vitae)*. He begins by acknowledging that a new state of affairs has given rise to questions which necessitate a re-examination of the Church's traditional teaching on artificial contraception.

In his relatively brief discussion of marriage and conjugal love, Pope Paul incorporates much of the material on marriage and the family in *Gaudium et Spes*. Much of what he says conforms with the majority report. Marriage, he states, is the wise intitution of the Creator to realize in mankind His design of love. "By means of the reciprocal gift of self, proper and exclusive to them, husband and wife tend towards the communion of their beings in view of mutual perfection, to collaborate with God in the generation and education of new lives."[33] Conjugal love is fully human, of the senses and of the spirit at the same time. Not only an instinct or a sentiment, it is an act of will intended to endure and to grow so that husband and wife become one only heart and one only soul. This love is not exhausted by the communion between husband and wife, but is destined to continue, raising up new lives. As Vatican II has said, the pope notes, marriage and conjugal love are by their nature ordained for the begetting and educating of children.

Paul VI proceeds then to rule out the use of artificial contraception, and repeats the traditional teaching that each and every marriage act must remain open to the transmission of life. He continues:

> That teaching, often set forth by the magisterium, is founded upon the inseparable connection willed by God and unable to be broken by man on his own initiative, between the two meanings of the conjugal act: the unitive meaning and the procreative meaning. Indeed, by its intimate structure, the conjugal act, while

most closely uniting husband and wife, capacitates them for the generation of new lives, according to laws inscribed in the very being of man and of woman. By safeguarding both these essential aspects, the unitive and the procreative, the conjugal act preserves in its fullness the sense of true mutual love and its ordination towards man's most high calling to parenthood. We believe that the men of our day are particularly capable of seizing the deeply reasonable and human character of this fundamental principle.[34]

The sequence of the argument seems to be as follows: first, marriage and conjugal love have both a unitive and a procreative meaning, the two being essentially bound together. Marital sexual relations should preserve the full meaning of conjugal love, and so should combine both unitive and procreative meanings. Artificial contraception prevents this from happening.

Why does Pope Paul's conclusion regarding artificial contraception differ from the conclusion of the majority report? On the nature of marriage and of spousal love, Paul VI seems to be in general agreement with the majority report. The difference seems to lie in two opposed ways of applying general norms to particular cases. Specifically, Pope Paul holds that artificial contraception is intrinsically evil and can never be allowed. This rules out any appeal to the totality of a marriage for reasons to justify artificial contraception in particular cases. It rules out allowing artificial contraception as a lesser evil in certain situations.

The encyclical does not give reasons for adopting the notion of intrinsic evil or for rejecting an appeal to the total good of the marriage or for not allowing contraception as a lesser evil. These provide an important area for theological investigation, because they constitute the apparent reasons for Pope Paul's rejection of the conclusions of the commission.

Why did he hold to these views against the advice of the majority report? He states that the conclusions of the commission were not definitive, but required his personal further study ". . . above all because certain criteria of solutions had emerged which departed from the moral teaching on marriage proposed with constant firmness by the teaching authority of the Church."[35] Therefore, although he does not dwell at length on the question of tradition and magisterial authority, this seems to be an important reason, perhaps the primary reason, for his conclusions concerning contraception.

Paul VI agrees with *Gaudium et Spes* that parents should be responsible in deciding the number of children ". . . either by the deliberate and generous decision to raise a numerous family, or by the decision, made for grave motives and with due respect for the moral law, to avoid for the time being, or even for an indeterminate period, a new birth."[36] When there are legitimate reasons for avoiding pregnancy, periodic abstinence may be used for that purpose. Paul VI argues that periodic abstinence is significantly different from artificial contraception. The former makes legitimate use of a natural process, whereas the latter impedes the development of a natural process.

Declaration on Sexual Ethics

In December, 1975, the Congregation for the Doctrine of the Faith published the *Declaration on Certain Questions Concerning Sexual Ethics*. Its main purpose was to warn against certain contemporary errors.

The declaration insists that there are objective moral standards which accord with the nature of human beings. These standards are known by a natural law written in the hearts of men. Revelation gives further knowledge of moral standards. Certain moral norms, including certain sexual moral norms, are immutable exigencies of human nature, not mere products of a culture which change as cultures change.

According to the declaration (and here it is following *Gaudium et Spes*, Section 51) the objective moral standards governing sexual acts are those which preserve the full sense of mutual self-giving and human procreation in the context of true love. That is, sexual norms are valid if they preserve the full sense of mutual self-giving and human procreation in the context of true love. Once again, the unitive and the procreative are bound together.

From this basis the declaration proceeds to an evaluation of various types of sexual behavior. It condemns premarital sex, because only in stable marriage can the full sense of mutual self-giving and human procreation in the context of true love be maintained. Premarital sex cannot be properly procreative because it lacks the stable family unit in which children can be properly nurtured. Only in the stable commitment of marriage is there assurance of sincerity and fidelity, protection against whim and caprice.

The same basis is used to condemn homosexual actions. They are wrong because they do not provide for a full sense of mutual self-giving and human procreation in the context of true love. The same criteria rule out masturbation, which, the declaration teaches, is intrinsically and seriously disordered.

The declaration points out that psychology can help to show how various factors, such as adolescent immaturity, may reduce responsibility in the case of sexual sin. However, one should not go so far as to presume easily that people are not seriously responsible when they trangress in sexual matters. If responsibility is to be evaluated in particular cases, one should take account of the person's habitual behavior and his or her sincere use of the means necessary to overcome sexual sin. In other words, the declaration seems to say, if the person normally tries sincerely to do what is right, and seriously makes use of prayer and other means, then there is some reason to believe that a particular failure may not be fully responsible and so should not be considered a serious sin.

The declaration comments on the notion of fundamental option. It opposes the idea that mortal sin occurs only in a formal refusal of love of God or in a complete and deliberate closing of oneself to love of neighbor. Mortal sin can occur because of the rejection of God which is implied in choosing anything which is seriously morally disordered. Thus, a sexual sin can be a mortal sin.

Furthermore, it is possible for a mortal sin to occur in one act. On the other hand, the declaration points out, "it is true that in sins of the sexual order, in view of their kind and their causes, it more easily happens that free consent is not fully given."

The declaration goes on to point out that chastity as a virtue does not consist only in avoiding faults. It involves something positive. It is a virtue of the whole personality, regarding both interior and outward behaviour. An important point, in the declaration's view, is that chastity frees the person to more fully follow Christ.

Questions

From this brief outline of official Roman Catholic teaching since 1918, several questions emerge. I will note only three questions which bear on the tasks of this workshop.

First, what is the relation between the unitive and procreative aspects of marriage? More generally, why are sex and marriage essentially directed towards procreation? Vatican II, the majority

208

report of the papal commission, and *Humanae Vitae* all agree that sex and marriage are essentially ordered towards procreation. Such agreement is not automatic today, however, among Catholic theologians. Outside of the Church there is relatively little support for the Church's official teaching on this point.

The second question is: given the general orientation of sex and marriage towards procreation, why must we conclude that artificial contraception is wrong in each and every case? Why must we accept that artificial contraception is intrinsically evil? Why may we not appeal to the total good of marriage, to other values in a particular situation, to allow artificial contraception in particular cases, at least as a lesser evil? More generally, may not the demands of the situation justify exceptions to other rules of sexual ethics?

The third question is: what weight is to be given to the traditional teaching of the Roman Catholic Church in sexual and marriage ethics? Some hold that the condemnation of artificial contraception has been taught infallibly.[37] Others would limit the scope of the Church's authority to teach on morals infallibly to the area of general principles and to things certainly revealed in Scripture. The majority report seemed to distinguish two levels. On a level of fundamental values the Church's teaching continues unchanged. On another level change can be accepted without being unfaithful to tradition. Is this an acceptable middle position?

Notes

1. *Casti Connubii*, Paragraph 5. Quotations from *Casti Connubii* used in this paper are taken from the translation in *The Church and the Reconstruction of the Modern World, The Social Encyclicals of Pius XI*, edited by Terence P. McLaughlin (Garden City, N.Y.: Doubleday, 1957).
2. Paragraph 17.
3. Paragraph 11.
4. See Paragraphs 11-13.
5. Paragraph 59.
6. Paragraph 9.
7. Paragraph 7.
8. Paragraph 23.
9. Paragraph 23.
10. Paragraph 24.
11. Paragraph 18.
12. Paragraph 54.
13. Paragraph 37.
14. Paragraph 123.
15. *Vom Sinn Und Zweck Der Ehe* (Breslau: Osterdeutsche Verlag).
16. Published in New York by Sheed and Ward.
17. *The Meaning of Marriage*, pp. 87-88.
18. *Acta Apostolicae Sedis* 36 (1944): 103.

19. An English translation of the relevant parts of this sentence is available in *Love and Sexuality,* edited by Odile M. Liebard (Wilmington, N.C.: McGrath, 1978), pp. 71-83.

20. See, for example, his allocution to the Sacred Roman Rota on Oct. 29, 1941, *Clergy Review* 22 (1942): 84-88; his address to the midwives, Oct 29, 1951, in *Love and Sexuality,* p. 117.

21. See address to midwives, *Love and Sexuality,* p. 117, and address of May 19, 1956, *ibid.,* p. 175-76.

22. See, for example, his address of Nov. 12, 1944, in *Love and Sexuality,* p. 92.

23. See the address to the midwives, *Love and Sexuality,* p. 116.

24. *Love and Sexuality,* p. 113.

25. Address on Sept. 29, 1949, *Love and Sexuality,* pp. 96-100; address to the midwives, Oct. 29, 1951, *Love and Sexuality,* 117-18.

26. Address on May 19, 1956, *Love and Sexuality,* p. 177.

27. *Love and Sexuality,* pp. 240-41.

28. *Gaudium et Spes,* Section 49.

29. *Gaudium et Spes,* Section 48. Quotations from *Gaudium et Spes* in this paper are taken from *The Documents of Vatican II,* edted by Walter B. Abbott (London-Dublin: Geoffrey Chapman, 1966).

30. Section 48. See also section 50.

31. Because these words are central to our discussion and are often quoted, it will be useful to quote the Latin of the original text. That text, having noted that the moral judgment must not depend only on a sincere intention or an evaluation of motives continues: *". . . sed objectivis criteriis, ex personae eiusdemque actuum natura desumptis, determinari debet, quae integrum sensum mutuae donationis ac humanae procreationis in contextu veri amoris observant."* It might be argued that in emphasizing that the couple must preserve the *full* sense of mutual self-giving and human procreation in the context of true love, this text rules out artificial contraception. However, that can hardly have been the general understanding of the text by the Council Fathers. Having been instructed by Pope Paul VI not to pronounce on the issue of artificial contraception, they would not be likely to try to settle the issue even in principle.

32. The first, third and fourth documents were published in *The Tablet* 221(1967): 449-54; 478-85; 510-13. The first and second documents are available in *Love and Sexuality,* pp. 296-320.

33. *On Human Life* (Jamaica Plains, Boston: Daughters of St. Paul, 1968), Section 8.

34. Section 12.

35. Section 6.

36. Section 10.

37. See "Contraception and the Infallibility of the Ordinary Magisterium" by J. C. Ford and G. Grisez, *Theological Studies* 39 (1978): 258-312, esp. 312.

Chapter 10

Proportionalism As a Methodology in Catholic Moral Theology

The Reverend Paul E. McKeever, S.T.D.

The Emergence of Proportionalism

Proportionalism maintains that the concepts "direct" and "indirect" are inadequate tools for moral analysis of human action. Circumstances and intention play a decisive role in determining the moral quality of a concrete action. Consequently, the proportionalists distinguish between moral evil on the one hand and "ontic," "physical," or "pre-moral" evil on the other. Thus, killing a human being, telling untruths, or taking something that belongs to another are first of all "ontic evils."[1]

To determine whether those acts are morally evil we must attend to the circumstances in which they were committed and willed. The proportionalists then call on certain facts from theological history to show that killing has been justified in cases of self-defense; that telling an untruth has been justified in cases where telling the truth would violate another's certain rights; and that taking something that belongs to another has been justified in cases of an agent's overriding need. Those circumstances constitute the proportionate reasons for killing, telling untruths and taking something that belongs to another. If circumstances do not justify such actions there is no proportionate reason, and killing another becomes murder, telling an untruth becomes lying, and taking something that belongs to another becomes stealing.

It is generally admitted that recent attempts to revise the concepts of "direct" and "indirect" owe their principal origin to Peter Knauer's article, "The Hermaneutic Function of the Principle of Double Effect."[2] Proportionalism therefore functions within the context of the principle of double effect, about which two remarks can be made. It is "Catholic" and is identified with "natural law" thinking. Attempts to revise its interpretation therefore have been within the Catholic tradition. Whether or not the proposed revision of the principle of double effect is within the parameters of natural law thinking is, of course, disputed.

Factually, proportionalism has been proposed, developed and ardently defended by some of the Church's outstanding scholars. To mention only the most prominent: Peter Knauer, S.J.; Bruno Schüller, S.J.; Josef Fuchs, S.J.; Franz Böckle; Louis Janssens; Charles Curran; and Richard A. McCormick, S.J.[3]

On the other hand, the whole concept has been severely criticized by authors like William E. May, Gustave Ermecke, Germain Grisez, Donald McCarthy and G. Martelet. Many Protestant scholars are opposed to proportionalism because of its acceptance of teleology in opposition to deontology.[4]

I would summarize the criticisms of proportionalism under the following headings, devised for the sake of convenience. (1) It is anaytically unsound; (2) it is opposed to traditional Catholic moral theology and casuistry; and (3) it is irreconcilable with past and most recent teachings of the magisterium.

Each has collected around itself a whole literature of response, a literature impossible to summarize in one short paper. Here I will simply indicate some conclusions I have reached, and leave to a longer version of my paper whatever justifications are necessary.

I realize we are principally interested in a theological evaluation of proportionalism, but I must say I think the hub of the question is to be found in the first criticism just mentioned – is proportionalism analytically sound? That is basically a question pertaining to formal ethics or to systematic theological ethics. We must note that even though systematic theological ethics is founded on the Christian revelation, it is nevertheless the work of reason. Consequently there must always be an inner connection between philosophical and theological ethics.

Ethics and the Bible

Now it is a commonplace that we do not find in the Bible a formal or systematic ethical system. As a result we cannot state that proportionalism is either supported or refuted by an appeal to a biblical ethical system.

A re-reading of criticisms (2) and (3) above will suggest that they are basically theological in nature. To repeat: proportionalism is opposed to traditional Catholic moral theology and is irreconcilable with past and most recent teachings of the magisterium.

Now, if those two criticisms cannot be based on the assumption that the Bible contains an ethical system, they must be based on some other theological supposition or suppositions. To stay with Holy Scripture, one could suggest that though biblical injunctions and prohibitions are not part of a biblical ethical system, they nevertheless reveal concepts or presuppositions that run counter to proportionalism.

Here of course we must take account of modern biblical hermeneutics. Certainly the Bible prohibits murder, lying, stealing, adultery, incest, etc., and certainly those prohibitions are objective. We must notice, however, that those objective biblical rules do not define precisely what they prohibit. It seems rather to be taken for granted that people of the times had a general and therefore serviceable idea of what was meant. What was meant depended on the culture in which those words were written and to which they applied. And what was meant has meaning for today, and had meaning for all the ages of Christianity. But what was "taken for granted" at one time had later to be more precisely described and defined. Thus we find St. Thomas and a whole theological tradition struggling with the task of defining precisely such terms as murder, adultery, stealing, lying, etc., etc. Now to read back into the Bible definitions arrived at in a later

213

time would appear to be bad hermeneutics.

I have said that the meaning of biblical prohibitions and injunctions was "taken for granted." Many contemporaries think that so much to be the case, that we should apply to them the term "parenetic" rather than the term "normative." As Richard McCormick puts it, ". . . in discussing norms we must be careful to distinguish between parenetic discourse and explanatory discourse or moral reasoning. Explanatory discourse deals with the pros and cons of a position, with argumentation, with the normative validity of a precept. Parenetic discourse is not concerned with the normative validity of a moral command. Such validity is taken for granted and then the precept is used to pass judgment on a person's behavior." He continues, "Thus parenetic discourse makes use of rules to accuse, convict, condemn, urge repentence. Positively, rules are used to praise, advise, implore, encourage, strengthen. Such discourse can succeed only if genuine agreement exists on what is right or wrong."[5]

It therefore seems to me that if the practical moral prohibitions and injunctions of the Bible took for granted the practical moral prohibitions of the society in which the various books of the Bible were written, and if those rules are parenetic rather than normative, we have no biblical basis for judging the truth or untruth of "proportionalism."

Indeed, when we recall that the whole controversy centers around such technical and philosophical words as "intrinsic evil" and "direct and indirect," we may well question whether such terminology can be justified on a biblical basis.

We have so far been concentrating on a narrow issue, namely, the pertinence of Holy Scripture to the proportionalist controversy. Proportionalism is an issue of methodology, which is therefore an issue of formal or systematic ethics. But Holy Scripture does not contain a formal or systematic ethical system. As a result, it furnishes us no formal or systematic means of judging proportionalism.

Scripture texts do contain moral injunctions and prohibitions, but many contemporaries regard them as parenetic, and not precise as to definition. Such texts, therefore, would seem to offer little assistance in evaluating proportionalism.

We cannot, of course, neglect the overall moral thrust of both the Old and New Testaments. Indeed, the revealed word of God establishes once and for all the fact that the moral or ethical question is not just one question among many; it is the only question. Every man and woman born into this world is "called" by the Father and must give response. The response of Jesus is the ultimate model of all response and everyone is "called" to be His disciple. We are called to the Kingdom, to be God's people, and to participate in the "new and everlasting covenant." The pivotal dynamism of the covenant is love – love for God above all else and neighbor as ourselves. In the New Testament, therefore, moral and religious conversion converge. Commitment to value and to the love commandment is, as moralists say today, "the fundamental option."

Does it therefore not follow that if Holy Scripture gives us little theological assistance in evaluating "proportionalism" we must look elsewhere? And where else except to the traditional "natural law" philosophy?

Immediately we must ask the question, "What is the relation between philosophy and theology?" For each is an integral discipline of its own.

To do so we must unravel the two threads that make up the skein of natural law theory. One is anthropological, the other nomian.

Anthropology in Natural Law Theory

First of all, natural law is based on a fundamental anthropological assertion. Men and women are created by God and have a "nature" that remains intact despite sin. That nature is open to God – to the inner life of the Trinity – whether we call that openness "obediential capacity" or the more modern term, "supernatural existential." To be human in accordance with one's nature, everyone must "act" or "do," and the fundamental underivable first principle of human action is that "the good must be done and pursued, and the evil avoided."[6]

That quotation from St. Thomas must arrest our attention for a moment because it brings to the fore the anthropological question of "obligation." That question has great significance because answers to it shape our view of moral theology.[7]

Students of St. Thomas point out that there is a significant difference between Thomas' concept of obligation, and the concept of Francis Suarez . We cannot dwell overly long on this difference, but we can catch the difference from the two following quotations, one from Louis Billot, the other from Gilson. Billot once wrote, "Moral obligation in the absolute sense arises only in complete dependence

215

on a superior who obliges and a master who commands ... who commands the whole interior man, imposing on him by authority, the supreme authority, a collection of precepts. ...."[8] Gilson, in tandem with Father Sertillanges, wrote that the moral theology of St. Thomas is "a moral theology without obligation, if morality were to be considered as imposed from without." He further stated: "... the only obligation the Thomistic moral theology recognizes for man is that of being perfectly man, being assured that man will thereby be what God wants him to be."[9]

For Suarez and his tradition, the conclusion of a syllogism can tell us that "killing John is murder." But we need something from "outside" to tell us we should not kill John. That something else is God's command. For Thomas, on the other hand, the very perception that killing John is murder and therefore evil already contains, as it were, the prohibition. In speaking about good rather than evil, Gregory Stevens makes the point quite succinctly, "... the obligatory ... results from the goodness of an action, not vice-versa."[10]

Suarez' view seems a quasi-voluntarism, Thomas' not. It is therefore neither an accident, nor a mere pedagogical device, that Suarez organizes his moral theology around the commandments, and Thomas around the virtues. I believe the difference accounts for the confusion today among many people who tend to think of the Magisterium, for instance, "commanding" rather than exposing moral truth.

Now, everything I have mentioned here under the heading of the anthropological aspect of "natural law" has a direct relation to theology. I also believe it generally accords with the recent insights of such Transcendental Thomists as Bernard Lonergan and Karl Rahner. Rahner refers to the results of his transcendental analysis as "primary natural law" and makes what I believe to be an authentically Thomistic observation when he says that "... man is characteristically the being who has been handed over to himself, consigned to his own free responsibility."[11]

In a definite sense this anthropological concept of "human nature" is presupposed by theology, and therefore pertains to theology. It is foundational. Indeed, a Karl Rahner arrives at the concept of "human nature" via theological analysis. "Human nature" is a residual reality – what is left after one has taken account of the supernatural realities within which all men live and have ever lived.

This anthropology is the theological basis for saying that man can "hear" the Gospel, can respond to the call to love God and neighbor, can live the Trinitarian life, can "see" God.

Natural Law Precepts

There is, however, the other thread of natural law that requires consideration, namely, the "nomian" or "law" aspect. The anthropology just described, the principle that "the good is to be done and pursued and evil avoided," the foundational concept of human dignity, the very love commandment itself, do not as yet give us concrete norms, rules and principles. In St. Thomas' whole conception and presentation of natural law we see that principles, rules and precepts must accord with reason,[12] and that, by his own admission, causes problems of varying difficulty, some of which arise from the subject matter itself, some of which arise from personal impediments.

Here I would like to quote from St. Thomas: "And as every judgment of speculative reason proceeds from the natural knowledge of first principles, so every judgment of practical reason proceeds from principles known naturally, as stated above (q. 94, aa. 2, 4): from which principles one may proceed in various ways to judge of various matters. For some matters connected with human actions are so evident, that after very little consideration one is able at once to approve or disapprove of them by means of these general first principles: while some matters cannot be the subject of judgment without much consideration of the various circumstances, which all are not competent to do carefully, but only those who are wise."[13]

In the very same article St. Thomas says something that must arrest our attention, for it illustrates what he has just said in general terms: ". . . there are certain things which the natural reason of every man, of his own accord and at once, judges to be done or not to be done: e.g. 'Honor thy father and thy mother, Thou shalt not kill, Thou shall not steal.' " If I understand St. Thomas correctly, those precepts are actually principles, meaning that they are immediately known and underivable. It would seem, then, that Thomas arrived quite quickly at specific principles which specifically mention honor, killing, stealing, etc.

We must remember, however, that even principles must be examined for what they actually contain and what they do not. May I say something like this: those precepts or principles are generally specific but not specifically specific? But which I mean, Thomas does not in question 100 define the terms he uses. When he does, we will have what he considers to be specifically prohibited and commanded. So, for example, he will later define theft as "the secret taking of something that belongs to another."[14] He will discuss homicide, excluding from culpable killing capital punishment and just defense.[15] He will discuss lying in rather technical terms.[16]

In addition to the work of St. Thomas, we all remember that generations of moral theologians have attempted to refine the definitions of murder, lying, stealing, etc. (I think I once read that among relatively recent moralists we can find something like nineteen definitions of a lie.)

Should we not therefore say that the problem of defining terms like murder, stealing, and so forth, arises from the very subject matter and not from the personal impediments mentioned above? Is is not, therefore, "subject matter" to be examined by those whom St. Thomas calls "the wise"?

The basic question raised by the proportionalist controversy would seem to resemble that ongoing effort to find precise descriptions and descriptions of moral terms. St. Thomas, quoting Holy Scripture, considers killing to be evil and considers that truth self-evident. Yet he finds it necessary to take into account and to except from the prohibition against killing such acts as capital punishment and self-defense. Are those exceptions self-evident? When one reads his argumentation in question 64, article 7, of the II-IIae, one could easily conclude that he is not precisely in the realm of the self-evident. One is rather in the realm of careful argumentation.

Likewise, when one considers such terms as "direct" and "indirect" and "intrinsically evil" or "intrinsically disordered," one will find it difficult to think he is in the realm of the "self-evident."

Those terms would seem to be the result of a methodology and methodology is the work of reason. But the methodology behind such concepts as "direct" and "intrinsic" is precisely what the proportionalists have questioned.

The problem then inevitably arises – on what basis can we, in the name of theology, deny the right of reason to re-examine a "received" methodology? I am not saying that re-examination of the "received" methodology will yield results strong enough to replace or modify it; I am simply suggesting that both the older and newer methodologies must argue their case before the court of reason. Isn't that, after all, the fundamental thrust of the "natural law theory"? *Natura ut ratio.*

Those considerations can lead us further along the path of asking some questions about the relation between theology and philosophy. The Catholic tradition has never taken a cavalier approach to philosophy. Philosophy has for its sacred purpose the discovery of truth.The natural law theory is fundamentally a philosophical systematization and Catholic philosophers have argued strenuously for the integrity of philosophy and its independence from theology. At the same time they and Catholic theologians admit, since truth is one and cannot contradict itself, that theology can exercise a negative judgment with respect to a philosophical system or a philosophical conclusion. It can state that they are incompatible with revealed truth or dangerous to the faith.[17] It cannot of itself construct a philosophy.

Analytical Soundness of Proportionalism

I see then a two-edged question. On what basis can theology reject the methodology employed by the proportionalists? And, are the terms "intrinsic evil" and the definitions of "direct" and "indirect" matters that pertain to the faith – are they a necessary and accurate summary of scriptural teaching? If not, we are back to asking whether proportionalism is analytically sound. And that is a question for the "truly wise."

In addressing it I would like to mention my own personal reactions to the literature surrounding the subject. I have noticed, for instance, that for every criticism of proportionalism there has been an appropriate rejoinder. By appropriate I do not necessarily mean successful. I mean, rather, that proportionalism has not been collapsed by any single overwhelming objection. If I were to compile a list of the most serious objections to proportionalism they and their rejoinders would look something like this:

1. It is opposed to traditional methodology; to which defenders respond, it seems to be the basic approach of St. Thomas.

2. It is vitiated by subjectivism; to which the rejoinder has been, proportionalism insists on two factors which are clearly objective: (a) the existence of ontic evil; and (b) the necessity of a proportionate reason. Proportionate reason does not mean *any* reason – it means one

truly proportionate to the value sacrificed. McCormick insists that proportionate reason means three things: (a) a value at least equal to that sacrificed is at stake; (b) there is no less harmful way of protecting the value here and now; and (c) the manner of its protection here and now will not undermine it in the long run.[18]

3. It has been charged with violating the principle that evil cannot be done in order to achieve good; the rejoinder suggests that the criticism begs the question. "Evil" in the principle should mean "moral evil" and that is precisely what is at issue.

4. It has been accused of following a utilitarian calculus, with the assumption that utilitarianism is an inadequate moral system; the rejoinder rejects that criticism, for proportionalists admit and insist on the fact that human dignity, irrespective of a person's worth to the community, can never be disregarded as some readings of utilitarianism seem to suggest.

5. It has been accused of allowing a person to turn directly against a basic good; to which the rejoinder replies, we must first decide precisely what constitutes such a "turning against."

6. It has been charged with "extrinsicism" because it relies so heavily on taking consequences into account when deciding what is concretely good and evil; the rejoinder states simply that some consequentialists may be extrinsicists, but there is nothing in teleology that demands it.

Now I do not wish to suggest that these rejoinders, which I have summarized with extreme brevity, put an end to discussion and further criticism. Quite the contrary. Critics of proportionalism deny that St. Thomas can be used in support of proportionalism; insist that the agent's intention must be identified with the disvalue involved; insist that, no matter how many reservations are stated, proportionalism is reducible to utilitarianism for proportionalism attempts to commensurate the incommensurable; and they insist that no truly human good can be directly attacked.

We must notice, however, that the criticisms we have mentioned and their attendant rejoinders operate on the level of systematic and therefore philosophic analysis. In principle, therefore, unless it can be shown that proportionalism is incompatible with revealed moral horizons, with Christian anthropology, or the Word of God pertaining to specifics, the argument must continue on the analytic or philosophic level.

220

Conclusion

In saying that, I realize that I have not yet taken account of the magisterium of the Church. In suggesting that the issue of proportionalism is open to further and continued evaluation I seem to be ignoring the magisterium, which has continued to use the language of "direct" and "intrinsic." Before going further, however, I would point out that the magisterium has not dealt specifically – or, if you will, *data opera* and *ex professo* – with proportionalism.' I assume, therefore, that defending proportionalism is not directly contrary to the explicit teaching of the Church. There is no such explicit teaching.

On the other hand, magisterial language implies a position contrary to proportionalism, and that cannot be denied.

Here, then, we enter the cratered field of post-Vatican II moral theology – the role of the magisterium in moral matters. I would argue that there must be some latitude in interpreting Magisterial statements. For, in the first place, they are not on the level of infallible teaching and are therefore hypothetically open to revision. In the second place, the issues involved in such language as "direct" and "intrinsic" seem beyond the reach of the theological resources available to us, as I suggested when speaking about the relation of theology and proportionalism. In brief, it seems to me that the realities covered by such terms as "ontic" and "pre-moral evil" preserve the essence of scriptural injunctions and prohibitions.

In this paper I am not so much advocating proportionalism as proposing that we continue to evaluate it. That involves continued study of all the issues that make up the tangled skein of present-day systematic moral theology: Christian anthropology, scriptural hermeneutics, specific Christian morality, and analysis of the human act in all its dimensions.

Notes

1. Instead of repeating "ontic," "physical," and "pre-moral," we will settle for the term "ontic" throughout this paper.

2. *Natural Law Forum* 12 (1967): 132-62.

3. Articles on the subject have been collected into one volume by Charles E. Curran and Richard A. McCormick, and include such authors as Knauer, Janssens, Connery, Fuchs, Schüller, Scholz, Jeffko, De Ianni, Quay, McCormick and Curran: *Readings in Moral Theology No. 1* (New York: Paulist Press, 1979). See also, Richard McCormick and Paul Ramsey, eds., *Doing Evil to Achieve Good* (Chicago: Loyola University Press, 1978) and Richard McCormick, "Notes on Moral Theology," *Theological Studies* 39 (1978): 76-115.

4. See Paul Ramsey, "Incommensurability and Indeterminancy in Moral Choice," in McCormick and Ramsey, pp. 69-144. See also, Frederick Carney, "On McCormick's Teleological Morality," *Journal of Religious Ethics* 6 (1978): 81-107, and William K. Frankens, "McCormick and the Traditional Distinction," in McCormick and Ramsey, pp. 145-64.

5. "Notes on Moral Theology," *Theological Studies* 36 (1975): 84. See also Bruno Schüller, "Christianity and the New Man," *Theology and Discovery: Essays in Honor of Karl Rahner, S.J.,* edited by William J. Kelly, S.J. (Milwaukee: Marquette University Press, 1980), especially pp. 308-09.

6. St. Thomas Aquinas, *ST.* I, II, q. 94.

7. See Germain Grisez, "The First Principle of Practical Reason: A Commentary on the *Summa Theologica,* I, II, question 94, article 2, *"Natural Law Forum* 10 (1965): 168-201. See also Etienne Gilson, *Saint Thomas D'Aquin* (2d ed., 1925), p. 12; Gregory Stevens, "Moral Obligation in St. Thomas," *The Modern Schoolman* 40 (1961).

8. Quoted from Dom Odo Lottin, *Principes de Morale* 2 (Louvain, 1947): 74.

9. Gilson, *loc. cit.*

10. Stevens, *loc. cit.*

11. *Theological Investigations* 9: 277.

12. *ST.* I, II, q. 94 a. 1." . . . illi mores dicuntur boni qui rationi congruunt, mali autem qui a ratione discordant."

13. *ST.* I, II, q. 100, a. 1. Translation from *Summa Theologica, First Complete American Edition in Three Volumes* (New York: Benziger Brothers, 1947), p. 1037.

14. *ST.* II, II, q. 64, a. 4.

15. *ST.* II, II, q. 64, a. 7.

16. *ST.* II, II, q. 110, a. 1.

17. As Albert Dondeyne has put it, ". . . l'Eglise ne peut se désintéresse complétement de la philosophie; le cas échéant, elle devra récuser tel système ou telle tendance philosophique reconnus incompatibles avec la foi religieuse qu' elle a pour mission de sauvegarder et de protéger. Ce faisant, le magistère ecclésiastique ne joue pas au philosophe, il ne s'arroge aucune compétence philosophique proprement dite. S'il intervient en des matieres qui concernent la philosophie, *il ne le fait pas* pour raisons philosophiques ni à partir de fondements proprement philosophiques, mais à partir de la foi et en vue de la foi: I1 juge qu'une philosophie déterminée est en désaccord avec la foi ou dangereuse pour la foi et, loin de venir brouiller les cartes, il demande au chrétien de prendre la philosophie au sérieux et d'etre plus que personne fidèle aux exigences de la refléxion philosophique." *Foi Chrétienne et pensée contemporaine* (Paris: Desclee de Brouwer & Cie, 1951), 3.

18. "Ambiguity in Moral Choice," McCormick and Ramsey, p. 45.

Chapter 11

The Use of Moral Theory by the Church

The Reverend Benedict M. Ashley, O.P., Ph.D., S.T.M.

A Fundamental Principle

The magisterium has already established that the fundamental principle with regard to a Christian ethics of human sexuality is the inseparability of the unitive and procreative meanings of sex.[1] Paul VI in *Humanae Vitae* (n.12) formulated it thus:

> That teaching [against contraception], often set forth by the magisterium, is founded upon the inseparable connection, willed by God and unable to be broken by man on his own initiative, between the two meanings of the conjugal act: the unitive meaning and the procreative meaning. Indeed, by its intimate structure, the conjugal act, while most closely uniting husband and wife, capacitates them for the generation of new lives, according to laws inscribed in the very being of man and woman. By safeguarding both these essential aspects, the unitive and

procreative, the conjugal act preserves in its fullness the sense of true mutual love and its ordination toward man's most high calling to parenthood. We believe that the men of our day are particularly capable of seizing the deeply ʹreasonable and human character of this fundamental principle.

By this last sentence Paul VI did not mean that his teaching would receive ready acceptance, but that its highly personalistic theology of sexuality would eventually prove to be what our personalist age is looking for, and would finally be judged to have been prophetic, rather than reactionary.

Before Vatican II and Paul VI magisterial teaching on sexuality had tended to subordinate the unitive to the procreative meaning of the conjugal act, and to pass over any positive emphasis on the moral value of sexual pleasure. *Humanae Vitae* clearly avoided this subordination and presented the procreative meaning as the complement and fruit of the unitive meaning. In my opinion, this principle as formulated by Paul VI can be completed by adding to it the corollary of the inseparability of the value of sexual pleasure considered as a positive human good from the unitive and procreative aspects of sexuality, making explicit what is undoubtedly implied in the pope's words. Thus we can say that just as it is immoral to seek sexual pleasure apart from the love of one's partner, so it is immoral to seek the sexual expression of love with the exclusion of the fruit of that love by which joyful love becomes both social and enduring.[2] In our culture many defend not only the separation of love from the family, but even the separation of pleasure from love.[3]

This principle of inseparability has not yet been defined by the magisterium and probably will never be defined. Yet, as I will argue in this paper, it is so solidly founded in Scripture and tradition, that it may well be definable. In any case it is clear that it is of a different order of certitude than the detailed conclusions which have been drawn from it both by the ordinary magisterium and by theologians.

Theological Controversies which Confront the Magisterium

Why is human sexuality inseparably linked to procreation? To many today this linkage is by no means evident. To some theologians the unitive meaning of sexuality seems self-sufficient and the procreative meaning either entirely secondary, or even to be understood in a broad sense as "creative," i.e., bearing fruit not just in children but in other enrichments of life. Thus the study commissioned by The Catholic Theological Society of America, *Human Sexuality,* after claiming that Vatican II "took a major step forward when it deliberately rejected this priority of the procreative over the unitive end of marriage," proposed as a further development the following:[4]

> We think it appropriate, therefore, to broaden the traditional formulation of the purpose of sexuality from *procreative* and *unitive* to *creative and integrative.*
>
> Wholesome human sexuality is that which fosters a *creative* growth toward integration. Destructive sexuality results in personal frustration and interpersonal alienation. In the light of this deeper insight into the meaning of human sexuality, it is our conviction that creativity and integration or, more precisely, "creative growth through integration" better expresses the basic finality of sexuality.

Other authors suggest that the notion of "human sexuality" is best understood in the light of modern psychology in a broad way as a dimension of all interpersonal relationships. Nor does the term "sexuality" have to be limited to male-female relationships, but should be understood as including all human relations as incarnational, i.e., relations between human persons as they are *bodily* beings who necessarily relate to each other sensuously and emotionally. Consequently, a distinction has become popular between "genital" and "non-genital" sexuality, the latter being viewed as necessary for healthy relationships for celibates and between persons of the same sex.[5]

A number of reasons have led these theologians to think that a liberation of sexuality from too close a linkage to procreation is a necessary development in Christian insight which they are duty bound to urge the magisterium to adopt and approve. The first and most obvious cause is that in our technological culture a large family has become an economic liability and the "population explosion" has seemed to make the rigid control of procreation a moral duty. Many fear that if contraception, which they believe is the only realistic, rational and humane method of family planning, is not generally adopted there will be an increase in abortion and even of genocide.

A second cause for "the new morality" is the oft repeated

accusation that the Christian Church historically has been deeply influenced by false philosophical and pseudo-scientific notions about sexuality, so that it has generally failed to meet the actual problems of human beings in realistic compassionate ways.[6] Closely related to this accusation is the feminist charge that the Church's emphasis on procreation as the end of marriage has worked severely to the disadvantage of women, limited them to the domestic cloister, and sacrificed their sexual needs to men's.[7]

Another source of these doubts is the magisterium's use of such terms as "natural" and "unnatural" and its appeal to the teleology of the sexual organs. What is "unnatural" in our technological culture where we are daily remolding the environment, and even our own bodies to suit our own humanly determined purposes? Modern science seems to deny any teleology in nature. If there is to be any purpose or value in our world we must put it there by our own creative choices. Even if it is admitted that "naturally" speaking the biological function of sex was originally procreation, why cannot we now change its function to something more humanly advantageous in today's world?[8]

Again, there is a wide-spread belief that in the past the Church was overly occupied with issues of sexual morality and too concerned to bolster the family as a social institution. Today the Church should take more account of the needs of persons for a satisfactory sexual life under the conditions of urban society.

Finally, and most urgently, is the fact that it seems very difficult, even impossible, to apply the principle of inseparability to the solution of conflict situations which are so often met in modern life. How is the innocent party in a divorce, the constitutional homosexual who cannot marry, the adolescent or youth not yet able to support a family yet constantly subject to sexual stimulation, to live up to such an abstract ideal? And how are those who minister pastorally to such people, to help them as Jesus would have done?

How Certain Is This Principle?

Any responsible answer to these difficulties requires the pastors of the people of God first of all to devote themselves to understanding and explaining this principle, and the Christian use of God's gift of sexuality which this principle formulates, so as to make this magisterial doctrine truly Good News for our times. In my opinion as a theologian, this teaching of the ordinary magisterium bears clear and sufficient signs that it is a part of Christian revelation. I will not attempt to demonstrate this thesis in detail here, but only sketch the lines the argument might take.

If we look in the New Testament for Jesus' own teaching on sexual ethics, we find that He presupposes the teaching of the Old Law and (according to Mt. 5:17-20) confirms and completes it.[9] Hence He confirms the sixth commandment against adultery, abolishes the toleration of divorce, asserts the equal obligation to fidelity on the part of both the man and woman, and adds that sexual sin is a matter of interior attitudes as well as external acts. As Pope John Paul II has recently shown, this adulterous attitude consists in treating others not as sexual persons but as sexual objects.[10]

Recent scholarship has shown this teaching on divorce to be one of the best historically authenticated of Jesus' teachings.[11] It is found first in Paul (I Cor. 7:10-11), who explicitly calls it a "command of the Lord," i.e., of Jesus; in Q (Mt. 5:31-32; Lk. 16:18), and in Mark (10:2-12) with a parallel in Matthew (19:3-12). This strong attestation, together with the fact that this abrogation of the law of divorce was contrary to Jewish practices and an embarrassment to the early Church, make it certain that it is Jesus' own doing. Of course, it remains possible to argue that Jesus was addressing His own times and that these time-bound words no longer apply to our modern situation. When faced with this type of exegetical difficulty, I believe that the hermeneutical rule for a moralist seeking valid ethical instruction from the Scriptures should not be to repeat proof texts, but to look for the reasons which the Scriptures themselves give for a particular precept (if they give any). It is the reason behind a commandment that enables us so to interpret that norm in such a way as to free it from its historical conditions and perhaps to find its universal significance and relevance.

In this case Mark (10:5-8) records Jesus' own reason for rejecting divorce, and it is this reason which has provided the foundation for the traditional Christian teaching on the God-given meaning of human sexuality. In reply to the Pharisees' appeal to the words of Moses permitting divorce, Jesus replies:[12]

> It was because you were so unteachable, that he wrote this commandment for you. But from the beginning of creation *God made them male and female* [Gen 1:27]. This is why a man must

227

leave father and mother, and two become one body [Gen 2:24].
They are no longer two, but one body. So then, what God has
united, man must not divide.

Thus Jesus bases His interpretation of the sixth commandment
on God's original reason for creating the two sexes, because this
original purpose of God's is universal and enduring, transcending the
historical situations of particular human cultures, even those of the
Chosen People divinely confirmed in the inspired Law of Moses. Note
that Jesus conflates a quotation from the P document (chapter 1) with
one from the J document (chapter 2), thus blocking the attempt of
some theologians to find in the older J document a view of sexuality
free of any stress on the procreative purpose of marriage, so evident in
the P ("Be fertile and multiply," 1:28). Taken together, as Jesus does,
the two creation narratives are complementary, and provide a clear
teaching on what God intended human sexuality to be for all time, a
faithful union in love of a man and a woman which expands into the
ongoing life of humanity.

There is in the Scriptures, however, another way of looking at
human sexuality, which Jesus also seems to confirm, although in a less
direct manner, when He speaks of Himself as "the bridegroom" (Mk.
2:19; cf. Mk. 22:1-10; 25:1-13). Here the fidelity of man and woman
becomes a metaphor of the covenant-fidelity between God and his
people (Dt. 4:24; Is. 1:21-26; 50:1; 54:6-7; 62:4-5; Jer. 2:2; 3:1-12;
Ezel. 16 and 23; possibly *Song of Songs* and Ps. 45) or between Christ
and His Church (references above and I Cor. 6:15-20; II Cor. 11:1-4;
Eph. 5:25-33). Thus, the Messianic banquet of heaven (and the
Eucharist which prefigures it) is a wedding banquet, "the marriage of
the Lamb" (Rev. 19:7-9; 21 and 22). These texts seem to say that the
deepest meaning of sexuality is that God in creating humanity as
incarnate spirit fashioned in His own image (Gen. 1:27), divided the
species into males and females in order that by mutual self-giving of
the most intimate kind ("two in one body") a married couple might be
a symbol or sacrament manifesting that intimate mutual love between
God and His creatures, between the divine and human in Christ, and
between Christ and His body the Church.

This covenantal-sacramental theology of sex puts the accent on
the unitive meaning of the conjugal relation and it is undoubtedly
profoundly biblical provided that we observe two cautions. Firstly,
this understanding of sexuality as a symbol or sacrament means that

the sexual union is relativized because it points to a greater reality than itself.[13] Jesus taught, "When people rise from the dead, they neither marry nor are given in marriage but live like angels in heaven" (Mk. 12:25) and St. Paul clearly preaches celibacy as an anticipation of the resurrected state (I Cor. 7). Thus this sacrament relates sexuality to the temporal, not the eternal order. Sex cannot be so spiritualized as to remove it from the biological context of the cycle of birth and death. Outside this context it becomes meaningless and ceases to perform even a symbolic function. Secondly, the stress on the unitive symbolism of sexuality in reference to the love of Christ and the Church should not be used to negate its procreative meaning. The Church is not a sterile, but a fruitful bride. As St. Paul writes:[14]

> The Jerusalem on high is freeborn, and it is she who is our mother. That is why Scripture says, "Rejoice, you barren one who bears no children; break into song, you stranger to the pains of childbirth! For many are the children of the wife deserted — far more than of her who has a husband! (Gal. 4:26-27; cf. Rev. 12:17.)

Thus the teaching of Jesus confirms the teaching of Genesis. God created human sexuality as part of our bodily, temporal human nature, so that His love for His creatures might be in a special way manifest in the faithful and fruitful love of man and woman in whom His very image shines out. The rest of the New Testament, wherever the authors touch in a pastoral way on the problems of sexuality, is fully in harmony with this understanding of sex and they apply it in promoting married love (e.g., I Cor. 5 to 7; Eph. 5:22; 6:4; Col. 3:18-21; I Th. 4:1-8; Tit. 2:1-10; Pet. 3:1-7), and in rejecting adultery (Jas. 2:8-11), extra-marital sex (I Cor. 6:15-20; Eph. 5:5), homosexuality (Rom. 1:24-28), or masturbation (Mt. 5:30).[15]

I do not deny that the New Testament exhibits a considerable diversity of ethical attitudes and certain developments (e.g., the exceptive clause in Matthew 19:9, the so-called "Pauline privilege" in I Cor. 7:15-16) conditioned by local and occasional situations; but these do not manifest any other view of the nature of sexuality than the one already described. In the subsequent tradition of the Church this continues to hold true. While undoubtedly diverse influences from Greek philosophy affected the Christian attitude to sexuality, no one has demonstrated that they modified it essentially. It will not do to claim that the Stoic emphasis on the procreative purpose of sex is responsible for this feature in traditional Church teaching since, as I have just shown, this was already present in the New Testament. Nor did Neoplatonic or Manichaean influences succeed in getting the Church to deny that the sexual body is intrinsic to the human person antecedently to original sin. One has only to read John T. Noonan, Jr.'s detailed study, *Contraception: A History of Its Treatment by the Catholic Theologians and Canonists,*[16] to be convinced that the magisterium has steered a rather even course between the extremes of libertinism and Manichaeism, and that it has always maintained the intimate connection between the procreative and unitive meanings of sexuality. The development in recent times toward a greater stress on the unitive meaning which Noonan details is undoubtedly very important, but there is no reason to think that it will someday lead to a reduction of the procreative meaning to a secondary position. Vatican II still says in *The Church and the Modern World* (n. 48):

> By its very nature the institution of marriage and married love is ordered to the procreation and education of the offspring and it is in them that it finds its crowning glory. Thus the man and woman, who "are no longer two but one" (Matt. 19:6), help and serve each other by their marriage partnership; they become conscious of their unity and experience it more deeply from day to day. The intimate union of marriage, as a mutual giving of two persons, and the good of the children demand total fidelity from the spouses and require an unbreakable unity between them.

and then goes on to speak of the sacramental meaning of marriage.

We may not conclude, however, that because the principle of inseparability is an infallible element in the ordinary teaching of the magisterium, therefore the whole array of concrete moral norms which have been deduced from it by theologians or even by the magisterium itself have this kind of certitude. St. Thomas Aquinas warns us that *"materia autem moralis talis est quod non ei conveniens perfecta certitudo,"*[17] not because the supreme moral principles lack certainty, but because the minor premises which intervene between the principles and the conclusions depend on our accurate understanding of many complicated, variable, and obscure matters. Thus the conclusion of *Humanae Vitae* about the evil of the individual contraceptive act, or the numerous conclusions drawn from the same principle by the *Declaration on Certain Questions Concerning Sexual Ethics* of the Congregation for the Doctrine of Faith[18] present many difficulties.

230

Both theological and pastoral caution should lead us in teaching and counseling to distinguish clearly between the different levels of certitude in magisterial teaching about sexuality. In our zeal to give clear and firm guidance we may be tempted to treat all moral norms as of equal weight; but this kind of dogmatism will backfire in the long run by lessening the credibility of the magisterium. At the same time, it would be an even graver mistake to conclude that because these concrete norms lack perfect certitude that they can, therefore, be ignored or minimized. It is typical of a legalist mentality to think of moral norms as obligatory only when they are certainly binding, rather than to be grateful for whatever guidance they can give us, even if this is only probably correct.[19]

Priorities

Thus the first task of the teaching Church with regard to sexuality is to seize every opportunity and use every appropriate means to explain to the world of today, dominated by a very different spirit, Jesus' own teaching on the God-given purpose of sexuality in all its interrelated aspects. The chief reason that consciences are confused is our failure to bring this teaching effectively into our world, where a thousand voices and images are dramatizing a very different notion of sex, a notion which separates pleasure from love and love from generativity.

A second task of the bishops is to apply this understanding of Christian sexuality to the concrete, practical situations of modern life. To do this they must make clear that they really appreciate the problems people face. Too often our preaching sounds as if we speak from the lofty heights of a protected celibacy, and that we have not felt the wounds of battle. We should frankly admit that for many women traditional marriage is experienced as a trap, that many homosexuals feel unjustly condemned and rejected by the Church, that young people feel the Church lacks humanity because it wishes to deny them an expression of their need for love at a time when they are not yet ready to commit themselves to marriage as they see so many marriages failing.

Overfacile solutions to the tragic dilemmas of life which people are experiencing make the Church appear smug and silly. Although the magisterium cannot sacrifice principles to a false compassion, or be silent about the truth, it also cannot simply "lay down the law." It must be ready not merely to provide advice and warnings, but also to provide well-developed positive programs to help those struggling with sexual problems. If we fail to do this, we will also fall under the Lord's condemnation of those religious teachers who "lay a heavy burden on others but do not lift a finger to help them bear it" (Mt. 23:4).

A third task of the Church is to develop and encourage forms of spirituality which fully integrate into our notion of growth in holiness the potentialities of human sexuality. We need a spirituality freed from the ancient Neoplatonic tendency to picture Christian holiness as a process of disincarnation of the human spirit, rather than the incarnation of the Spirit in the human bodily temple (I Cor. 6:15-20; cf. 3:16-17; Rom. 5:5). I think that Catholics have been falsely accused of Manichaeism and Stoicism, but the charge of Neoplatonism is more justified.[20]

These tasks of the episcopacy are difficult to accomplish without the active cooperation of theologians. In bearing witness to the Church's traditions in unity with his fellow bishops and the pope, a bishop speaks with full and proper authority, but when faced with the problem of applying perennial principles to current conditions, he needs the assistance of research and scholarship. Today the trust of bishops in many of our most gifted and active theologians has been seriously shaken, because some of these theologians seem to be out of harmony with the magisterium. Thus bishops are tempted to ignore theologians and to content themselves with the safety of repeating papal documents without taking the risk of interpreting these documents to their people in the language of the people, or showing how the principles enunciated can actually be "made to work" in the concrete situations in which people live. To do that they need the cooperation of theologians, sociologists, psychologists, and journalists. Bishops have experienced that this can be a risky, embarrassing business.

If, therefore, bishops are to make an effective use of the expertise of theologians they must first undertake to establish in the Church of the United States an atmosphere of genuine dialogue not only between theologians and bishops, but also among the theologians themselves. Last year in this workshop I pleaded that bishops should invite theologians from the whole spectrum of opinion to meet under episcopal auspices in situations free of undue publicity to work out areas of general agreement, and to focus on points of difference for serious research, particularly as regards moral theology. An alternative would be for the bishops to sponsor publications on controversial topics in which they insure that all the main opinions are given an equal hearing and the discussion is kept focused on the principal difficulties to be solved.[21] I am still hoping for such undertakings where the bishops actively promote a legitimate pluralism in discussion; motivated, however, by an effort to increase the area of consensus. That this is not a hopeless task is evidenced by the fact that a considerable area of consensus already exists. From my reading I believe that almost all Catholic moralists in the United States agree at least on the following not unimportant points:

1. The incarnational character of all human relationships.

2. The need for a positive approach to sexual questions that goes beyond the repression of sins to the promotion of the positive values of sexuality for human life, while at the same time recognizing the value of voluntary celibacy.

3. The centrality of the unitive meaning of sexuality, i.e., that married love is not merely a means to the procreation and education of children.

4. The fundamental equality of man and woman.

5. The need for a compassionate pastoral approach to individuals caught in conflict situations based on respect for the subjective conscience of each person at each stage of his or her spiritual development.

6. The conviction that the reform of morals cannot succeed without reform of the social conditions in our society.

7. The need for methods of sex education which respect the primary responsibility of the parents but which also employ the best in current psychology and medicine.

Compared with this broad area of agreement, the disagreements, although serious, are relatively narrow. In fact the disagreements do not so much concern the goals of Christian life, nor even the principal means to obtain these goals, but rather the manner of resolving certain conflict situations, which we must honestly admit no one knows how to solve very satisfactorily.

Conflict Situations

At the present time the methods used by American moralists to solve ethical conflict situations can be broadly reduced to four. The first is based on a deontological concept of ethics, i.e., an ethics which justifies its norms by an appeal to the authority of the legislator, whether that legislator is God, the Church, the State, or, as for Immanuel Kant, the autonomous good will of the rational individual. For Christian ethics this usually means an appeal to the will of God or of the bishops having their authority from God. In such a method conflicts are solved by "casuistry," by an effort to determine the obligation of the law in given cases. This system dominated post-Tridentine Catholic theology, with the result that moral reasoning tended to be assimilated to the legal method more proper to Canon Law.[22] Protestant ethics, because of its biblicism, and its suspicion of all philosophy (except that of Kant) has been largely deontological.[23] Deontological ethics is defended today by the very capable Protestant moralist Paul Ramsey[24] and by the philosopher William Frankena.[25] The merits of such a system are its objectivity and its reliance on precedence, undoubtedly a very important guide in ethics which depends so much on historical, social experience.

Since the Thomistic revival initiated by Leo XIII, however, deontologism has steadily lost ground among Catholic moralists because: (1) it was a product of the voluntarism of late medieval nominalism with its Pelagian tendencies; (2) it seems incompatible with the New Testament vision of God not as an oriental despot, but as loving Wisdom; (3) it tends to legalism and thus runs counter to Jesus' teaching on the New Law of the Spirit.

Aquinas teaches that the New Law is the guidance of the Spirit dwelling in the Christian Church and in each of its members.[26] This guidance is not merely deontological but teleogical, i.e., it guides us to seek God, the true goal *(telos)* of our life by prudent choices of appropriate means. In such an ethics the supreme principle is the goal itself, union with the Father in the Incarnate Son by the Spirit in the human community of the Church, and this principle is expressed by Jesus in the Great Command of the love of God and neighbor, even of the enemy.[27] All other norms receive their authority from this supreme principle and must be interpreted in its light. Finally, this principle is not merely an abstract rule but is embodied concretely in Jesus Christ Himself, so that the Christian life is "the following of

234

Christ" by the grace of Christ, His Holy Spirit.

In a teleogical ethics, conflict situations are solved not by casuistry in the proper legal sense, but rather by an analysis of the *priority of values* judged in terms of the relation of human acts, as means to an end, to that end and to each other. The judgment of conscience is not merely the work of abstract reason, but of prudence, a virtue which also involves the rectitude of the will (i.e., what today would be called "healthy, sensitive, integrated, mature feelings") along with a depth of moral experience — all these human powers being elevated in the Christian by faith, hope and love.

Most Catholic theologians today are agreed on such a teleological, prudential methodology, but they are divided as to how to determine this priority of values. Why this diversity? The basic reason is well stated by Charles E. Curran in a critique he made of the *Declaration on Certain Questions Concerning Sexual Ethics.*[28] He complains that this magisterial document presupposes

> a more deductive methodology based on the eternal, universal principles found in human nature. The Declaration cannot and does not employ the methodology of the Pastoral Constitution on the Church in the Modern World of the Second Vatican Council which begins its consideration of each question with a reading of the signs of the times – a much more inductive methodological approach which gives greater recognition to historical and cultural developments as well as to ongoing human creativity.

It seems to Curran and to many other theologians today that a moral theology built, as Aquinas' was, on the conviction that human reason can arrive at a noumenal understanding of a universal human nature which transcends historical and cultural conditions rests on sand. Modern philosophy generally denies the possibility of such noumenal knowledge; the scientific theory of evolution undermines it; the social sciences seem to demonstrate the contrary; and modern biblical scholarship seems to show that it is not confirmed by the Hebrew understanding of what it is to be human. Consequently, many moralists are attempting to reconstruct moral theology on some more secure foundation. Curran is proposing that we begin with "the signs of the times" or as others say, "what God is doing in our world today."

In the effort to reconstruct moral theology two "new" versions of teleological ethics have been put forward. One is "Situation Ethics"[29] which argues that there can be only one universal moral norm, namely the Great Command of love. All other ethical generalizations have a purely relative character, so that in concrete moral decisions they do not bind. This system has been severely criticized by Protestant and Catholic moralists alike as reducing in practice to an act-utilitarianism, an ethical system generally recognized by philosophers as inadequate. I know of no Catholic theologian today who defends Situation Ethics.

A second, more cautious form of teleological ethics has been put forward by Josef Fuchs of the Gregorian University and is to be found in a great many recent publications, namely what is being called "Proportionalism."[30] The Proportionalists point out that the classical Principle of Double Effect which has been our main guide in solving conflict situations has two principal conditions: (1) we may never perform an act which is intrinsically evil; (2) if an action is not intrinsically evil it may be performed in conflict situations if the proportion of the foreseen good effects equal or outweigh the foreseen and bad effects. Now, they reason, the first of these conditions rests on the presupposition that we can determine that some acts *by their very nature* are *morally* evil. While it can be easily granted that some acts considered in themselves involve some pre-moral evil, e.g., an act of killing is physically injurious; how are we to determine in the abstract, apart from a knowledge of the circumstances or the intention of the agent, that they are *morally* evil? An act of killing can be morally virtuous or sinful depending on whether it is an act of a soldier in a just war, or a terrorist. The Thomistic answer to this question was to refer the nature of the act to the human nature of the agent; but this is to suppose that we can arrive at a knowledge of that nature which transcends history, the very point which is now in doubt.[31]

Consequently, Proportionalism has abandoned the first condition of the Principle of Double Effect and the notion of the *malum per se,* and contends that all moral decisions in conflict situations must be solved simply on the grounds of the proportion between the values and disvalues which are foreseen to follow. This does not mean, be it noted, that Proportionalists, like the Situationists, reject all moral norms except the Great Commandment. They (at least the more cautious Proportionalists) accept the validity of all the traditional Christian moral norms as useful guides to the weighing of values and disvalues; but what they insist on is that there are (theoretically at least) no absolutely universal, exceptionless moral norms, since no matter how gravely evil an act may appear (considered pre-morally apart from the circumstances and the intention of the agent) in its moral actuality under special circumstances and in view of the agent's intention it may happen that its human values outweigh this evil. Thus, while Jesus' command against divorce has general validity, in some cases divorce and remarriage can be not only morally permissible, but even a duty. In all fairness to Proportionalists I want to emphasize that this methodology does not *necessarily* lead to solutions contrary to the magisterium. A Proportionalist might very well come to the conclusion that all those acts traditionally forbidden as intrinsically evil, are also forbidden on the grounds that in most cases they involve greater disvalues than values.

The third type of teleological ethics seeks to retain the notion of the *malum per se,* i.e., that in moral decisions it is *sometimes* possible to judge that certain acts are forbidden from the nature of the act itself, antecedent to any modification of the act by the circumstances, including any *circumstantial* intention of the agent.[32] What is in question here is not merely the pre-moral nature of the act, as Proportionalists sometimes assert, but the nature of the act considered as a *moral* reality, i.e., as placed by an intelligent, free, human person in view of that person's authentic goals in life. Thus, in the example given above, the moral nature of the act of killing is not the mere physical action, but this same action as a specific kind of *means* to the agent's end. The soldier in a just war uses force as a means to prevent aggression; the terrorist as a means of propaganda. Nor can this moral difference be reduced to the circumstantial intention of the agents, because the intention of defense or propaganda is intrinsic to the act and not merely circumstantial. Thus if a soldier engaged in a just war should have a personal motive of private revenge, that intention would be circumstantial.

It follows that for this type of teleological ethics some actions are always morally wrong in themselves, and can be so judged antecedent to any knowledge of the circumstances. Hence, we can (contrary to the Proportionalist position) formulate some universal, exceptionless ("absolute") moral norms. Note, however, that this does not reduce this type of ethics to deontology, although deontological ethics also defends exceptionless norms. The absolute value of such norms for this type of teleology does not rest on the authority of the legislator, but on the objective nature of the act in question as it is a moral act, i.e., seen as a means to achieve those goals which inhere in the nature of the human person. Need we feel insecure, as the Proportionalists contend, in claiming to know what human nature is, with its basic needs? Can we determine, for example, what the intrinsic meaning of human sexuality as an essential dimension of human nature is, in a way that transcends the meaning given to human sexuality by different cultures in history? Curran is obviously correct in saying that the magisterial documents use a methodology which presupposes that we do in fact have such an understanding of human nature.

I cannot in this paper undertake a defense of the validity of this type of teleological ethics based on a culturally transcendent anthropology. I would only note two things. First of all, such an anthropology need not defend a "static," ahistorical, "essentialist," or non-personalistic view of human nature. It can take all these aspects of human nature into full account and still maintain that human beings all belong to a single species and a single historical community with the same fundamental needs. Second, although Thomism provided an anthropology and an ethics of this type, such a view of humanity and human morality does not depend on any particular philosophy, but rests on the data of revelation. We are children of Adam, and we are restored by grace to brotherhood with Jesus, in the new Adam. Jesus, in recalling in Mk. 10:1-12 what God intended us to be in the beginning, appeals to this original vision of humanity from which sexuality takes its primordial meaning, a meaning which transcends the variations of history, and demands eschatological fulfillment.

It seems, therefore, that the magisterium has been justified in formulating the principle of the inseparability of the unitive and procreative meanings of sexuality as an exceptionless negative norm: *It is never licit to perform sexual acts except in order to express the lifelong, self-giving love between a man and a woman open to the transmission or fostering of the fully human life of a new generation of persons.* This negative norm, however, is only a reflection of the positive meaning of the gift of human sexuality through which human persons can achieve their total fulfillment as persons for this earthly life. In a teleological ethics the only reason that limits are placed on some forms of sexual activity is because such acts are misuses, abuses of sexuality by which sexuality is turned against itself and becomes an obstacle to its own fulfillment.

238

Conclusion

I have tried to show that the magisterium ought to continue to preach from the housetops the fundamental principle of sexual ethics, namely the principle of the inseparability of the unitive and procreative meanings of the conjugal act, patiently educating the Christian people in the biblical truth that true sexual fulfillment is to be found only in faithful and fruitful marriage. It must also apply this principle to the solution of concrete ethical problems with prudence and compassion, showing why some forms of sex considered by our society as necessary for sexual fulfillment are in fact intrinsically opposed to such fulfillment and, therefore, never objectively justified.

At the same time the magisterium must not reject nor neglect those persons whose subjective conscience does not permit them as yet to see the practical truth of the Church's teachings on these difficult matters. Above all the pastors of the Church must keep in mind how difficult our disordered society makes it for people either to understand or to live this high Christian ideal, and must join actively in bringing about social change in support of family living.

Notes

1. Cf. Bernard Haring, "The Inseparability of the Unitive-Procreative Functions of the Marital Act," in *Contraception: Authority and Dissent,* edited by Charles E. Curran (New York: Herder and Herder, 1969). For a commentary on the formulations of *Humanae Vitae* by an author rumored to be one of its drafters, see Gustave Martelet, *L'existence humaine et l'amour* (Paris: Desclee, 1969). Also cf. Carol Wojtyla (John Paul II), *Amour et responsabilité* (Paris: Stock, 1978), pp. 211-24 (written in 1962 before the encyclical). Note also the statement of this principle in *The Church in the Modern World:* "Marriage and married love are by nature ordered to the procreation and education of children. Indeed children are the supreme gift of marriage and greatly contribute to the good of the parents themselves. . . . But marriage is not merely for the procreation of children: its nature as an indissoluble compact between two people and the good of the children demand that the mutual love of the partners be properly shown, that it should grow and mature. Even in cases where despite the intense desire of the spouses there are no children, marriage still retains its character of being a whole manner and communion of life and perserves its value and indissolubility"(n. 50).

2. I have attempted to formulate the principle as follows: *"Principle of Personalized Sexuality:* The use of human sexuality must be in keeping with its intrinsic specifically human teleology which is (1) the loving, pleasurable, bodily expression of the complementary union of a male and a female person and (2) the perpetuation and expansion of this personal communion through the family they beget and educate." Benedict Ashley and Kevin O'Rourke, *Health Care Ethics* (St. Louis: The Catholic Health Association, 1978), pp. 211-17.

3. Hugh Hefner's notorious *Playboy Magazine* has repeatedly defended its "philosophy" according to which sexual pleasure need have no connection with love between the partners. Interestingly, the study which it commissioned, *Playboy Report on American Men,* conducted by Louis Harris Associates, 1979, Playboy Enterprises, shows that American men on the average are looking for married love and a faithful spouse.

4. Anthony Kosnik *et al., Human Sexuality: New Directions in American Catholic Thought* (New York: Paulist Press, 1977), p. 86.

5. Donald Goergen, *The Sexual Celibate* (New York: Seabury, 1974). "Being sexual, therefore means many things . . . Among other things, it means sexual differentiation, being female and male. It also means being relational – structured for another – incomplete by oneself – inescapably social. Sexual existence is social existence. In my social life I encounter other sexual beings of my own sex and other sexual beings of the other sex. Being sexual also means being bodily, physical. My body is a sexual reality and is involved in what I do and how I act" (p. 5). These statements are a bit ambiguous. To be sexual is to be social, perhaps; but is to be social to be sexual?

6. E.g., Vern L. Bullough, *Sexual Variance in Society and History* (New York: John Wiley and Sons, 1976) labels Christianity as a "Sex Negative" religion and says, "The Church Fathers regarded sex as at best something to be tolerated, and evil whose only good was in procreation. Western attitudes have been dominated by this concept ever since" (p. 196).

7. Thus Mary Daly in her *Gyn/Ecology: The Metaethics of Radical Feminism* (Boston: Beacon Press, 1978) devotes chapter 2 to a demolition of "Christian myths" and chapter 6 to "European Witchburnings: Purifying the Body of Christ in an effort to show that "Christianity is just another phase of the cruel war of patriarchy to enslave, torture, mutilate, and destroy women physically and psychologically. This should take its place alongside the efforts of Nietzsche to show that Christianity is a religion aiming at male castration.

8. The basic cause of the modern rejection of the concept of "nature" is this rejection of teleology by modern science, beginning with Galileo and philosophically justified by Kant. It rests on a misunderstanding of the notion of teleology, identifying it with (1) conscious purpose; (2) with some kind of occult efficient cause. See my article, "Teleology," *New Catholic Encyclopedia* (1967) 13:979-81.

9. For detailed discussion of this question and bibliography, see John P. Meier, *Law and History in Matthew's Gospel* (Rome: Biblical Institute Press, 1976), and the summary of his conclusions in his *The Vision of Matthew* (New York: Paulist Press, 1978), pp. 62-66.

10. General Audience of Wednesday, Oct. 8, 1980; in *L'Osservatore Romano* (English edition), October 13, 1980.

11. Meier, *Law and History*, pp. 140-49.

12. Jerusalem Bible. Cf. Hugh Anderson, *The Gospel of Mark*, New Century Bible (London: Oliphants, 1976), pp. 241-243, who notes that "one body" might mean either "whole person" or "kindred." For the attempt to give preference to the J theology of sexuality see Helmut Thielicke, *The Ethics of Sex* (New York: Harper and Row, 1964), pp. 3-16, and Derrick Sherwin Bailey, *Sexual Relations in Christian Thought* (New York: Harper and Sons, 1959), pp. 265-67. Bailey's numerous books on the theology of sexuality have been widely influential, and exhibit a remarkable ingenuity for suavely "explaining away" the "hard sayings" of the Bible. On "canon criticism" see Bevard S. Childs, *Introduction to the Old Testament as Scripture* (Philadelphia: Fortress Press 1979), pp. 72-83.

13. See the brilliant little essay of Ida F. Gorres, *Is Celibacy Outdated?* (Westminster, Md.: Newman Press, 1965). On the historical context in which the Christian concept of celibacy developed see Abel Isaakson, *Marriage and Ministry in the New Temple* (Lund: C. W. K. Gleerup, 1965).

14. Vatican II, *Dogmatic Constitution on the Church*, n. 6.

15. Of course each of these texts taken in isolation is open to various exegetical difficulties. It is the general, developmental consistency in which one text explains another that is most significant. Against the way in which these texts are often treated today I would cite the criticism which George T. Montague made of the study *Human Sexuality* (reference in note 4 above), "In general, though the study repudiates the method of proof-texts, it tends to espouse the same method in reverse, by its nagging insistence that there are no absolutes regarding sex in the Bible, and, in places, by an unconvincing attempt to explain away the rather obvious meaning of the text. This method is deficient in its appreciation of the progressive character of biblical revelation, lumping under a statement that the Bible has different views about sexuality, texts that come from different periods and show a distinct evolution in teaching on sexuality." "A Scriptural Response to the Report on Human Sexuality," *America*, Oct. 29, 1977, p. 284.

16. *Contraception: A History of Its Treatment by the Catholic Theologians and Canonists* (Cambridge, Mass.: Harvard, 1965). This pioneering work is somewhat deficient in its treatment of the patristic period where not enough allowance is made for the complexity of the relations between biblical and hellenistic thought or the literary form of patristic pronouncements. A good general treatment of the patristic theology of sexuality still remains to be written.

17. *Sententia Libri Ethicorum* (Leonine ed.) I. 3. 1094a.15.

18. Sacred Congregation for the Doctrine of the Faith, *Declaration on Certain Questions Concerning Sexual Ethics* (Jan. 22, 1976), *Catholic Mind,* April, 1976, pp. 52-64.

19. On the history of post-Tridentine moral theology see Bernard Haring, *The Law of Christ* (Cork, 1963) 1:11-34. and *Free and Faithful in Christ* (New York: Seabury, 1978), 1:45-58.

20. The negative effect of this Neoplatonic spirituality (it had many positive effects also) was that it was Logos-centered, but not Incarnation-centered. Middle Platonism had already permeated Hellenistic Judaism (Philo, *Wisdom)* and the early Church (Gnosticism, Justin Martyr), culminating in Origen (third century). In the systematic form of Neoplatonism beginning with the pagan Plotinus (perhaps a fellow student with Origen), it spread through the Cappadocian Fathers to Evagrius Ponticus, the Pseudo-Dionysius, and Maximus the Confessor. The works of Pseudo-Dionysius were commented on by John Scotus Erigena in the ninth and Albert the Great in the thirteenth centuries. From Albert it influenced Meister Eckhart, Suso, Tauler and Luther (!) and from Suso the great Spanish mystics.

21. A remarkable example of this type of symposium is furnished by the magazine *Current Anthropology* (University of Chicago) which regularly invites an expert or a team of experts to produce a paper on a topic of current interest in the field. This position paper is then submitted, before publication, to the outstanding specialists of all countries and schools of thought for specific critical comments. Then all views are published together, permitting the reader to judge for himself on the basis of reasoned evidence.

22. On this influence of Canon Law see the references in note 19 above.

23. James M. Gustafson, *Protestant and Roman Catholic Ethics* (Chicago: University of Chicago Press, 1978), gives a very fair discussion of these differences and growing consensus. Significantly, however, he tends to cite as evidence of convergence Catholic authors who are proportionalists.

24. Charles E. Curran and Paul Ramsey, *Politics, Medicine and Christian Ethics: A Dialogue* (Philadelphia: Fortress Press, 1973).

25. William Frankena, *Ethics,* 2nd ed. (Englewood Clifss, N.J.: Prentice-Hall, 1973).

26. St. Thomas Aquinas, *Summa Theologiae,* I-II, qq. 106-8. Very helpful on the role of prudence are the appendices by Thomas Gilby, in the McGraw-Hill edition of the *Summa,* vol. 16, pp. 184-86; vol. 33, 174-84. Cf. also Reginald Doherty, "The Judgement of Conscience and Prudence" (unpublished dissertation, Aquinas Institute, 1961).

27. Cf. Gerard Gillemann, *The Primacy of Charity in Moral Theology* (Westminster, Md.: Newman Press, 1959), and John Piper, *"Love your enemies": Jesus' Love Command in the Synoptic Gospel and in the Early Christian Paraenesis* (Cambridge: Cambridge University Press, 1980).

28. Charles E. Curran, "Sexual Ethics: Reaction and Critique," *Catholic Mind,* Jan. 1977, pp. 41-56; p. 49.

29. Joseph Fletcher, *Situation Ethics* (Philadelphia: Westminster Press, 1969); cf. Harvey Cox, ed., *The Situation Ethics Debate* (Philadelphia: Westminster Press, 1968).

30. See the presentation of Proportionalism by Richard C. McCormick, S.J., in *Doing Evil to Achieve Good,* edited by Richard McCormick and Paul Ramsey (Chicago: Loyola University Press, 1978), along with several critical essays by Charles E. Curran and Richard A. McCormick, S.J., in *Readings in Moral Theology,* no. 1, *Moral Norms and Catholic Tradition* (New York: Paulist Press, 1979). A strong criticism, with reference to other criticisms, will be found in William May, "An Integrist Understanding," in *Dimensions of Human Sexuality,* edited by Dennis Doherty (New York: Doubleday, 1979), pp. 95-124; and May and John F. Harvey, "On understanding human sexuality: a critique of the C.T.S.A. study," *Communio,* Fall 1977, pp. 195-225.

31. Some proportionalists argue that unless we consider the intention of the agent along with the nature of the act, the act remains pre-moral and cannot be judged as either morally good or evil. In the classical theory, however, by the term "intention" in the specification of moral act

was meant one of the *circumstances,* i.e., a circumstantial intention (e.g., the giving of alms in order to be admired by others), not the intention which is intrinsic to the moral object itself and which specifies it as moral, i.e., to benefit a poor man by alms, nor the intention of the ultimate end which enters into every human act. Thus a soldier in a just war kills the enemy with the immediate and specifying intention of stopping an act of aggression. It is this intention intrinsic to the act which gives it its moral species. However, in some cases the soldier may have a further, circumstantial intention, such as revenge, or a display of his skill, which modifies the moral character of the act but does not specify it.

32. A very clear presentation of the classical theory of the moral specification of human acts can be found in Germain Grisez and Russell Shaw, *Beyond the New Morality* (Notre Dame, Ind.: University of Notre Dame Press, 1974).

Being, 140-42, 145, 148-50
Benjamin, Harry, 82
Bergson, Henri, 142, 145
Bernardin, Archbishop Joseph, 159
Bernardine of Siena, St., 56, 57
Bestial intercourse, 48, 55, 56, 58, 65
Bible, 15, 27, 213, 214
Bieber, I., 82
Billot, Louis, 215-16
Biology, 15, 102, 117, 140, 152, 155;
    biological: constitution, 115;
    determinism, 115; factors, 86, 108,
    115, 117, 127; influences, 79, 80;
    predisposition, 106; sciences, 109;
    understanding of sexual behavior,
    86; biologistic: approach to
    contraception, 196, 199, 204; basis
    of marriage, 201, 226
Biophysic influences, 79, 80
Birth control, 15, 26, 186
Birth defect, syndromes, 72
Birth rate, 63; see also Population
Black Death, 57
Brain, 81, 83, 85, 91, 93, 97, 100-03;
    development to conceptualize,
    100-02; developmental periods,
    103; fetal brain programmng, 98
Breadwinner, 88
Brown, Bertram, 133
Buber, Martin, 142

Caesarius of Arles, St., 47
Cajetan, Cardinal, 56, 57
Callewaert, R.S., 46
Calvin, John, 58; calvinism, 61
Canon Law, 41, 99, 197, 199, 200;
    canonical prohibitions, 99
Casti Connubii, 192, 193
Castration, 24, 25, 60
Casuistry, 59, 235
Catherine of Aragon, 58
Catholic Church, 62, 108; authentic
    teaching, 13; Catholic: moral
    theology, 212, 236; philosophers,
    147; theologians, 198; tradition,
    219, Church teaching, 176, 184; see
    also, Roman Catholic
Catholic Theological Society of
    America (CTSA) 174, 185, 225
Celibacy, 13, 30, 40, 55, 58, 161, 231,
    233

Celibates, 8, 40, 225
Central nervous system, 81, 100
Change, 140, 209
Chardin, S.J., P. Teilhard de,142
Charity,45
Chastity, 158, 175, 208
Child, brain development, 100-06;
    development, 99-108; rearing, 99;
    see also, Offspring; Procreation
Christian, Church, 98, 108, 226, 234;
    humanism, 55; life, 233, 234; moral
    norms, 236; prophetic tradition
    (Hebrew Christian), 133;
    psychiatrists, 108; psychologists,
    108; revelation, 213, 227; sexuality,
    231; thinkers, 162; writers, 86
Chromosomal, aberrations, 72; errors,
    102; sex, 71, 72
Church, 6, 30,39, 62,63,159, 161,
    162, 175, 183, 192, 204; American,
    173, 174; magisterial teaching, 11;
    sexual ethic, 180; teaching, 176,
    184, 231, 239
Circumstances, 211, 212, 237
Civilizations, 112, 116
Clarke, W.N., 148
Clement of Alexandria, 40
Clitoris, 75
Code of Canon Law, 11, 169, 191,
    192, 194
Cohabitation, 111, 123, 124
Cohorts, homgeneous, 89
Coitus interruptus, 60-63, coitus, 126
Commitment, 130; as individuating,
    132; level of, 126, 129
Community, 187, 188, 220, 238
Concepts, 101, 107, 113,
    conceptualization, 99-102; of
    culture, 115
Conception, 102
Concubinage, 18
Concupiscence, 42, 191; *remedium
    concupiscentiae,* 43
Conditioned reflex, 115
Condoms, 61, 63
Configuration, of behavior 115; of
    culture elements, 114, 121; through
    reintegration, 131, 132
Conjugal love, v, 191, 192, 194, 201,
    203, 205-06

201, 230; institutional change, 123
Intentionality, 142
Intercourse, see Sexual intercourse
International Monetary Fund, 186
Intrinisicism, 169, 174-75; intrinsic
  evil, 182, 203, 206, 214, 218-19,
  236.
Intepersonal: behaviors, 95;
  impersonal interaction, 132;
  relations, 154
Intersubjectivity, 151

J.T., 103-06
Jacklin, Carol N., 127-28
Janssens, Louis, 212
Jansenism, 58-59, 61
Jesus, 4, 27, 29-32, 133, 186, 215,
  227-28, 234, 237-38
John XXIII, Pope, 200
John Paul II, Pope, v, 227
Johnson, Virginia E., 126
Jost, A., 76-77
Jung, Carl, 98
Justification, 58-59

Kallman, F.J., 80, 83
Kant, Emmanuel, 133, 140, 234
Killing, 211-212, 217, 236-37
Kingdom of God, 29, 215; of heaven,
  37
Kinsey, Alfred C., 90-91, 126; Kinsey
  Scale, 91-93
Kinship, 118, 120
Klinefelter syndrome, 72
Knauer, S.J., Peter, 212
Knaus, H., 196
Knights of Columbus, vi
Knowledge, 140-41, 148, 154, 204
Lambeth Conference, 192
Kolodny, R.C., 81
Kosnik, Anthony, 160

LH, 81, 83
Labia: majora, 75; minora, 75
Labor, division of, 121, 131
Lactation, 46
Language, 114, 116, 161-63; empirical
  and metaphysical,134; see: Syntax
Lasch, Christopher, 184-85
Lateran Council, Fourth, 40
Law, 12, 27-28, 152-54, 156;
  Decalogue, 28; for divorce, 18;

moral laws, 12; Mosaic, 19, 26-28,
  31, 228; natural, 19, 49, 53-54,
  152-53, 170, 175, 178, 207,
  215-19; New Law of the Spirit, 234;
  of gradualness, v; of the Most High,
  23; Old Law, 26, 39, 227; Old
  Testament, 19-20, 27
Learning, 99; social, 117
LeMaistre, Martin, 56-57
Leo XIII, Pope, 63, 193, 234
Levirate law, 46
Leydig cells, 79, 85
Libido, 118
Life-styles, alternative, 127
Lonergan, S.J., Bernard, 216
Lorenz, Konrad, 115
Louvain, 59
Love, 17, 42-43, 48-49, 60, 101-102,
  139, 154, 157, 176-78, 182, 186,
  228, 231; commandment of love,
  28-29, 215, 234, 236; God is love,
  101; law of love, 32; of neighbor,
  24; ordered and disordered, 42-43;
  total love of God, 44; see: Conjugal
  love; Charity
Lust, 56
Luther, Martin, 58
Lysis, 74, 79, 85
McCarthy, Donald G., 212
McCary, James, 89, 94
McCormick, S.J., Richard A., 212,
  214, 220
McGinley, J., 81
Maccoby, Eleanor E., 127-28
Magazines, 105-06, 127;
  pornographic, 105-06
Magisterium, 11, 191, 212-13, 216,
  221, 223-24, 226-27, 230-32,
  237-39
Maine, Henry Sumner, 122
Major, John, 57
Male chauvinism, 120-21
Maleness, 88-89; male dominance,
  115, 118-20
Mammals, 102
Manichees, 41-42, 46-47;
  Manichaeism, 170, 174, 183-85,
  230, 232
Marcel, Gabriel, 143, 175
Marcuse, H., 145

248

Social confusion, 112
Social differentiation, 118, 128-29,
    131-34; see: Differentiation
Social interaction, 123
Social issues, 108
Social skills, 95-96, 102, 108;
    behaviors, 95-96
Sociobiologists, 115, 118, 128
Sociocultural factors, 81, 87, 98; in
    masculinity, femininity, 122, 127; in
    sexual inequality, 115; sociocultural
    completion, 115
Sodomy, 23, 25, 29
Sorokin, P., 132
Soto, Dominic, 57
Soul, human, 156; male and female
    soul, 156
Spanier, Graham B., 126, 128
Spermatids, 85
Spirit, 27-29, 114; see: Sociocultural
    definition, 114; see: Holy Spirit
Spiritual relationship, 39
Spirituality and sexuality, 232
Sterilization, 46, 186-87
Sterility, 41, 46, 60
Stoic philosophers, 41; influence, 229,
    232
Strawson, P.F., 145
Suarez, S.J., Francis, 215-16
Subculture, 113, 120
Subjectivity, 142, 144, 148
Subsistence, 142
Substance, 70, 140-49
Supposit, 147, 150
Symbolling, 114, 116; symbols, 116;
    symbolic universe, 117; sex as
    symbol, 188, 228-29
Synod, Fifth International, v, vii, 179;
    "Message to Christian Families," v
Syntax, 114, 116

Tactile stimulus, 105-06; sensitivity,
    128
Teachers, authoritative, 108
Teenage years, 104; teenagers, 108
Teleological ethics, 234-38
Template, 98
Tertullian, 37
Testicular feminization, 72, 83
Testis, 71-72, 74, 76-78, 81, 84-85
Testosterone, 77, 79, 81, 83, 85;

testosterone metabolites, 80
Theology, 158, 161; theological ethics,
    213; of love, 178; and
    methodology, 218-19; theological
    sciences, 109
Thomas Aquinas, St., 12, 38-39,
    44-45, 47-49, 54, 58, 145-46, 148,
    153, 156-57, 175, 197-98, 215-17.
    219-20, 230, 234-35
Thomas More, St., 55
Thomism, 141, 238; Thomists, 148,
    171, 175; Thomist revival, 234
Thought, 142-43, 145, 149, 155
Tollison, C. David, 95, 105
Traits: cultural, 152; elements of
    cultures, 113; "macho," 121;
    masculine/feminine, 98
Transcultural, basic of *humanum,* 70,
    163
Transsexualism, 69, 80, 82-83, 97;
    male to female, 97-98;
    phenotypically normal male
    transsexual, 98; transsexual errors
    in gender role identification, 73
Trent, Council of, 57-58
Tubercle, genital, 75, 78-79
Turner, Ralph, 133
Turner, Syndrome, 72
Tylor, E.B., 114

Unchastity, 30-31, 188; see: *Porneia*
Unitive meaning of marriage and
    sexuality, 197-98, 200-04, 223-25,
    233
Urethral folds, 75
Urogenital tract, 77
Uterus, 74
Utilitarian: calculus, 220; thought, 120

Vagina, 71, 74
Valla, Lorenzo, 54
Values, 117, 120, 144, 153-54, 156,
    204, 209, 220; communal, 120;
    conflict of, 169, 180, 234-36;
    cultural, 116, 121, priority of, 235;
    tolerating different, 127; weighing
    of, 236
Vas deferens, 74, 78
Vatican, 60, 63; First Vatican Council,
    63; Second Vatican Council, 162,
    170, 176, 200, 205, 208, 224-25;
    see: *Gaudium et Spes*